The Astute

Speculator

This book is dedicated to the referenced practitioners, academics, and especially academic-practitioners who are my masters and mentors on stock market speculation.

The Astute Speculator

Eric L. Prentis

Houston

Prentis | Business

Houston, Texas
prentisbusiness@earthlink.net
www.theastuteinvestor.net

The intended purpose of *The Astute Speculator* is to present faithful and
useful information concerning stock market speculation. Common stock buy,
sell, or hold recommendations are not made in this book and should not be
assumed. Professional services — such as legal, accounting, tax, insurance, or
registered investment advice, etc. — are not offered in this text. If
professional services are desired, please contact legally-licensed
professionals directly.

Prentis | Business | is a registered trademark (pending)

Jacket photographs by James Sweet

Publishers Cataloging-in-Publication Data

Prentis, Eric L., 1948-
        The Astute Speculator / Eric L. Prentis - 1st ed.
        p. cm.
        Includes glossary, bibliographical references, and index.
        1. Speculation–United States. 2. Common Stock–United States.
        3. Money Management. I Title.
        ISBN-13: 978-0-9759660-2-0
        ISBN-10: 0-9759660-2-2

Library of Congress Control Number: 2007923368

10 9 8 7 6 5 4 3 2 1

Contents

Contents

Graphs

Tables

Websites

Contents

Introduction

EARNING +33 PERCENT PER YEAR speculating in the stock market, in both good times and bad, and retaining the profits once earned are challenging but realistic goals and the focus of this book. Trying to beat the stock market with what is learned in other professions and a smattering of Wall Street lore is almost certain to fail, as approximately 95 percent of new speculators regrettably discover.

Few acquire the correct speculative expertise prior to trading, trial and error are often used and experience becomes the initial teacher. Speculating in the stock market without the necessary understanding and practice is often a harsh, perplexing and expensive way to learn.

Eleven key scientific speculative factors, three speculative arts and ten speculative bylaws necessary for correct stock market speculation are presented. Success when speculating is best achieved by first becoming a knowledgeable stock trader, then practicing using simulator trading, next performing odd-lot trading with limited funds and only then graduating to trading in round lots.

Speculative Experience

The majority of speculators find out about the stock market the hard way, simply by doing. Learning by doing, while common in many other endeavors, is a dreadfully expensive way to learn how to speculate in the stock market. By reading this book and applying its lessons well, novice speculators avoid many ruinous pitfalls which await those who begin speculating without first learning how.

Experience by itself does not inform on the lesson learned. Events merely appear without a frame of reference. If speculators are unaware of what to observe, during what can be a very stressful trading experience, they will not understand the important signs appearing right before their eyes even though they think they see what is happening. The significance of what the important data and information are becomes hidden among the thousands of other distracting facts and opinions.

Some will say, "Yes but, experience is the best teacher and he or she will do much better next time." Nevertheless, if the losing novice speculator is so traumatized by the bad experience that they never want to see or hear about the stock market again, then this good learning experience is wasted.

Learn First, Before Doing

The man or woman who masters the knowledge of stock market speculation, as presented in this book, is exceptional because few accomplish this task before they begin trading. Speculators should take a pledge to shun Wall Street until they are entirely convinced, using their own intelligence, that they are doing the "right thing" and the "thing right." Before speculating in the stock market, first learn about one of the most all-encompassing, strategic, fast paced and complex professions in the world.

Perhaps in no other professional activity will correct understanding pay higher dividends than learning beforehand how to trade properly in the stock market. Correct speculative theories, strategies and methods presented in this book succinctly explain how to make money in the stock market.

A positive approach is used to explain stock market speculation. The goal is to point speculators to crucial and essential speculating knowledge

2

and to what that knowledge means. The stock market, more than anything, is a mental game—as discussed next.

Mental Game

Stock market buying and selling is a mental game based upon the perceptions of participating traders. Taking advantage of market inefficiencies and winning on Wall Street are the province of those with the correct knowledge, foresight, patience, humility, iron nerve, discipline, judgment and have the courage to take proper action.

Failure in the stock market is thinking in an intellectual rut. Only after most or all is lost do beaten speculators finally realize they have to think completely differently to be a success when trading common stock. For this reason, losing speculators are required to change their beliefs, desires, decisions and actions to achieve speculative success.

It is expected that beginning speculators will develop a reference for both understanding and feeling comfortable trading common stock. *The Astute Speculator* is self-empowering and helps speculators feel confident in taking control of their own money when speculating.

Speculative Overview

Stock market speculation is both an art and a science. The study of eleven key scientific speculative factors include what stage the market is in, the market's trend, whether the market is undervalued or overvalued and how to calculate a corporation's margin-of-safety multiple. The three speculative arts are: 1) how to time stock buying or short selling over the intermediate-term using turning points and trigger points; 2) how to sell or cover a stock position by taking the emotion out when using stop-loss orders and money management rules; and 3) knowing yourself and what strategy will work best for you based on your character, personality and lifestyle.

Learn why short selling is not un-American and has to be mastered to be a successful speculator. Making a purchase commitment on a stock is more complicated but less emotional than concluding it, how to best accomplish both are presented. Recognize that sectors and industries have a major influence on how a stock within that industry will behave over the intermediate term.

Price action indicates but is secondary in importance to trading volume which validates the stock market's buy-side advance or sell-side decline. How to use tape reading to recognize trigger points to capitalize on market turning points is explained. Speculative bylaws and money management rules are presented and should be followed to become a successful speculator. Speculative strategies have to fit the speculator's character, personality and lifestyle in order to be effective—learn how this is accomplished.

Speculating in the stock market is a first-class profession, i.e., no outside office is required and no employees or clients are necessary. A computer with an Internet connection is all that is required and that may be located anywhere in the world. Many want to enter this unsurpassed speculative profession but few take the time to properly learn and practice prior to beginning and, predictably, they fail.

Speculative Goals

Challenging but reasonable goals when speculating are to earn three times the average super long-term S&P 500 Index return of approximately +11 percent per year, i.e., +33 percent per year and then be able to retain the profits which is the real end game. The most significant goal in stock market speculation is to have money available at the end of your trading career for a new life interest, leisure, or for a comfortable retirement.

Do Not Force The Stock Market

The market cannot be forced to fit your needs. Those who want the stock market to pay their weekly bills by trying to scalp full-or-half point moves in a stock are destined for failure. Trying to make the stock market pay for an upcoming expense or a particular bill is futile. Invariably, the timing is wrong resulting in impulsive or unreasoning trades.

Astute speculators are advised to take what the market gives them on the market's terms. Determining the objective truths of "what, when, who and where" of stock speculation should be thought of as detective work and going on a journey of discovery.

How To Succeed On Wall Street

There is a saying on Wall Street, "Persons who act like stock market speculation is the road to riches frequently go broke, however, persons only wanting a reasonable profit on their money have the best chance of becoming rich."

Speculators learn that correct trading is not a random activity, nor mere chance or luck; but, a rigorous undertaking that requires the elimination of risk as much as possible prior to taking a stock position. This is accomplished by relying on a strategy suitable to the speculator, calculation, analysis, evaluation, good judgment and the courage to act properly.

Know the proper trading principles and follow the ten speculative bylaws for speculative success. Know yourself, do not overreach, practice first using simulator trading, start trading initially using odd-lot trades with limited funds and only then graduate to regular round-lot trading. Do not take unduly large risks in the stock market.

The purpose of this book is to point readers toward crucial and essential speculative knowledge and to what that knowledge means, thereby transforming novice speculators into astute speculators—as described next.

What Is An Astute Speculator?

An astute speculator has foresight, a cool temperament, a clear mind, patience, iron nerve, discipline, is shrewd, humble, keenly aware of what information and data are the most significant in the field of stock market speculation and has the courage to act properly.

Astute speculators plan and know where to locate data necessary to make necessary model calculations and how to interpret these results for proper decision making. Astute speculators are seekers of truth, possess market vision, speculative intelligence, can take appropriate action and have practical stock market experience.

How To Become An Astute Speculator

Those who do best at stock market speculation are persons who are truly interested in learning as much as possible about how to trade. Speculators should ask themselves if they are excited by market or stock price movements and cannot wait to understand why they are occurring, if so, these persons could delight in speculating.

To become a speculative professional and make a living from the stock market, it is imperative that traders take their calling seriously. Success in the stock market entails earnest in-depth study and only then taking proper action.

Trading stock looks deceptively easy to the uninformed, however, speculation can be very trying. It is an axiom that one tends to get out of life an equal measure of what is put into it. Since the goal is to make outsized profits in the stock market by having money work extra hard, it is necessary that speculators work extra hard because no one earns something for nothing in life.

How speculators implement the information presented and the effort put forth when speculating ultimately establishes how successful they become when trading. Knowing what is in this book and applying it correctly, compared to others who are ignorant of its content, makes knowledgeable individuals speculative winners. To be an expert stock market speculator requires first being an expert investor, as described next.

Be An Expert Investor First

It is required to first be an expert on investing prior to attempting to speculate in the stock market. An outstanding investor knows whether the overall stock market is undervalued or overvalued, if the market is in a long-term upward trend or long-term downward trend, what is the most promising stock to buy and what interest rates to monitor.

Astute investors use investment models, know where to locate data on the Internet to make calculations, understand what the results signify, can properly take action and are familiar with the following concepts:
1. Understands the difference between systematic risk and unsystematic risk.
2. Knows how the stock market acts as a discounting mechanism.
3. Fully understands diversification versus concentration of a stock portfolio.
4. Knows whether the overall stock market is either undervalued or overvalued.

5. Knows how the rational, non-rational and irrational behavior of stock traders affects their actions.

6. Can determine which of four stages the stock market is in and how that affects strategy.

7. Understands corporate intrinsic value, market value capitalization, bargain values and how to use margin-of-safety multiples to evaluate common stock.

8. Knows the political-economic conditions and how they affect the stock market.

9. Can determine interest rate spreads and how yield curves affect the stock market.

10. Understands how expected and unexpected news are used in the stock market.

11. Knows the contrarian methodology and how it is applied.

12. Can implement the practical ten-step method for investment success.

Only after feeling comfortable making investment decisions and performing properly on diversified portfolios over the long term of 1, 2, 3, 4, 5 years or more, should novice speculators attempt to make judgments and perform successfully on concentrated portfolios over the intermediate term of 1, 2, 3, 4, 5 months or more. For those new to stock trading or for those who would like an investment refresher course, the above topics are fully covered in *The Astute Investor* by this author—please see the bibliography for the specific reference.

Stock Market Stages

Correctly identifying with 95 percent certainty which of four stages the stock market is currently in is paramount to good speculating. The following four stock market stages are named and are referenced throughout this book:

Stage 1: Mark-Down – Downtrend
Stage 2: Accumulation – Bottoming
Stage 3: Mark-Up – Uptrend
Stage 4: Distribution – Topping or Rounding Over

The S&P 500 Index Nine Month Moving Average Trend Line with confirming indicators, as discussed in chapter 4 of *The Astute Investor*, are used to help determine the four stock market stages.

Do Not Rely On Luck

Speculators learn that correct speculating is not mere chance or luck but an activity relying on proper strategy, analysis, foresight, patience, character, discipline, good judgment and timely action. Thus, competing against those whose beliefs and methods rely on the luck of the market gives the advantage to astute speculators.

Practical day-to-day solutions to the problems of speculating are presented and Internet websites on where to find the appropriate data for speculators to run current models for themselves are specified. Fundamental speculative questions are asked which are vitally important to stock market traders and discussed next.

Speculative Questions

Stressing only the answers to stock market speculation is often short sighted. Speculators repeatedly find it more instructive to be taught the correct questions they should ask rather than to be given a momentary correct answer, such as in a market newsletter. The correct answers are only for a specific time and place, while the correct questions and solution methodologies transcend both dimensions and are universal.

The Astute Speculator helps speculators answer, for themselves, the following fundamental speculative questions:

1) What speculative principles are important?
2) Why is being a good short seller crucial in speculation and what are trigger points?
3) Why is the buy decision so complex and timing so critical?
4) Why is the sell or covering decision so emotional and how can trades be successfully completed?
5) What aspects of trading volume are vital when identifying turning points?
6) How can sectors and industries be used to help recognize intermediate-term speculative momentum?
7) What character traits do winning speculators have and what are the ten speculative bylaws for trading success?
8) What money management rules reduce risk and ensure a profitable retirement?

9) Why do speculative strategies have to be matched to each speculator's character, personality and lifestyle?

10) What are the strengths and weaknesses of participating in the futures and options markets?

Each of the chapter topics in *The Astute Speculator* support speculators by helping him or her answer the above fundamental speculative questions for themselves, as explained next.

Speculative Questions Answered

The following chapter synopses highlight the solution methodologies presented to allow speculators to answer the above ten speculative questions.

1) Speculative principles cover both the art and a science of speculation. The eleven key scientific speculative factors are presented and the three speculative arts and techniques for solution are explained. Learn why the stock market is called the "unbeatable game" and how it can be beaten. A stock market taxonomy is presented and categorizes the stock market for better communication and understanding.

2) The vast majority of speculators trade on the long side of the market. Astute speculators are encouraged to trade on the short side of the market, as well. Learn how to sell stock short at the appropriate time using trigger points.

3) The ability to "say no" to a stock purchase is key. Learn whether to buy now or later on, what type of stock to buy and what price should be paid. Patience is crucial when making the buy decision, learn why. Making a purchase commitment is more complicated but less emotional than concluding it. Learn why keeping a cash reserve is imperative.

4) Learn how best to sell or cover stock. Once having purchased a stock, it is emotionally difficult to sell it—even for professionals. The stop-loss order is certain protection against a speculator's human weakness when it comes time to sell or cover. The effect use of stop-loss orders is presented.

5) Price action indicates, whereas trading volume validates. Learn how to read the tape. Trend changes are anticipated by using price and volume transactions that show up on the tape. Turning points indicate a stock market losing intermediate-term momentum, either up or down. The first goal is to recognize the turning point and then to speculate on the correct side of the market.

6) Momentum speculating is different from momentum investing. Sectors and industries typically either lead, lag or are coincident with the overall stock market's long-term trend, consequently, the intermediate-term momentum of stock may be determined. Industry high and low rankings help specify the leading stock within the industry that should be purchased or the lagging stock that should be sold short.

7) The character traits of the best speculators are specified. Astute speculators should follow the speculative bylaws when trading. Why using simulator trading is a good first step when practicing is explained. Start with limited funds to reduce emotional stress when trading with money, only when successful, graduate to trading in round lots.

8) Money management issues force speculators to prepare for possible trading downside losses. Money management rules focus on position size or how many units or shares should be acquired in relation to the total amount of risk capital available to the speculator. Money management is about determining the risk of the trade based upon the percentage of the total risk capital put into each trade. Focus speculating, drawdown, emotional trading zone and calculating the reward-to-risk ratio are explained.

9) How each speculator responds to the pressures of trading in a volatile stock market is unique, therefore, it is required that each speculator devise a speculative strategy that works best for their character, personality and lifestyle. The three strategies presented are: 1) panic or contrarian specialist; 2) box theory; and 3) tandem trading. Each speculator may select one of the presented strategies to implement, or mix and match different aspects of the three to find a strategy that works best for themselves.

10) Futures and options exchanges are described. Different call and put strategies are explained. Good options strategies with the possibility for unlimited gain and for limited loss are recommended. Why the futures and options markets are problematic for astute speculators is explained.

Who Should Purchase This Book?

This book should be purchased by:

1) Speculators who need to understand a seemingly puzzling and enigmatic stock market, and those who desire gaining essential trading knowledge grounded in the science of speculation.

2) Those who desire a systematic approach to stock market speculation that includes becoming an expert investor first. Speculators learn important website addresses and how to find current data on the Internet to do the necessary model calculations for themselves.

3) Speculators who demand more than just description and theory; but, also how best to gain practical experience.

4) Financial services professionals who are required to fully comprehend and explain the stock market to their clients.

It is difficult to know with certainty exactly what the stock market is going to do, however, probabilities are put in the speculator's favor by purchasing, reading and correctly implementing what is presented in *The Astute Speculator*.

Website Commands

Current market data are vital for speculators to run speculative models for themselves. Therefore, websites with defined commands necessary to find specific current data and information are identified in bold letters. The website logon address is given first and then, as explained in the brackets, where to look on the computer screen is given, or what to click on, or as sometimes required what to type in is also specified. The following is an example:

> **Logon:** http://finance.lycos.com
>
> **Where:** [Where to look on the computer screen (e.g., on the top heading, along the left column, or in the main body) and the name of what to look for]
> **Click:** [What specifically to click on the computer screen to find the next screen or the necessary data]
> **Type:** [Sometimes it is required to type in information]

Many steps may be required, consequently, the **Where, Click** and **Type** instructions are frequently repeated.

Bibliography & Glossary

The Astute Speculator incorporates the essential speculative wisdom from classic, practical speculative books and journal articles which are presented in the bibliography section. This saves individuals considerable time when learning how to speculate in the stock market. The glossary contains a financial dictionary of speculative words. Speculative principles are discussed next in chapter 1.

1

Principles Of Speculation

Introduction

S PECULATION IS DEFINED. The similarity of stock market
speculation to business speculation is presented. Stock market
speculation over the intermediate term is both an art and a science, learn
the eleven key scientific speculative factors and the three speculative arts
that determine success.

Why the stock market is inefficient, and therefore necessary, is
emphasized. The importance of markets and exchange to the welfare of the
economy is explained. Why stock market speculation is a socially necessary
profession responsible for directing funds to high value opportunities, i.e.,
the leading companies in the highest ranking industries, is highlighted.

Stock market speculative theories and principles are presented. The
stock market is called "the unbeatable game," ironically, the stock market
does not beat speculators, instead, learn why it is the speculators' unique

unreasoning instincts that cause their own failure. How speculators should counteract their natural but incorrect trading tendencies is explained.

Speculation Defined

Speculate, from Webster's dictionary, is derived from the Latin word "speculari" which means "to spy out, look out, observe and examine." A speculator is a risk taker who contemplates the past, present and the future, understands a priori what objective and subjective truths portend—using premises without benefit of scientific experimentation—has vision into the future and acts to position himself or herself properly prior to an uncertain but expected end result.

Speculation first occurs on a philosophical or perceptual level and then progresses to a practical or commercial reality. Speculators take responsibility for their actions and strive to be included in the "knower group" rather than be in a sheepish crowd of simple "believers" who follow others' opinions.

The following are required for speculative success, speculators must: 1) know and properly analyze objective and subjective truths affecting the nature of the endeavor and its expected outcome; 2) interpret correctly what this analysis means and arrive at a prudent judgment; and 3) take proper action to successfully apply and accomplish practical or commercial endeavors—balancing patience with swift action is often necessary during step 3.

Business And Stock Market Speculation

The American dream of achieving a better life through hard work, daring and resolve is alive and well in the United States (U.S.). Consequently, Americans, by their temperament, are risk takers and naturally love to speculate. There is nothing unique about speculation, it takes place in many fields of business that are new to the individual just beginning the enterprise.

A speculative opportunity may be identified in agriculture, mining, manufacturing, retailing, the arts, or the stock market. The new product, process, marketing and financial conditions are systematically analyzed and determined to be beneficial and lucrative for the speculator. Because the business endeavor is new, it may seem hazardous; but, the expectation is that the new product or service is either wanted or necessary and has the probability of profit when presented for sale in the marketplace.

Americans speculate regardless of the risks, as a result, using laws and legislation to protect speculators from attempting seemingly unwise endeavors is impossible. Since the way is open for all Americans to speculate, it behooves all speculators to acquire as much knowledge prior to attempting the speculative task to secure the best chance for success.

The probability for business success increases exponentially by the amount of pertinent understanding speculators have prior to the commencement of the speculative act. Stock market speculation is but a subset of business speculation and perhaps requires the most specialized knowledge for persons to be successful, as discussed next.

How Business And Stock Market Speculation Are Alike

The underlying rule for success in the stock market is no different than in any commercial enterprise. One's speculative profits depend, like any store merchant, on the ability to sell purchased goods at a higher price than acquired. Therefore, common stock should be thought of as a speculator's merchandise.

This principle applies to real estate, retailing and all lines of business, not just on Wall Street, and the objective is simple—"buy low, sell high." Consequently, it is best only to buy common stock with sound fundamentals that are going up in price and are expected to be sold at a profit. Promotion is important in business as well as the stock market, as explained next.

Business And Stock Promotion

Businesses get customers to purchase goods and services at higher prices by advertising and promoting the benefits of these products and services. Any flaws in the products or services are only reluctantly discussed and even then, only with a positive spin to present any drawbacks in the best possible light.

Promotion is also used in the stock market. On Wall Street, the most effective promotion takes place in the news media, therefore, speculators take advantage of this fact by using correct buying and selling trigger points based on the daily news, as discussed in chapter 2.

Markets Are Required

Economic society develops markets, typically where people congregate in towns and cities, to aid distribution through exchange. Markets, at a specific location or under the auspices of an institution, determine where buyers and sellers may come together to transact business. Markets bring order out of disjointed hit-or-miss exchange operations. Speculative exchange differences make markets necessary.

Exchange is the engine of social progress. Exchange takes place between people and the natural physical world, as well as solely between people. Production of products or services and distribution at exchange markets are symbiotic, production cannot exist without distribution at exchange markets and distribution at exchange markets cannot exist without production. Cooperation via exchange is cultivated between people and nations and is a major force unifying the world.

Speculators are necessary for the proper functioning of exchange markets. Business speculators attempt to equalize the exchange of the business supply and demand, and by so doing the resulting price range is smaller and fluctuations are less abrupt than they would be without speculative activity. The stock market is but a subset of exchange markets and is never in equilibrium for long, as explained next.

Stock Market Disequilibrium

A stock market always in equilibrium and therefore efficient is unattainable. Grossman and Stiglitz explain that it is impossible for the stock market to always be in equilibrium and therefore efficient because traders have different endowments, beliefs and preferences. Therefore, the stock market is not in equilibrium for long, nor is it efficient.

Human progress constantly throws the economic supply and demand equation out of balance which then becomes the speculator's challenge. The inefficiency of the stock market not in equilibrium is good for astute speculators, because, stock positions can now be exploited to earn outsized returns.

If exchange markets were always in equilibrium and efficient, markets would not be needed. A government agency is all that would be required to set quality, quantity, delivery and price conditions for every commodity, product and service needing distribution. Even during wartime, markets are required, i.e., government price control agencies do not work well for long—as explained next.

Why Markets Are Required: An Example

John Kenneth Galbraith (1908-2006) is the "price czar" administrator of wage and price controls at the Office of Price Administration during World War II. Price controls grew more and more controversial as industry representatives began complaining long and loud about Galbraith's price setting during the second world war.

The process of setting wages and prices by government fiat became increasingly dysfunctional and, consequently, Galbraith is forced to resign in 1943. Galbraith says of his experience, "I reached the point that all price fixers reach, my enemies outnumbered my friends." Markets are impersonal and ensure that managers respond rapidly to unbalanced conditions where the resulting new prices communicate necessary future production, distribution and exchange operations.

Stock Market Speculation

The speculator's challenge in the market is that human progress constantly throws the economic supply and demand equation out of balance. Intelligent stock speculation is both an art and a science and is not frivolous gambling but a reasoned endeavor to foresee and profit from an economic future state of affairs.

The stock market is only a barometer that registers what political-economic conditions are likely to be. A security market does not cause what happens in business, in government, or world affairs, but is merely a financial record of coming events.

Speculators should always be looking forward to visualize what will happen three-to-six months into the future and not fixate on past or present events. This separates speculators from business managers and those in government who because they are focused upon current conditions are often blind-sided by sudden changes.

Stock Market Musical Chairs

Participating in the stock market is a little like playing a children's game, i.e., musical chairs. When the music is playing and the chairs are not needed they seem plentiful, therefore, the game is easy and even enjoyable for all to play.

Similarly, when the good financial and economic news is in the media, speculators walk around with "stock not for sale signs"—stock bids at higher and higher prices seem plentiful. But let the pleasing financial and economic good news stop, then speculators rush to sell all at once and the high-priced stock bids are pulled away and there are not enough bids for all except at appalling low prices.

This is the importance of anticipating the end of the wonderful financial and economic good news, prior to its ending. Looked at another way, it is also important to begin speculating by purchasing stock before the good-news starts. Knowing when to get in or out of a stock position, in relation to promotional financial and economic news, is the speculative key.

Stock Market Speculation Requires Foresight

Stock market speculation is a venturesome, risky and deliberate choice made in a timely manner with the belief that an extraordinary profit may be expected. Speculation requires foresight into coming expected events, correct observation, the intellectual exertion of planning and scheduling, knowledge of political-economic conditions, arriving at proper conclusions and then taking timely action.

The investing public does not look forward to foresee coming events in the stock market but concentrates, instead, on past stock prices and the current financial and economic news. The present conditions are made the only benchmark, consequently, daily financial and economic news does not move the stock market as expected by the investing public. By this process, stock market movements are characteristically promoted by the daily news leading to crowd or herd behavior.

When greed or fear gets the upper hand and the ignorant and unsophisticated, who look upon the stock market as little more than a gigantic gambling casino, begin to trade impulsively—losses almost assuredly follow. Comprehension of correct stock market speculation reduces emotional stock trading risk to a minimum.

What Defines A Good Stock Market Speculator?

The stock market requires research to delve into the facts that eventually determine stock price movements. Speculation is not merely blind luck, which is the province of gambling, but making expenditures on enterprising positions where risk is effectively reduced to a minimum.

The "when" of buying or selling short is more significant in determining speculative profits than the "what" to buy or sell short or the price, i.e., the "how much" of the transaction. Timing of the purchase or short sale is the primary speculative art, or the "art of arts." Speculative profits in the stock market are first the result of precise timing when buying or short selling, second, the result of what to buy or sell short, and only third, the transaction price.

Patience when speculating in the stock market is often overlooked, but is paramount for success. It is worthy of note that a correct conjecture by a speculator on a common stock is easier to attain on Wall Street than having patience when speculating. Allowing a beneficial major stock price move to play out completely requires infinite patience and staying power.

Speculative Outcomes Vs. Expectations

Worldly wealth increases at a slow measured pace while speculators assume that their speculative stock positions will increase in value at a higher compound growth rate. Consequently, the growth of worldly wealth does not match speculative expectations. Therefore, speculators are required to be proactive to be successful in earning above average returns at reduced risk in the stock market.

Absolute safety and surety in life as well as in the stock market are imaginary, they do not exist. The New York Stock Exchange (NYSE), National Association of Securities Dealers Automated Quotation (NASDAQ) and American Stock Exchange (AMEX) make available a regulated, impersonal setting for the trading of stock. Speculative mistakes should not be blamed on the stock exchanges.

If speculative outcomes do not match expectations, it is necessary to change one's approach to the stock market. Thinking in the same inferior rut produces speculative losses, consequently, to change results for the better, speculators should improve their thinking based on correct stock market knowledge. Amateur speculators often have misplaced beliefs, as discussed next.

Amateur Speculators

Tyro speculators look at the whirling stock market and begin to concoct fantasies of great wealth. The callow speculator quickly makes a bet on a stock that is recommended by a market pundit on the nightly news, by an investment strategist reporting in a newspaper or newsletter, based on a "hot tip" from a friend, or they purchase on price-to-earnings ratios that they have been taught are a good indication of a company's value. The new speculator then says, "Even when the stock price declines initially, I hold on until the stock makes money." This tyro investment strategy ultimately leads to disaster for as many as 95 percent of new speculators.

Eventually the stock price declines below the purchase price and our fearless—only because he or she does not know any better—novice speculator holds on for a while but eventually sells out near a market bottom in a fit of panic selling. At that point all the profits and maybe most of the speculator's principal are lost and our now fearful speculator feels that the stock market is overly risky, mysterious and not to be trusted. Many sold out tyro speculators, after this sad experience, vow never to return to the risky stock market again.

The royal road to success is not possible in other forms of business and is certainly not possible on Wall Street, either. The initial monetary stake when speculating need not be large, what is vitally important, however, is that speculators begin trading with the correct stock market knowledge.

Market's Siren Song

The siren song to new stock market speculators is to make a vast amount of money in a short space of time, all while risking a small amount of capital and without having to work very hard. Amateur speculators desire bragging rights for an easy road to financial riches and are almost invariably disappointed when their haphazard dabbling in stock speculation, instead, loses money.

New speculators, without a basis for understanding the stock market, get drawn into an advancing overall stock market and find it easy to make money on paper. It becomes exciting to make money by speculating and novice speculators begin to believe that they have the whole speculating problem solved and wonder why no one else has recognized the obvious solution. But this naïve winning condition does not last for long.

Amateur speculators are particularly susceptible to trading with money needed for living expenses and, consequently, do not have a clear mind. Speculating with money required for pressing needs, such as, for the doctor, paying credit cards or the landlord, should not be attempted. Many amateur speculators trade who cannot afford to lose, consequently, they become frightened at the first perceived sign of trouble and begin to trade impulsively which invariably leads to disaster.

Common stock held by the investing public and amateur speculators are in "weak hands" because they trade on impulse. Weak handed crowds are easily spooked into doing the wrong thing at the wrong time because crowds scarcely think, but instead, react impulsively. Amateur speculators often look at speculation as just gambling, which it is certainly not, as presented next.

Stock Market Speculation Is Not Gambling

Stock market speculation, when performed properly, is not gambling. With gambling, contrived and needless risks are artificially created for escape, entertainment, or for the most likely reason, the need for action. The possibility is for financial gain with immediate gratification, typically with poor odds for the player and advantageous odds for the house or casino.

Stock market speculation, on the other hand, is a socially necessary endeavor. Production, distribution and exchange risks are already present in the economy, the only question for a businessperson is, "who shall assume these risks?" Speculators bear risks that business persons wish to lay off on others. Unlike gambling, both sides of a stock market trade may profit from the exchange over a period of time.

Stock market speculators take risks because their judgment convinces them they will profit by their actions. Speculators' knowledge, experience, character and courage are tested in the stock market and by their action the collection of capital for industrial use is made more secure and the overall economy is served.

Efficient Market Hypothesis

The efficient market hypothesis (EMH) and random walk theory of stock prices, where it is assumed that speculating in the stock market is like betting on American roulette in a giant gambling hall, is scientifically proven to be incorrect (please see Prentis (forthcoming)). Unfortunately, amateur speculators continue to falsely believe that stock market speculation is simply gambling.

Gambling in the stock market is absolutely the wrong way for amateur speculators to operate. Rather than fearing that a small run-up in a stock's price will be lost, one should hope that a small profit will eventually become a very large profit. Rather than hoping the stock once down in price returns to its purchase price, one must fear that a current small stock loss will develop into a major loss.

Amateur speculators have things turned upside down, i.e., they hope when they should fear and fear when they should hope. Learn to fear that a small loss will turn into an large loss, instead of being a risk taker during a stock price decline. Learn to hope that a small profit will turn into a large profit, rather than being risk averse during a stock price advance.

The correct policy is: 1) keep the stock position for a large gain only when winning; and 2) when losing, only lose a small amount. A taxonomy to understand the overall stock market is presented and explained next.

Stock Market Taxonomy

The stock market taxonomy is first presented in *The Astute Investor* and the subject material in categories 1, 3 and 4 are covered there, i.e., how to use an asset allocation, dollar-cost averaging, buy-and-hold strategy to invest over the super-long-term of 20 years or more, and in the S&P 500 Index and common stock of individual companies over the long-term of 1, 2, 3, 4, 5 years or more.

Table 1 – 1: Stock Market Taxonomy category 6, the shaded area, is the subject category addressed in this book where speculative decisions on common stock of individual companies over the intermediate-term of 1, 2, 3, 4, 5 months or more is the focus.

Table 1 – 1: Stock Market Taxonomy

S&P 500 Index	Individual Company Stock	Time Dimension
1 ***	2	Super Long-Term: 20 Years or More – Use Yearly Data
3 ***	4 ***	Long-Term: 1,2,3,4,5 Years or More – Use Monthly Data
5	6	Intermediate-Term: 1,2,3,4,5 Months or More –Use Weekly and Daily Data
7	8	Short-Term: 1,2,3,4,5 Days or More – Use Daily and Hourly Data

*** Categories covered in *The Astute Investor*

The X axis depicts the S&P 500 Index and individual common stock. What can be said about the S&P 500 Index versus an individual common stock is different due to the differences in their systematic and unsystematic risks. The Y axis is the time dimension on Table 1 – 1, covering super-long-term, long-term, intermediate-term and short-term planning horizons.

Graphs & Charts

Graphs and charts present a historical picture and are a good way to visualize what has occurred on the stock tape. Perspective and the use of monthly charts are recommended for long-term decisions concerning the S&P 500 Index.

Weekly charts include more historical data on one chart at a single glance than daily price charts. Consequently, the perspective of a weekly chart is recommended for intermediate-term decisions on common stock of individual companies.

Use weekly Japanese candlestick price charts with trading volume bar charts to get a good picture of common stock intermediate-term pattern recognition. Watch for double top or bottom or head and shoulders top or bottom reversal patterns. Also, higher highs, higher lows, and lower highs, lower lows are easier to identify on weekly charts.

Support and Resistance

Support is that point on the graph or chart where the price decline holds as buyers materialize on the downward price reaction. Resistance is that point on the graph where the price advance stops as traders begin selling on the upward price bulge. Support and resistance are further discussed in chapter 5 as a result of potential supply and demand for stock.

Resistance becomes support, if instead of sellers appearing, the price significantly, by more than one percent, breaks above the previous resistance level. Thus, in a long-term and intermediate-term upward sloping market, higher highs and higher lows are in evidence.

Support becomes resistance, if instead of buyers, the price significantly, by more than one percent, breaks below the previous support level. Thus, in a long-term and intermediate-term downward sloping market, lower highs and lower lows are in evidence.

Support and resistance levels revealed on weekly charts, and then on daily charts to confirm specific price levels, are important when setting stop-loss order price points. Use intraday prices rather then closing prices when setting stop-loss order points, as explained in chapter 4.

Speculative Theory

Stock market speculation is an effort to reduce risk through knowledge and then to balance being suitably venturesome without overreaching. Unfortunately, human nature errs on the side of making fools of ourselves in groups and being too timid when on our own. To fight timidity, gain the knowledge necessary to proceed with courage when acting alone. Resign yourself to be humble in the face of the stock market, but not be beaten by it.

The stock market should not be thought of as a frivolous game that is dependent upon luck, but a serious endeavor that through the speculator's efforts help determine the well being of a public company, an industry and the overall economy. The duty is upon the speculator to select the most promising stock positions and to set economic priorities which help shape future social conditions.

Speculators want both to beat the stock market game and to feel they are special in some way. Perversely, speculators often use the same mistaken procedures that others have used so that they can feel somehow superior and prove themselves extraordinary. Do not fall prey to this losing impulse. Instead, learn what successful speculators have employed in the past to beat the stock market, as discussed here, and then feel comfortable using these time-tested winning techniques yourself.

Play To Win

To be a successful speculator requires the mindset to play to win rather than to take a strictly defensive position of playing not to lose. Buying seemingly safe stock, based on conventional wisdom or on surface conditions alone, is normally a terrible mistake. The fear of losing, looking silly and losing face are strong in all of us, however, letting these non-rational and irrational emotions dominate our speculative operations is speculative suicide.

One way speculative profits are achieved on Wall Street is to trade in good common stock and buy when no one else wants these shares and sell when everyone else does, i.e., simply be a nice person. Mayer Amschel Rothschild (1744-1812) perhaps said it best, "I buy cheap and sell dear."

Astute speculators do no sit passively by and wait for something good to happen, instead, they train their eyes and/or ears to recognize opportunity coming just before it arrives. When stock market speculative opportunity is recognized, reach out and grab it for your advantage. This is accomplished when speculating on Wall Street by reading, understanding and properly implementing the strategies and techniques presented here.

Speculation: Both Art & Science

Stock market speculation is both an art and a science. The scientific method helps achieve the goal that science desires which is objective truth and knowledge. Art is, or should be, imaginary or creative use of truth, knowledge and facts to produce subjective or desired social awareness, change or effect.

Art is best employed when what is artistically presented is beautiful and/or entertaining and seems more real and/or advantageous than reality itself, so as to persuade the audience what might be achieved upon acceptance of the artistic vision. The intended social progress is best accomplished by using an artistic approach that seems natural and does not draw attention to itself or said in another way, "Art that is so artful, it's artless."

Astute speculators are shown how to excel at both the art and the science of speculation. Scientific analysis for speculation in the stock market requires the study of the following eleven key speculative factors:

1) Knowing the difference between systematic risk versus unsystematic risk.

2) Knowing what stage the overall stock market is in and knowing the long-term stock market trend.

3) Determining whether the stock market is either undervalued or overvalued.

4) Yield curves, interest rate spreads and what affect they have on the stock market.

5) Knowing the political-economic conditions and how they affect the stock market.

6) Appreciation of human nature and trader psychology.

7) Understanding how the investing public responds to the news and the discounted news theory (DNT).

8) Knowing crowd psychology and when to be contrarian.

9) Intrinsic, true, or fair value and the margin-of-safety multiple calculations for common stock evaluation.

10) Understanding the discounted market hypothesis (DMH).

11) Identifying industry rankings and intermediate-term trends using turning points.

All of the eleven key scientific speculative factors are clearly presented in *The Astute Investor*, by following the practical ten-step method for investment success, or in this book.

The three speculative arts are crucial to becoming a successful stock market speculator. When mastered, the following speculative arts help ensure stock trading success:

1) How to time stock buying or short selling over the intermediate-term using turning points and trigger points.

2) How to sell or cover a stock position by taking the emotion out when using stop-loss orders and money management rules.

3) Knowing yourself and what strategy will work best for you based on your character, personality and lifestyle.

The methodology for approaching and techniques for solving these three speculative arts are presented here so that astute speculators can make money in the stock market. The practical approach to solving the three speculative arts should be internalized so the mastering of these speculative arts, while extremely difficult, looks effortless to outsiders and astute speculators feel natural while trading.

Thinking Vs. Action

The public may be divided in those who delight in thinking and those whose main aim in life is action which may be defined as "the soul of progress." While the distinction often blurs, those who make the best speculators love to both "think and to act."

Speculation is an intellectual pursuit requiring correct thinking and analysis and, as importantly, requires a person with energy who has the will power to act properly in a timely manner. The successful speculator has self-control and manages his pursuits with ease. Correct methodology is the watchword and the reliance on "luck" is ridiculed. A correct balance of determination versus flexibility is required to profit from stock market trends, fluctuations and changing conditions.

A Wall Street saying is appropriate, "Bulls make money, bears make money, but hogs get butchered." It is careless to remain in a stock position beyond the cutoff point warranted by the risk entailed. However, there should be no reason to sell a stock that has done nothing wrong. Balance is key, do not overreach.

Accurate speculative theories are budding facts, the worth to the trader lying solely in their appropriate application. For stock market speculators, Rene Descartes (1596-1650) puts speculative success another way, "It is not enough to have a good mind, the main thing is to use it well." The correct application or proper implementation of the theory during trading is most crucial.

There are an infinite number of ways to fail, but only a very few ways to make something a success—especially in the competitive field of stock market speculation. How to find the winning approach that works best for you is discussed next.

What Is Needed To Win In The Stock Market?

Speculating in the stock market is a numbers game. Even if the speculator is an expert, only approximately six stock trades out of ten earn money. The requirement here is to let the winners run and only sell winning positions if the stock does something wrong, i.e., the stock behaves poorly. For the expected four out of ten stock losers, sell them quickly for small losses.

Speculators make the trends in the market and normally borrow money when going long and borrow stock when going short. As interest rates increase, the cost and therefore the difficulty in borrowing money triggers speculative sales, and when borrowing stock is a problem this triggers speculative buying. Thus, the importance of knowing about stock float and how interest rates affect the stock market—as discussed in the next chapter.

To be an astute speculator requires permanently graduating from the gambler class to the professional class which requires using intelligent foresight, good judgment and following a written plan and schedule. Speculators who are correct in the stock market have two things going for them: 1) the fundamentals of the speculative situation; and 2) speculators who are wrong. Persons in other businesses or professions typically are poor stock speculators, as presented next.

Other Professionals Find Stock Speculation Difficult

Persons with commercial training and experience in other businesses or professions, e.g., mining, retailing, manufacturing, or the arts, and the legal, academic and medical professions all have difficulty translating their area of expertise into practical stock market success. Commercial business or a professional knowledge and skill set does not automatically translate into success when buying and selling common stock, an example follows.

Enron Bankruptcy Example

Kenneth L. Lay, founder, chairman, director and chief executive officer (CEO) of Enron Corporation presided over, as this is written, the second largest corporate bankruptcy in U.S. history, on December 2, 2001, of approximately $63 billion dollars. Lay was found guilty on securities and wire fraud and conspiracy for lying to investors about Enron's corporate well being prior to its scandal-ridden collapse. Those responsible at Enron caused many billions of dollars of investor losses and took away the retirement savings and employment of their workers.

Reportedly, during Enron's final months, Lay had most of his investments in Enron stock even though his financial advisers requested he diversify his holdings. During the trial, Lay's defense said that fraud was not the real reason for Enron's demise but the stock was brought down because of short selling and bad news reports. Lay seemed delusional, blamed the messenger for his problems and when the castle-in-the-air perceptions (discussed in chapter 2) collided with the reality of a recession and bankruptcy—stock market reality clearly prevailed.

What happened at Enron is inexcusable, management has a duty to know what is going on within their companies and to be forthcoming with shareholders. However, it is interesting to note that top business persons seem blinded to their own business conditions, and additionally, know relatively little about the stock market.

Insiders often hold on to their corporation's stock even when it is clear to stock market professionals that their stock should have been sold long ago. Lay probably remained overly optimistic about the company he founded and continued to maintain high expectations while fighting for Enron's financial survival. Ken Lay did not see because he did not want to see and probably did not know what to look for in the stock market, in any case.

Consequently, the required undoing of the businessperson or professional's current market beliefs and then special training are often necessary for success when trading in the stock market. Business persons in the financial services industry who keep up to date with interest rates, credit conditions, political trends and the business situation are typically the most successful part-time speculators.

Speculative Principles

The stock market is pure capitalism at work. Astute speculators should never think of the stock market as a overly friendly place where everybody wants everyone else to get rich, in fact with two sides to every trade, the truth is just the opposite. Instead, be a cynic concerning everyone's motives and intentions in the stock market. The stock market game is merciless and played by professionals using survival instincts that are always complex and sophisticated.

Speculative professionals have the advantage when playing against the investing public, because, the investing public typically does the wrong thing at the worst possible time. However, the game is balanced because professionals risk their great wealth by relying on their judgment of future political-economic conditions.

The stock market is populated by speculators whose actions keep enormous amounts of money vigorous, liquid and available. Speculators, not the investing public, determine the intermediate-term trends in the stock market. To operate profitably, it is the speculators' duty to direct funds to high value opportunities when purchasing stock, e.g., the best companies in the highest ranking industries.

Speculative Goals: +33 Percent Per Year & Retain Profits

The basis of stock market speculation is to increase capital by exchange alone, without benefit of material or labor, which makes it an intellectual pursuit. Speculation requires the formulation of theories based on facts, assumptions based on observations, correct premises, and coming to a conclusion using reasoned inference concerning the underlying forces that determine future stock prices. This is the proper development of market foresight making the stock market a discounting mechanism.

The speculator's approach, whether over the long-term or intermediate-term, is to be in step with the market trend by either purchasing or covering short positions on declines and selling or selling short on price bulges.

This requires immense courage with the ability to act in a timely manner based on knowledge and judgment.

A challenging but reasonable goal when speculating is to earn three times the average super-long-term S&P 500 Index return of approximately +11 percent per year, i.e., +33 percent per year. Try not to overreach, to expect to earn more than +33 percent per year, especially in the beginning of a speculative career, is unrealistic. Once the money is earned, the second goal and real end game requires retaining the profits by using stop-loss orders and money management rules.

Stock Market Imperfection

The stock market is an imperfect game, it is impractical to live up to a standard of perfection. Market timing, i.e., expecting to purchase common stock at the very bottom price and to sell at the very top price on any intermediate or long-term move is impossible. Speculators, do not chastise yourself for not being able to do the impossible. Feel comfortable in being close enough and attaining the more secure middle two thirds in any market move.

Rather than expecting perfection in our stock market operations, think in terms of predicting the future based on conditional probabilities. Astute speculators expect to put the probabilities in their favor prior to making a commitment, but then live graciously with the results.

Nothing is achieved by being greedy and attempting to secure 100 percent of the stock market gain on any intermediate or long-term move. Think of any price range movement as a yardstick—be pleased to capture the center twenty-four inches. The famous and very successful speculator, Mr. Rothschild, never tried to time the exact bottom or top of a market move; but instead, always wanted and planned only for the fair middle portion.

Keep The Mind Clear

Keeping the mind clear, balanced and unprejudiced is paramount for trustworthy judgment. To be successful in the stock market requires not fixating on the fear of losing. Outside pressures of fixed time limits, debt, or bills needing payment directs the speculator to attempt, either consciously or unconsciously, not to lose rather than to win which is a sure path to defeat. Stress clouds the mind and adversely affects trading performance.

A clear mind allows for speculative market-poise which is a belief and confidence that market action will result in a profitable outcome. A speculator with poise possesses dignity, equanimity and steadiness while dealing with the stress of emotional stock market circumstances.

As an example of an unclear mind, a famous speculator experienced continuous heavy losses which unnerved him and he could not think clearly. He felt he was being influenced by rumors, tips and outside influences, therefore, he quarantined himself away from everyone else. Orders were sent to the stock trading floor, but no communication from any outside source came in to him except through a stock tape machine. The isolation method worked to clear this famous speculator's mind and his profitable trades, as a result, resumed.

Go Long Or Short, As Conditions Demand

To be an astute speculator requires the flexibility to go both long or short as market conditions demand. If speculators feel they must be either long or short all the time, this makes them an underdeveloped one-way speculator and change is required. A biased long or short mindset makes speculators' judgments unqualified because they are colored by a preset long or short opinion.

Being either in a long or short position sways the speculator to that side of the market because, subconsciously, our judgment supports our actions. Instead, speculators should forget their current stock position. If long in a declining market, sell. If short in an upward trending market, cover. Only one speculator in a thousand is so proficient as to completely conquer the effect that his or her long or short position in a stock exerts upon his or her judgment and resulting actions.

Human Impulses

Human impulses cause speculative calamities. Speculators should never act rashly or impulsively, but instead plan and schedule everything necessary to reach their speculative goals.

Successful traders have to control their feelings, disregard hopes, fears and greed and consistently follow a plan and schedule of operation that works for them. The speculative position should be well thought out and entered into unemotionally, with composure and with forethought.

Study your own character with an eye to compensate for routine mistakes of judgment. If too impulsive, learn or even force yourself to reflect and wait an extended period prior to making another commitment. Triumph or losses in the stock market rests squarely on the speculator's character and personality, as discussed in chapter 8.

Snap Judgments

Amateur speculators make snap judgments on faith based on market surface appearances without forethought or a plan. Consequently, naïve speculators operate blindly and often blame Wall Street for mistakes they bring on themselves.

Surface appearances on Wall Street are deceptive and often contrary to what is actually occurring. Instead, look for the undercurrents that determine the true force and core tendencies in the market. Train yourself to examine the obvious which repeatedly goes unnoticed and to study the past for clues about future conditions.

Ironically, for novice speculators without the necessary knowledge, doing the exact opposite of what their inclinations and snap judgments dictate earns them money. Said another way, the uninformed need to be seemingly illogical to earn money on Wall Street.

Do Not Take Tips

Sentimentality and the stock market are not compatible. Just because the person giving you a tip is an old school friend, relative, or in a position of authority is no reason to rely on their judgment. The stock market is a pure form of capitalism—enter into it with a minimum of trust in others, a reliance on yourself and with your eyes wide open.

A successful stock trader looks behind the news by employing scientific analysis, making calculations and being skeptical of all opinions. Each speculator basically receives the same news and information, consequently, winning or losing on Wall Street is determined on how the news and information are interpreted and utilized.

Speculating, to do it properly, requires an enormous amount of time to think about and plan. Profits are not assured on Wall Street, many give their professional lives to the stock market without making a living at it. It is futile to blame others, tip taking, or the stock market for mistakes you make yourself. Instead, use any misstep as an object lesson and try never repeat the same mistake twice.

Stock Journal

Speculators should study the market behavior of stock market indexes, industry indexes and common stock by keeping accurate daily journal records. Intrinsic value, market value capitalization, bargain value, margin-of-safety multiple and the ten additional crucial factors should all be known and evaluated for each stock position entered into (please see chapter 6 in *The Astute Investor*).

Keeping a written journal forces planning prior to making a commitment, reduces problem trades and promotes speculative poise after the decision is made. A tangible document is now available to reference and to record profits and losses. Going through the planning and scheduling process in a journal guards against making impulsive decisions which normally result in trading disasters.

Record significant actual events in your journal, i.e., the daily opening, high, low and closing price data, the trading volume data, why the trade was entered into and why it worked or did not work. Along with volume data, record volume in terms of dollars, i.e., the number of shares traded that day times the stock's price, to get better feel for the dollar volume figures.

Keep track of the reasons why a stock was purchased and later sold, try to determine why a trade either did well or lost money. Serious study of the market is required in order to make a success of stock speculation. Because a very limited number of people are willing to work hard by thinking and keeping a journal, success in the stock market goes to the few.

Write down in a journal all the pertinent data, results, reasons and conclusions to try to improve your future trading technique. Trading memory is notoriously unreliable and trading information is too important not to write down. An undependable memory often results in large speculative losses.

A journal is an enormous help in making the infinitely more stressful sell decision, i.e., determining when to exit a long or cover a short position. Knowing exactly why a stock is purchased or sold short is an important factor in knowing when to end the commitment. Being able to describe in writing if the trade is either profitable or not and why, often determines if and when the stock should be sold or covered.

Use Cash Accounts

Cash accounts are preferred to margin accounts for purchasing common stock. Margin money is lent by brokerage firms to traders, often at a high interest rate. Carrying charges of interest and other expenses are, in addition to commissions, charged to the margin account holder. Consequently, speculative profits are hard to come by when using brokerage margin accounts.

The securities in the margin account act as collateral for the loan and are listed in the Street or nominee name, and can be lent out to short sellers by the brokerage firm which may not be in the speculator's best interest. Those in a long stock position using margin are at the mercy of their creditors which clouds their judgment.

Margin accounts at brokerage companies typically are too expensive and should be avoided. Astute speculators, instead, should open a cash account at a discount brokerage firm when purchasing stock.

Chronic Trading

New speculators are drawn to the stock market by fantasies of easy riches. The attraction is so alluring that speculators feel compelled to chase the latest price move and, accordingly, trade constantly. Stock market success, however, is only determined by the amount of money made and kept, not by how frequently stock trades are made.

Novice speculators are obsessed with the idea of having their money working all the time. Incorrectly, they believe that being out of the market is a sign they are not working hard enough. Regrettably, this strategy is sure to fail because no one can do better than the market by always being invested.

Speculators often expect too much too quickly from their operations in the stock market. A speculator may be able to beat a particular stock or the market for a period of time, however, it is impossible to beat the stock market all the time. Always being in the market and having to continuously play the game is a sure way to be average, at best.

To trade stock just because cash is at hand is an inexcusable blunder. Speculators do not need to always be in the stock market to earn outsized profits, if fact, the only way to earn outsized profits is to trade sparingly. The better strategy, resulting in higher returns, is to wait until the probabilities are in the speculator's favor prior to making a commitment. Instead, concentrate on the correct timing for buying and selling the best stock at the right price.

Chronic trading is an easy habit to fall into. A large stock market profit makes even the most professional speculator believe they are invincible and they quickly try to duplicate their recent fantastic gain. The endorphin rush to a speculator that comes from making a killing in the stock market inspires immediate duplication. Aggravatingly, in accordance with the Law of Compensation, the largest stock loss often comes right after the largest stock gain.

After an immensely profitable trade, take at least a week off from trading while you carefully plan and schedule your next move. Do not rush back into trading with reckless abandon, or profits will disappear. The market is ongoing and if a good opportunity is not here today, one will surely arise tomorrow or next week.

Also, a spate of poor trades may cause the speculator to be overanxious in trying to recoup their losses all at once. Traders typically trade in larger amounts to quickly earn the loss back. Speculators should recognize they are getting into an agitated condition and are over trading. Instead, clear the books by going to a neutral cash position and take some time off to clear the mind. When trading resumes, trade very small amounts of money until you again have a winning tradition.

Many brokerage firms designate chronic traders as active traders who are required to make a minimum number of trades per month so that a maintenance fee is not charged to their account. To feel pressure to trade clouds the mind and is detrimental to successful trading. Do not relinquish the management of the number of trades per month by agreeing to a fixed schedule of trading instituted to benefit a brokerage company.

It is futile to try to force the market to produce excessive profits through chronic trading, instead, only buy into an expected large gain at the right time. Being patient and letting cash remain in a neutral cash position is preferable to "always being invested," as discussed next.

Neutral Cash Position

A neutral cash position allows the speculator to view the market through an unbiased lens without having a stock position to justify. Trade only on real opportunity which is clearly seen and judged with a focused mind best attained by being in a neutral cash position while the pressure is off. Knowing and following this rule is the difference between amateur and professional speculators.

When the stock market is not acting correctly and a speculator has grave doubts, sell or cover at the market and go to a safe neutral cash position. This is described as being in a non-action position. Being out of the market may be stressful because of the feeling of not being part of the action and maybe missing something, however, nothing will be lost either.

When the market does not look or act right, get out immediately. When speculators are trading cold and things just do not seem to be going their way, accept this and go to a neutral cash position. Periods of being in a neutral cash position are unquestionably constructive for the mental well being of every speculator.

During critical points, judge the stock market and an individual stock both by what happens as well as by what does not happen. If the stock market or a stock is acting in an uncharacteristic manner, that is a clue to future price action and perhaps a good reason to remain in or now be in a neutral cash position.

Never go directly from a long position to a short position without first going to a neutral cash position. Impulsive chronic trading without having a well thought-out plan is almost certain to fail. Planning and scheduling takes time and effort but are necessary for success. A trader who permits being rushed into any market decision will undoubtedly regret it.

Do not push the market to your schedule. If the market is doing something that you are not comfortable with, go to a neutral cash position and sit back and just watch. When the market is enigmatic, know not to participate.

Trader's Market

No well defined upward or downward long-term trend is in evidence during a trader's market. A trader's market occurs during two distinct market stages: 1) during stage 4 when distribution is ongoing at a market top as the market transitions from a long-term upward trend to a long-term downward trending market; and 2) during stage 2, as the market transitions from a long-term downward trending market to a long-term upward trending market and accumulation is ongoing.

A trader's market is also in evidence during one or more intermediate-term moves that run counter to the overall movement during a stage 3 long-term advance and during a stage 1 long-term decline. Look for trader's markets and analyze them by watching for the price to breakout of the trading range on increased volume and then go with the trend.

Know whether it is a long-term upward trending market in stage 3, then buy on the reactions and sell on the bulges. Rather than hoping to catch the exact market top, sell all stock on extraordinarily active bulges to lock in profits when the market seems to be in its "roman candle stage."

During transition stage 2, astute speculators prefer to buy on the reactions and sell on the bulges. The accumulation of stock during stage 2 is an excellent time to sell stock when the bulges occur. Do not feel that stock prices will get away from you at this stage. If the mistake of buying on a bulge occurs then the stock will have to be carried during the next one or two reactions which cuts into trading profits.

During a general long-term decline during stage 1, sell short on the bulges and cover on the reactions. And during transition stage 4, prefer to sell short on the bulges and cover on the reactions. During stages 2 and 4, whenever in doubt concerning uncertain conditions, quickly go to a neutral cash position to clear the mind.

Floor Traders

The focus here is on speculating in corporate stock of individual companies experiencing intermediate-term swings in the market. It is felt that exchange members or floor traders have the best opportunity to speculate successfully in short-term swings of 1, 2, 3, 4, or 5 days or more in a particular stock because they do not pay commission costs.

Short-term stock market movements are typically just daily chatter, or trader caprice. Trying to catch short-term trends for an individual stock is difficult and best left to floor traders who have all day every day to watch the market. Also, short-term trading in individual stock shares promotes chronic trading which astute speculators shun.

Off-floor speculators may be tempted to perform short-term day-trading with acceptable results for awhile. However, it is felt that over many years time the short-term in-an-out activity will shred the speculator's confidence and not leave the mind clear for more potentially successful intermediate-term trading.

Intermediate term moves are more reliable and dependable then short-term daily stock market chatter. As long as stock positions are protected using calculated stop-loss orders, daily unexpected price fluctuations are less material to intermediate-term market success.

The Unbeatable Game

Wanting to beat the stock market which is often called "the unbeatable game," seems universal. The adage on Wall Street is, "The market does what it pleases and proves the greatest number of traders wrong in the process."

Market prices, especially on the down side, may change, in only a few days, more than a few years worth of stock dividends. Consequently, speculative stock price changes merit waiting for rather than simply selecting high-dividend common stock for purchase.

Speculators, if expert, can beat a certain stock or group of common stock for a period of time. However, it is impossible for a speculator, no matter how good, to always beat the stock market. What that means is that speculators who are chronic traders and always in the market taking positions, can never do better than the stock market because they are the stock market. In order to do better than the stock market, speculators have to bide their time in a neutral cash position and buy or sell short common stock only when all the crucial factors are judged to be in their favor.

The readiness and strength of character to keep money in a cash account until just the right opportunity comes along is a major factor in the ability to earn excess returns in the stock market.

Our Most Formidable Competitor Is Ourselves

Astute speculators are competing with the investing public, with amateur traders and with professional speculators, who presumably are knowledgeable about their vocation, but in the final analysis the most formidable competitor that we have is ourselves. The ways to lose are many because we defeat ourselves, the ways for us to win are very few indeed.

Speculators often beat themselves out of profits because as human beings, we are subject to all the human frailties. Also, because we are all different, we have to find a style of trading that matches our own character, personality and lifestyle which is discussed fully in chapters 8 and 9.

How much stress a speculator can handle should be analyzed prior to starting to trade. Review your emotional trading zone, as discussed in chapter 7, to determine the stress level that you can tolerate. For those fitful traders who cannot sleep at night, the adage on Wall Street is, "sell down to the sleeping point."

Ironically, in the final analysis, the stock market never conquers the speculator. Rather it is the speculator's own unreasoning instincts and inherent ruinous predispositions that cannot be prevailed over that are ultimately the catalyst for his or her speculative failures.

Computer Graphs

Computer graphs are important when speculating. A typical graph or chart is developed using Google Inc. (GOOG) as an example. Custom graphs are developed using the BigCharts.com & MarketWatch.com research and investment website. As this is written, the Quotes Tab when clicked brings speculators to a computer screen that allows for stock symbols to be saved so that selected price quotes can be retrieved whenever requested. The News Tab is a link to MarketWatch.com for all the latest investment news.

The Industries Tab brings speculators to ranking lists of the ten-best and ten-worst Dow Jones industries. The Historical Quotes Tab is useful when a stock's prior volume and pricing information are required for previous dates. The Big Reports Tab identifies common stock with the largest price or volume percentage changes and those hitting 52 week high or low prices.

For the purpose of *The Astute Speculator*, the Home Tab is required and automatically accessed when the speculator logs on to the Internet website for BigCharts.com & MarketWatch.com at http:// bigcharts.marketwatch.com. To create the Google Inc. weekly Japanese candlestick price graphs with 10 and 40 week moving average trend lines and trading volume bar charts, logon to the BigCharts.com website to retrieve current market data that are vital for speculators to run investment models for themselves.

Website individual commands, as this is written, necessary to find BigCharts.com & MarketWatch.com current data and information are identified—first, where to look on the screen is given, then either what to click on or what to type in is specified. First, look to the right-hand column to get started—and after the sample chart is pulled up on the screen—all of the information is found in the left-hand column to properly setup the BigCharts.com & MarketWatch.com computer site.

Logon: http://bigcharts.marketwatch.com

Where: Right Column – find My Favorite Charts
Click: The Red Sample Icon
Where: In the left column find the white box labeled Enter Symbol or Keyword
Type: GOOG

Click: The dark blue "time frame" box (if not already opened)
Where: The white box labeled Time
Click: The blue down arrow at the right side of the Time box or the box itself
Where: In the resulting drop-down list find 1 Year
Click: 1 Year

Where: In the white box labeled Frequency
Click: The blue down arrow at the right side of the Frequency box or the box itself
Where: In the resulting drop-down list find Weekly
Click: Weekly

Click: The dark blue "compare to" box
Where: In the white box labeled Index
Click: The blue down Arrow at the right side of the Index box or the box itself
Where: In the resulting drop-down list find <None>
Click: <None>

Where: The white box labeled <u>Symbols</u> is left empty

Click: The dark blue "indicators" box
Where: The white box labeled <u>Moving Averages</u>
Click: The blue down arrow at the right side of the
<u>Moving Averages</u> box or the box itself
Where: In the resulting drop-down list find SMA (2-Line)
Click: SMA (2-Line)

Where: Just to the right of the above <u>Moving Averages</u>
box (may have to move slide to the right at the bottom
of the column to see this box) there is a separate small
white box that is not labeled
Click: The mouse cursor in this small white box to
allow the typing of:
Type: 10,40 (Only these two numbers, separated by a
coma, should now be in this small white box – remove
any other numbers if listed)

Where: The white box labeled <u>Upper Indicators</u>
Click: The blue down arrow at the right side of the
Upper Indicators box or the box itself
Where: In the resulting drop-down list find <None>
Click: <None>

Where: The white box labeled <u>Lower Indicator 1</u>
Click: The blue down arrow at the right side of the
<u>Lower Indicator 1</u> box (may have to move slide to the
right at the bottom of the column or the slide down
along the side of the column to see this box) or the box
itself
Where: In the resulting pop-up list find Volume near the
top of this list
Click: Volume

Where: If <u>Lower Indicator 2</u> and <u>Lower Indicator 3</u> white boxes already indicate <None> skip to "chart style," if not continue:

Where: The white box labeled <u>Lower Indicator 2</u>
Click: The blue down arrow at the right side of the Lower Indicator 2 box or the box itself
Where: In the resulting pop-up list find <None>
Click: <None>

Where: The white box labeled <u>Lower Indicator 3</u>
Click: The blue down arrow at the right side of the Lower Indicator 3 box or the box itself
Where: In the resulting pop-up list find <None>
Click: <None>

Click: The dark blue "chart style" box
Where: The white box labeled <u>Price Display</u>
Click: The blue down arrow at the right side of the <u>Price Display</u> box or the box itself
Where: In the resulting drop-down list find Candlestick
Click: Candlestick

Where: the white box labeled <u>Chart Background</u>
Click: The blue arrow at the right side of the Chart Background box or the box itself
Where: In the resulting drop-down list find Default
Click: Default

Where: The white box labeled <u>Chart Size</u>
Click: The blue down arrow at the side of the <u>Chart Size</u> box or the box itself
Click: Medium, Large, or Big (i.e., the largest size that best fits your monitor)

To Draw the Google Inc. Chart:

Where: Go back up to the top of the column (may have to move the slide at the side of the column up)
Click: In the big red box labeled "Draw Chart"

Once setup, speculators should save the above settings on http:// bigcharts.marketwatch.com so the Google Inc. graph can be easily redrawn with new or current data whenever requested. To save the newly created Google Inc. graph for future updating and use:

Where: Along the top of the GOOG Chart highlighted in blue find add to favorites
Click: add to favorites

Where: An Add Favorite box appears and in the white box
Type: Astute Spec
Click: OK
Where: My Favorite Charts box appears
Click: OK

To check if the chart is properly saved:

Where: Along the top of the GOOG Chart highlighted in blue find list favorites
Click: list favorites
Where: My Favorite Charts computer screen appears
Click: The Red Icon in the Astute Spec box.

On the computer screen a weekly graph of the Google Inc. should now be visible, with the 10 week moving average (MA) trend line represented by a orange line and the 40 week MA trend line shown in blue. The computer graph represents weekly price data using the figurative Japanese candlestick charting technique. Trading volume is the Lower Indicator bar chart.

BigCharts.com & MarketWatch.com, when appealed to by the author, does not as a rule grant permission to reproduce their website graphs for use in other publications. Consequently, the graphs presented in *The Astute Speculator* are produced using Microsoft Excel.

Graph 1 - 1: Google Inc.

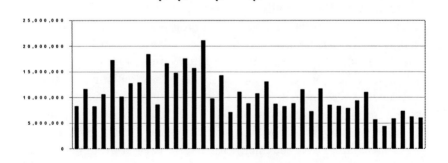

10 Week MA Trend Line (Dashed Line)
40 Week MA Trend Line (Solid Line)

Graph 1 – 1: Google Inc. is shown above for weekly data from August, 2005 to April, 2006. The intermediate-term trend is upward with the 10 week moving average (MA) trend line identified as the dashed line and the solid line representing the 40 week MA trend line. Trading volume, represented by bars in the lower half of Graph 1 – 1, increases significantly during the fast run up in Google's stock price during October and November of 2005.

Summary

Speculate, from Webster's dictionary, is derived from the Latin word "speculari" which means "to spy out, look out, observe and examine." The underlying rule for success in the stock market is no different than in any commercial enterprise, i.e., "buy low, sell high." Common stock should be thought of as the speculator's merchandise, only buy common stock with sound fundamentals that are going up in price and are expected to be sold at a profit.

The "when" of buying or selling short is more significant in determining speculative profits than the "what" to buy or sell short or the price, i.e., the "how much" of the transaction. Timing of the purchase or short sale is the primary speculative art, or the "art of arts." Astute speculators should feel comfortable going either long or short, as conditions demand.

Speculative differences make markets necessary. A stock market always in equilibrium and therefore efficient is impossible because traders have different endowments, beliefs and preferences.

Speculation is a socially necessary profession. The speculator's challenge in the markets is that human progress constantly throws the economic supply and demand equation out of balance. To operate profitably on the long side, it is the speculators' duty to direct funds to high value opportunities, i.e., the best companies in the highest ranking industries.

Amateur speculators hope when they should fear and fear when they should hope. The correct strategy is: 1) keep the position for a large gain only when winning; and 2) when losing, only lose a small amount. Stock market speculation over the intermediate term is an effort to reduce risk through knowledge and then to balance being suitably venturesome with not overreaching.

Do not engage in chronic trading. Keep the mind clear, human impulses cause speculative calamities, instead, plan and schedule everything necessary to reach a financial goal. Keep a journal and list the reasons a stock is purchased and later sold, try to determine why a trade either did well or lost money. Challenging but reasonable goals when speculating are to earn three times the average super-long-term S&P 500 Index return, i.e., a speculative +33 percent per year and then be able to retain the profits which is the end game.

Stock market speculation is both an art and a science. Scientific analysis for speculation in the stock market requires the study of eleven key speculative factors. The three stock market speculative arts are: 1) how to time stock buying or short selling over the intermediate-term using turning points and trigger points; 2) how to sell or cover a stock position by taking the emotion out when using stop-loss orders and money management rules; and 3) knowing yourself and what strategy will work best for you based on your character, personality and lifestyle.

Wanting to beat the stock market which is often called "the unbeatable game," seems universal. Ironically, in the final analysis the market never defeats us. Rather it is the speculator's own unreasoning instincts and inherent ruinous predispositions that cannot be prevailed over that are ultimately the reasons for his or her speculative failures. To change your success rate, change your beliefs and stop thinking in an intellectual rut.

2

Short Selling

Introduction

SELL HIGH, BUY LOW describes the correct procedure when short selling. Speculators typically trade on the long side of the market. Astute speculators should trade, at the right time, on the short side of the market, as well. The three steps in a long-term downward sloping stock market are presented, how to sell short on the first technical rally is explained.

Stock sold short has to conform to Securities and Exchange Commission (SEC) regulations. Buy ins and short squeezes are downside hazards for short sellers who should know the stock's float, short interest, short-interest-to-float and short-interest ratio prior to taking a short position.

Short sellers use 10-K and 10-Q reports to analyze the corporation's business plan and to identify crucial financial numbers to monitor. Why short sellers have the advantage over security analysts on Wall Street and the six telltale signs of a short-sale stock candidate are presented.

Speculators should delay shorting a weak stock until reality, either good or bad, is confirmed at a trigger point. Trigger points represent a fulfillment of what is expected and help with speculative short-sale timing. General Motors Corporation (GM) is analyzed and expected trigger points on when to short its stock are listed and discussed.

Most Speculators Trade Long, Not Short

The American investing public and most speculators, in their heart, feel more comfortable trading on the long side of the market rather than on the short side. Americans in general are optimists, believe in progress and in the future prosperity of the American economy. During a long-term downward trending stock market the investing public, if they are not forced out in a margin call, typically only waits and hopes for things to improve—as explained next.

Investing Public

The investing public almost always shuns market trading except for a stock advancement and generally believes that short selling is very risky, incomprehensible, unpopular, unpatriotic and unnatural. In addition, during economic contractions when the stock market is in a long-term downtrend, reduced economic activity results in falling stock prices highlighting the retrenchment of all aspects of money making—including stock market speculation.

It is estimated that 99.8 percent of the investing public trades on the long side of the market when buying and selling common stock. As this is written, reportedly only 29 mutual funds, out of approximately 12,500 mutual funds available to the investing public, trade exclusively on the short side by selling stock shares short and/or by purchasing put options (options are discussed in chapter 10).

Consequently, approximately 99.8 percent of the investing public hopes, expects and roots for stock prices to increase. When a stock moves below the investing public's purchase price, they typically wait for the stock price to recover in price to get out even, perhaps over a period of four years, or they get out of their position during a panic selling at a long-term market low.

When common stock come off their price highs, after a long-term market climax, the public assumes the stock is on sale at a bargain price and will purchase stock over an extended time period with the expectation that stock prices will quickly regain their prior price peaks. This, incorrectly, is the investing public's attempt to "buy low and sell high" which ultimately leads to speculative losses.

Selling at a loss wounds the investing public's pride and saving face is the most important consideration for most investors and speculators. The investing public and amateur speculators concern themselves with not looking foolish in front of others and especially, to themselves.

Saving face or high self regard is what 99 percent of those trading on Wall Street try to protect, even to the detriment of making money. Astute speculators, on the other hand, should learn to value money more and to protect capital through good defensive play which is explained in chapters 4 and 7. How speculators operate on the short side of the market is explained next.

Short-Sale Speculators

A very high percentage of speculators trade on the long side of the market, as well. A March, 2006 report from the NYSE at www.nyse.com gives the following data: the NYSE market capitalization is $13.9 trillion dollars; the average share price is $37.55; the total number of NYSE shares outstanding is approximately 370 billion shares; and the total short interest on the NYSE is approximately eight billion shares.

Consequently, as this is written, the NYSE reports only about 2.2 percent of the total number of shares outstanding have been sold short. Therefore, the vast majority of all investors and speculators trade on the long side of the market.

Consequently, since approximately 99.8 percent of the investing public and 97.8 percent of speculators are on the long side of the market, short sellers have to wait for those long to help with stock selling before shorts can earn a significant amount of money selling stock short. There are many hazards with short selling which have to be understood prior to entering a short-sale position, as discussed next.

Short-Selling Caveats

Short sellers have the moniker "plunger" because a corporate stock's price can drop sharply in a very short period of time. The timing of the stock price plunge is always the major issue, i.e., many short sellers have gone broke in the interim while waiting for their stock panic day to arrive.

Selling short is risky and can be economically hazardous. Long stock positions can only lose -100 percent of the investment if the price drops to zero. Persons selling short must revisit the stock and purchase an equal number of shares they previously borrowed at the then current market price. Common stock may increase in price by +500 percent or more, consequently, being liable for unlimited risk justly frightens stock market participants, so shorting common stock is only infrequently used by the investing public as well as by speculators.

Crowds may be comforting to longs on long-term stock advances, however, nothing is more perilous for shorts than to have too much additional short-sale company crowding into their short-sale positions. Consequently, short sellers are typically tight lipped about stock they are currently selling short.

Super-Long-Term Investors

Over the super long term of twenty years or more, long investors are more likely to make money than short sellers because the United States continues to progress and grow economically which eventually enhances future corporate values. The expanding economy and human progress ensures higher earnings and shareholder profits over the super long term. Consequently, it is said, "A habitual short seller is an eventual loser."

The habitual short seller repetitively takes a position against human progress. This gives rise to the saying, "Do not sell America short." The short seller's outlook is on the side of calamity, mishap, management duplicity and incompetence rather than being confident of a measured enhancement of business dealings and U.S. political-economic conditions. The correct time to be an optimist or a pessimist concerning the stock market's outlook is discussed next.

Optimists Vs. Pessimists

Traders who are always on the short side of the market are perpetual pessimists who fail to recognize positive political-economic conditions. Pessimists seem always to be finding fault and worry about all the possible bad things that may befall companies or the overall economy. Stock valuations always seem too high in the opinion of the permanent short-sale trader. Predictably, even when permanent pessimists have good reasons for their position they, like Cassandra from Greek mythology, are generally ignored.

Speculators who are always long are eternal optimists about the stock market condition and never see a market top. As high as stock prices rise, it is felt they will continually increase in value. Because ceaseless optimists are always long in the market, reasons for staying long are always sought and, consequently, believed. Billions of dollars are made on a long-term upward market move, only to have it lost during the long-term market reversal. Synthetic optimism as a market comes off its long-term top price is often spread by politicians and business persons, as explained next.

Synthetic Optimism

Synthetic optimism should first of all be recognized and then guarded against by astute speculators. The timing of this synthetic optimism is usually after the first major stock market price break coming after the long-term market peak high and prior to the beginning of a long-term economic downturn.

When the news is full of synthetic optimism about the stock market or the economy, be wary. Political and business leaders usually are so involved with present day worries they do not have time to perform a clear-sighted political-economic evaluation, and therefore, cannot foresee the future correctly.

Normally, an optimistic political-economic prediction is what the public wants to hear anyway—so rosy scenarios are freely given by politicians and business leaders. Rather than listening to politicians and business leaders, after the first major stock market price break, depend on the S&P 500 Index Nine Month Moving Average (MA) Trend Line to supply evidence as to the market's condition, as explained next.

S&P 500 Index

Rely on the stock market as a discounting mechanism, represented by the value weighted S&P 500 Index which is a broadly diversified portfolio of the foremost U.S. companies selected based upon market capitalization size, common stock trading liquidity and from all the S&P industry groups. The S&P 500 Index has only systematic risk and responds solely to overall political-economic conditions and not to the unsystematic risk associated with an individual company.

The direction of the S&P 500 Index Nine Month Moving Average (MA) Trend Line reflects the analysis, judgments, decisions and actions of millions of stock traders who are properly situated to see everything, hear everything, and generally, to know everything. The S&P 500 Index Nine Month MA Trend Line is scientifically proven to help identify long-term trends and stages in the stock market.

The time to be a pessimist or a contrarian is at a market top, when the S&P 500 Index Nine Month Moving Average (MA) Trend Line turns down. Be assured that this foreshadows a future wide-ranging weakening of the economy—perhaps in the next six-to-twelve months. This is the time that the longs will be helping the shorts by selling their positions in response to the now poor political-economic news.

Short-Sale Traders

"Sell high, buy low" describes the correct procedure when short selling. The same objective as long buyers follow, however, the actions are in reverse order. Short sellers constantly test the long stock positions and the direction of the market to find the truth of the market.

The speculator, on the short side, is planning to profit from a drop in the stock's price. An astute short seller is skeptical of conventional wisdom and uses facts, analysis and good judgment to make timely short trades. A cool temperament, a clear mind, iron nerve and the courage to act properly are the main attributes of a successful short seller.

A major market break begins in a market that may be characterized as peaceful or even tranquil, followed by an unexpected swift panic of plunging prices. Once a long-term downward sloping market is underway, all stock market sectors and industries are sooner or later dragged down in price.

While short selling is very difficult, successful short traders make large profits more quickly than long traders because it typically takes a long-term downturn only half the time necessary for the preceding long-term upturn. Stock market history records colossal fortunes made swiftly by going short in common stock in times of panic on Wall Street. Sadly, the number who manage to retain their outsized earnings are few—they give it all back and then some. How to guard against this common peril is explained in Chapter 7: Money Management. Why short-sale traders are often unjustly maligned is discussed next.

Short Sellers Vilified

Selling short is considered un-American and just not nice by many. Short sellers are often vilified by the investing public and by politicians, especially after a stock market crash. This has happened in the past and is expected to persist in the future.

Politicians have outlawed short selling, beginning with the Dutch in 1610. Napoleon Bonaparte railed against short sellers, thought their actions treasonous and had the Paris Bourse prohibit short selling. Germany outlawed short selling in 1897.

In the United States, short selling was outlawed in 1812 and restricted in 1864. President Hoover tried to investigate whether short-selling raids occurred in the great stock market crash of 1929 with the assumed short-selling goal to impair his presidency.

Fortunately, all of the above short-sale restrictive laws were later rescinded as unworkable. Even today, as we saw in the Enron example presented in chapter 1, short sellers are unreasonably vilified. Just the opposite is true, however, short selling is necessary to a viable stock market—as discussed next.

Short Selling Vindicated

The NYSE economist J. Edward Meeker, in his book *Short Selling*, explains and astute speculators concur that without short selling, markets would be even more volatile then they are currently. Short selling deflates boom-bubble buying at market tops and buying to cover creates trading liquidity at panic-selling market bottoms.

Bernard M. Baruch also believes that short selling calms market prices, and it is the individual short-seller's judgment that is being tested rather than the operations of an unfair manipulative short-selling cabal. Baruch goes on to say that restrictive short selling laws cannot protect traders from themselves. Short sellers, instead, help the markets, as discussed next.

How Short Sellers Help The Market

A large short interest in a stock offers support during its price decline as traders cover their positions. A considerable short interest represents underlying buying power that otherwise would be unavailable during times of panic. Investment grade stock issues may break badly and have five points between sales while common stock with a large short interest will typically experience an orderly price decline.

Market makers, specialists and block traders regularly sell stock short to increase liquidity in the stock market. These professionals, in an attempt to reduce price volatility, increase stock trading supply using short selling. Even speculators making short-sale mistakes help the market, as explained next.

How Speculators Make Short-Sale Mistakes

A speculator who has sold out a position in a stock and then goes short is responsible for a large percentage of the short interest in a stock. This is human nature working against being able to make money in the stock market.

An amateur speculator may purchase a stock at $30, sell it at $40 and then watch it advance to $75. The speculator's pride is vexed and decides that the company must be very overvalued and therefore shorts the stock. Wanting to get "even" in the stock, the object is to hold it until it declines to $40. Every reaction is cheered and every advance deemed a mistake. Perhaps the speculator is obligated to cover at $95, but whether a profit or a loss, the speculator is drawn to the short sale in order to save face.

The short-seller's "will to believe" vanity is destructive to the speculator's pocketbook, but helps the stock market's liquidity and contributes to a more orderly market.

Being Either Consistently Long Or Short Is Dangerous

Both the consistent short seller and long trader eventually come to pain and misery because they are unaware when to cease speculating on their preferred side of the market. Success on the favored long or short side of the market generates a mental bias that over a period of time is almost impossible to overcome.

Prejudices blind perennially long or short speculators, consequently, political-economic danger signals are missed. When growth seems constant in the economy and stock prices rise higher and higher, remember that "trees do not grow to the sky." Everything in the span of human events eventually comes to an end. Knowing when the end is and how to take advantage of it is the astute speculator's job.

Astute Speculators Trade Both Short And Long

Astute speculators feel comfortable trading on both the long and short side of the market, at the appropriate time. For speculators who attempt to make the long-to-short transition, be careful, often those who have completely sold out their long positions because they think the market is topping long term now expect that it is time to be short and secretly want everyone else to also think so. Correct timing for a long or short stock position is always the issue, as discussed next.

Technical Rallies

Normally, there are three steps in a long-term downward sloping market. The first step is the initial break where prices decline stunningly swiftly but soon recover during the first technical rally. The second step is a steady stock market decline as business conditions and earnings continually weaken. During the third step, terrible business conditions are evident to all—resulting in suspended dividends, bankruptcies, mass layoffs and talk about tax cuts by politicians.

The first technical rally, after a first step breaking long-term downward sloping market begins, lulls the investing public into a false hope that this decline is just temporary. After all, business earnings are generally still good and even increasing at many companies. This is where the investing public incorrectly attempts to "buy low and sell high" after the first break.

Rather, the first technical rally in a long-term down market is the safest time to go short. As the market rallies back close to its market high, the ability to short common stock at an advantageous price presents itself. Watch this first technical rally for a gradual reduction in total shares traded and the failure of stock prices to regain their prior highs, this is the indication that the next price trend will be down on much heavier trading volume.

Oversold And Overbought Markets

Technical rallies, during a long-term downward market, are the result of markets becoming "oversold." The short traders, who helped bring the market down, rush to cover while the long traders buy, as a result, they both plan to profit from a "quick turn" in the market. When most speculators have purchased stock and are long, the market is described as "overbought" and susceptible to an eventual reaction.

On good news, when the investing public is frequently buying on bulges, the professional speculator is normally making a short sale. Overbought and oversold markets are unbalanced equilibrium conditions that are soon rectified. The sharp rallies in a long-term downward trending market and abrupt reactions in a long-term upward trending market are the result of oversold and overbought conditions.

At the end of the long-term third step down in prices is when astute speculators should be considering purchasing stock. Cover any short positions if the market no longer declines on bad news or the S&P 500 Index Nine Month MA Trend Line begins to point upward. The mechanics of how a short sale actually takes place is presented next.

Short-Sale Mechanics

On the long side, when purchasing common stock, the stockholder is the owner and the shares may be delivered to his or her account. On the short side, common stock shares are borrowed from a brokerage firm and sold in the market to an unknown third party.

The short seller is required to pay all dividends paid on the stock to the account from which the stock is borrowed and to eventually return the stock to the broker. The short seller never takes possession of the stock which puts him or her in a rather precarious position.

Since a sale has taken place, cash is the result of a short sale. Large-scale professional short sellers have arrangements with their brokerage firms to pay interest on the short-sale cash balances in their accounts. In effect, large-scale professional short sellers are paid interest while they position themselves for an eventual stock price decline. Unfortunately, this same advantageous practice is not extended by brokerage firms to small-scale short sellers.

Regulation T

A short account at a brokerage firm must be a margin account and the short seller is required to supply at least 50 percent of the money for the short sale. The 50 percent margin limit satisfies Regulation T (Reg-T) of the Federal Reserve. The reason a margin account is necessary for shorting stock is because stock is being borrowed from someone else. This is similar to the concept for a margin account for long purchases where, instead, money is being borrowed.

If the price of the stock moves down, more stock may be shorted in the short position account. If the price of the stock moves up and the equity in the account falls to below 50 percent, this constitutes a restricted account and Reg-T requires the account to be brought up to 50 percent equity within seven days. If the equity in the short account further falls to 35 percent, typically the brokerage firm will make a maintenance call that requires the short account to be immediately brought up to 50 percent equity, or the broker will buy the shorted stock to cover the position. Brokerage houses normally place further limitations on accounts that short inexpensive stock priced below $5 dollars per share.

SEC Uptick Rule

Assuming the stock shares can be borrowed, the Securities and Exchange Commission (SEC) uptick rule 10a-1 of the Securities Exchange Act requires the short sale to take place on a plus tick (increase in price) or zero-plus tick (unchanged price) from a prior transaction price. A trade completed on a plus tick or uptick is prompted by the buyer while a trade on a minus tick is prompted by the seller.

The uptick rule restricts short selling in a declining market and prevents the shorts from forcing a stock's price straight down. The NYSE has a comparable uptick rule 440B which applies to member brokerage firms and specialists on the trading floor.

Due to the uptick rule, a stock price that is plunging in price on the tape should not be shorted "at the market" because it is likely to result in a very poor order fill price. Also, the uptick rule often causes the stock price to increase for awhile after a short order is executed, therefore, be prepared for that eventuality.

Buy Ins And Short Squeezes

Normally, brokerage fees for going short are the same or only slightly higher then when going long. Short sellers needing or wanting hard-to-borrow stock may have to pay as much as 15 percent of the total short sale amount to begin or to remain in the short position.

As more stock gets shorted in a particular company, the once easy to borrow stock may become hard-to-borrow. This is where the precarious hard-to-borrow short position becomes real, as discussed next.

Buy Ins

The first problem facing the short seller is that the stock wanting to go short on may not be available. A separate department at a brokerage firm is responsible for locating short-sale stock. Shares are borrowed from another customer's long margin account that has its stock in the street name of the brokerage house holding the certificates. There may be no stock shares available at that brokerage firm, causing the search to be expanded to other broker dealers on Wall Street.

A "hard-to-borrow" short condition indicates that this stock has a very limited floating supply. Float refers to the number of stock shares available to the public for trading. More on float later in this chapter.

With stock that cannot be borrowed or with a very limited supply available, the broker informs the short seller of required higher fees to remain short or warns that a "buy in" is now possible. Unless the short seller can locate stock to borrow on their own which is very unlikely, the brokerage house covers the stock on the short seller's behalf in the open market without the short seller knowing about the transaction until the next business day.

Often the buy in is done at the worst possible time in the market for the short seller. This may seem unfair, but buy ins are a reality. The covered stock is then returned to the brokerage firm that originally lent the stock and the transaction is now complete. Short squeezes are another hazard for short sellers, as discussed next.

Short Squeeze

Another downside to shorting hard-to-borrow stock is the "short squeeze" where those in long positions try to pressure shorts to quickly cover which results in a sharp stock price increase. Examples of events that can squeeze shorts are brokerage house upgrades, Wall Street buyout or merger rumors and intermediate-term swings in the market that go against the short position. Also, individual company management may get antagonistic toward short-sellers—as described next.

Companies may get proactive in trying to squeeze short sellers in the following ways: 1) they write to their stockholders of record urging them to move stock out of the street name so that shares may not be lent by brokerage houses and thereby creating a hard-to-borrow condition; 2) they contact major institutional holders to restrict lending with the goal of forcing buy ins; 3) the company purchases their stock on the open market in an attempt to increase the share price which may drive shorts out of their positions; 4) companies place large quantities of stock where it cannot be borrowed; 5) companies issue different stock classes such as A and B shares which have different voting rights; 6) companies declare a one time stock dividend at a critical point to try to force up the stock's price; and 7) companies announce a subsidiary sale, leveraged buyout (LBO) or possible merger.

Short squeezes are hazardous to the short seller and a very real possibility, consequently, the importance of knowing the stock's float, short interest, short-interest-to-float and short-interest ratio can lessen the possibility of this occurrence—as discussed next.

Float, Short-Interest-to-Float And Short-Interest Ratio

Float represents the number of shares in the investing public's hands available for trading, the higher the float the better the stock's liquidity and ease of shorting. A company with a large percentage of shares held by management or owners reduces float because they are less likely to trade their shares. Also, stock holders with brokerage cash accounts may not allow their shares to be shorted by removing them from the street name of their broker's borrowing account which further reduces float.

Buy ins and short squeezes are the reason that short sellers should know the float, short interest, short-interest-to-float and short-interest ratio prior to taking a short position. Since the stock market is always changing, brokerage buy ins and short squeezes are forever a possibility and should look to be avoided during the planning stage of a short-sale operation.

The pain in seeing one's short position price rise +25 percent in one day on suspected phony news can severely rattle a speculator's nerves. Buy ins and short squeezes almost never happen with large capitalized companies having a huge stock float and is the reason that astute speculators limit their shorting activity to these types of corporations.

An example of stock not to short are stock on pink sheets, because the float is normally very limited. Pink sheets are in fact pink and list wholesale price quotations, typically by one market-maker dealer, for usually small, low-priced stock companies in the over-the-counter (OTC) market. Low priced OTC common stock are highly risky and astute speculators, either on the long side or short side, should stay clear of them.

Short-Interest-to-Float

The total number of a company's shares that are currently sold short defines short interest. The short-interest-to-float is the short interest divided by the company's stock float. A high short-interest-to-float percentage is dangerous for short sellers because it shows that a large short position is already in the stock and short sellers, when putting on a short sale, prefer not to have too much short-sale company.

Short-Interest Ratio

A small capitalization stock with a limited number of shares outstanding with a small float may have a high short-interest which is the number of shares sold short but not yet covered or repurchased. The short-interest ratio divides the average daily trading volume into the short interest to show how many days would be required to cover all short-sale shares.

High short-interest ratio stock are more hazardous to sell short because the short position may be too crowded.

A better strategy for hard to borrow stock with small float is to use the options market. Unattainable stock that are hard-to-borrow or experience buy ins in the stock market may be available for a synthetic short on the options exchange, i.e., buying a put or selling a call, as discussed in chapter 10.

Short Selling

Timing is the primary speculative art and the "art of arts" and is called the short-sellers nightmare. Typically, the short-sale speculator sees many warts on a company's financial statement, a worsening market for the company's products due to increased competition and management turmoil—and incorrectly believes that it is also readily apparent to everyone else, consequently, the stock is shorted prematurely.

Mistakenly, the short position is put on only to have the stock remain in a close trading range for as many as two years. The speculator may take the short position off and then watch in horror as the stock suddenly plummets in price. To counteract untimely shorting, resolve to remain watchful but not overly farsighted when selling stock short. Ways to overcome the timing problem are discussed in "short sale trigger points," presented later in this chapter.

Overlooking Company Negatives

When economic times are good and money is easily available, company negatives are often overlooked. However, in inflationary times when money is being restricted by the Federal Reserve, Wall Street can and will abandon poor performing companies to their sorry fate.

It is interesting to note that companies go into bankruptcy not just because of company negatives, but also because the access of additional funds from Wall Street is denied. Also, shrinking Wall Street equity values during a long-term downward sloping market further restricts capital flowing into the markets, making bargaining for monetary access that much more intense, thus, increasing borrowing costs.

Selling Short And Market Stages

Always know what long-term stage the stock market is in and follow the long-term trend when trading, either long or short. It is estimated that the systematic risk of political-economic conditions that affect all equities account for 50 percent of a common stock's price. The industry that the company belongs to accounts for another 10 percent of its price. Specific unsystematic risk associated solely with an individual company accounts for the remaining 40 percent of its share price.

When the stock market is in Stage 3: Mark-Up - Uptrend, trade only on the long side of the market. During Stage 1: Mark-Down - Downtrend, trade only on the short side of the market. The trading markets of Stage 2: Accumulation - Bottoming and Stage 4: Distribution - Topping or Rounding Over may have both long and short trades but the preference is to be only long during stage 2 and only short during stage 4.

In this way, the overall political-economic conditions and systematic risk that make up approximately 50 percent of a stock's price are always in the speculator's favor and helping his or her long or short position. If things do not work out as quickly as planned when trading on the favorable side of the market, wait patiently for prices to move in the speculator's direction. The astute speculator wants all factors on his or her side, therefore, trade short only when overall market, industry and company circumstances are all weak.

Laggard Short Sale Candidates

Common stock to sell short, during stage 1 in a long-term downturn, are in troubled industries and are lagging second or third-tier companies facing stiff competition from an industry leader, have poor or even fraudulent management who cannot execute their business plan, practice accounting chicanery, have an outmoded product, flat or negative revenue growth along with rapidly increasing inventories, report negative earning surprises and have a highly leveraged balance sheet with massive debt. Any combination of the above negative points may be enough to make a laggard stock a short-sale candidate.

Common stock shares that have already fallen sharply in price and are very weak may be the best common stock to short. Rarely do weak low-priced stock of large capitalization companies rally significantly in price when the long-term trend in the overall market remains downward.

Short only overvalued widely held stock in weak hands or held by large mutual fund institutions and laggard companies with a large market value capitalization and a sizeable floating supply of stock that are easy to borrow. Preferred, also, are relatively few shorts in the issue and the stock currently making an all-time low price.

Watch the stock leaders that have pulled the market off its prior long-term lows, they are the first to decline at the next long-term market top and indicate that the market has entered Stage 4: Distribution - Topping or Rounding Over. It is preferable that once a long-term downward market has been determined, only short positions or neutral cash positions are maintained—any long stock positions at this time will only cloud and distract the mind which instead should be kept sharp, focused and clear.

Naked-Short Position

Stock sold short must conform to the following SEC requirements: 1) the exchange handling the trade must be informed that the order is a short sale; 2) the sale execution must be in conformance with the short-sale uptick rule; and 3) the brokerage firm handling the sale must have borrowed the stock to make delivery at the time of the sale.

During a naked short transaction, one or more of the above SEC requirements are deficient. Presumably, the most egregious short-sale rule broken is shorting without having first borrowed the stock, i.e., the stock is simply shorted with the borrowing function handled later by the brokerage firm.

Another description of the naked short is a position in a stock that is not hedged. If the speculator does not own the stock outright or does not own call options on the stock then the short position is termed naked.

Also, to sell short a security already owned in this year, to carry the tax gain forward next year for tax purposes, is a transaction called going "short against the box." The Internal Revenue Service (IRS) has rules which now makes this procedure much less profitable.

Amateur Speculators And Short Selling

To short stock successfully requires iron nerve to endure the stress of short selling which few amateur speculators possess. Amateur speculators typically sell stock too soon, capitulate and repurchase the same stock at a higher price, buy more stock as the price sinks during a market downturn and finally lose money by selling everything on an impulse at a market bottom.

Amateur speculators do not take the time to weigh facts, learn conditions, or think through the consequences of their actions. Ironically, data are plentiful—so much so that it overwhelms, misleads and confuses tyro speculators, consequently, they often give up looking for suitable information because they do not know where to look.

Amateur speculators believe that chance or stock tips dominate activity in the stock market, willingly overtrade on margin with inadequate capital, take profits too early, trade impulsively and become chronic traders because they love the action of trading. Amateur speculators work on incorrect theories or principles that are completely at odds with demonstrated successful practice and scientific research.

To be successful, stock market traders must either do the opposite or not do what the amateur speculators do. Speculation requires remaining suitably enterprising without becoming imprudent or ridiculous and the aspect of risk should be reduced and quantified in whatever venture is undertaken.

Good Times And Bad

During the stock market boom times in 1999, before the market crash during 2000-2003, experts and market pundits were telling the investing public that a "new era" was in place and that prior standards of stock price valuation no longer hold any validity, i.e., the stock boom should go on forever. Most people like being liked and the vast majority are naturally optimistic, therefore, the investing public wants to believe rosy prognosticators.

During times of economic uncertainty, the public craves assurances that everything will be all right. Government and business leaders' statements of optimism and upbeat falsehoods are carried in the press and on television to show that they are doing everything in their power to straighten things out. Leaders who did otherwise would be branded as defeatists, quickly replaced and berated throughout their lifetime by the majority of people. The crowd only sees what it wants to see and desires to take notice of only agreeable news in both good times and in bad.

Telling The Truth

Telling the truth in public is often dangerous to one's health. Many now celebrated truths, (e.g., the earth rotates around the sun, evolution of the species, love your neighbor as yourself) have resulted in disgrace, mockery, legal trials and even death for those brave enough to express these truths in public.

Telling truth to power is always risky and even inconvenient minor truths are often times reacted to harshly by those in charge. Consequently, take with a grain of salt everything one hears from politicians and business leaders just prior to an economic downturn when reality is often easy to ignore.

Instead, conclusions that astute speculators come to after looking at the facts and doing the requisite analysis are paramount for success. Learning what to look for when going short is imperative for professional short-sellers, as presented next.

Professional Short Sellers

Kathryn F. Staley explains that professional short sellers enjoy delving into the corporate financial statement numbers in 10-K and 10-Q reports and reading proxy statements that are sent along with the request for a signed proxy from existing stockholders prior to the annual stockholder's meeting with management.

The 10-K and 10-Q financial reports are submitted to the SEC and give details on the company's business plan. Professional short sellers match the financials to this plan to identify the crucial numbers to monitor. Key variables such as inventory buildup, debt to equity ratio, research budget, same store sales, asset liquidity and legal or political problems may be important, depending on the company.

Proxy Statements

Professional speculators thoroughly review proxy statements and SEC 10-K and 10-Q financial reports to find out about the current management and their possible exorbitant salaries, retirement programs, severance packages, stock option compensation, insider stock sales or purchases and the stance management takes toward the treatment of stockholders.

Proxy statements, if viewed over a series of years, identify management turnover which often goes unannounced in the media. If the proxy statement is poorly written and seems to obfuscate more than clarify, so that a speculator has to read the proxy statement more than twice, a good short candidate may be identified.

Investigate The Company

Professionals learn as much as possible about the company through reading newspapers, trade magazines and brokerage reports. Read the competitors' annual reports, ask competitors and vendors how good the company being investigated is. Read Value Line or Standard & Poor's industry information to put the company's information in perspective.

Make store checks to review décor, customer traffic and to talk with store managers. For companies dependent upon commodity prices, study the commodities market prior to shorting the company's stock. Check the institutional ownership percentage of the stock, if this number is very high, a stock price breakdown is expected to run concurrently with unanticipated poor corporate events. Know the stock's float, short interest, short-interest-to-float and short-interest ratio to determine how likely a buy in or short squeeze would be.

Journals

Professionals keep a journal of why a stock is shorted, what the anticipated profit is and what the downside risk is on the stop-loss order. The reward-to-risk ratio should be equal to or greater than four, expect to make at least four times what is being risked on the stop-loss order, as explained in chapter 4.

Short sellers, after making a mistake, should spend time and energy studying what went wrong, without recrimination, with the sole purpose of analyzing the trading mistake and how to improve in the future.

Why Short Sellers Are Secretive

Professional short sellers are a secretive lot, especially about their positions in common stock with float less then 10 million shares. Too many amateur speculators on the short side of a stock make the stock's price very volatile, which frightens the longs who do not participate by buying the stock to give price support, just when the speculator is attempting to establish a short position.

Normally, when a professional short seller informs the media about a good short-sale idea they are hoping for a quick break in the price as a result so they can cover their existing short position at a larger profit. Why security analysts are not, as this is written, a threat to professional short sellers is explained next.

Security Analysts

Professional short sellers have an advantage over security analysts on Wall Street because analysts, while handsomely paid to supply future earnings estimates, seldom bother to scrutinize financial statements. That is because security analysts are mainly compensated to support Wall Street promotional operations, not to argue by arriving at an independent decision based on in-depth analysis of 10-K and 10-Q reports.

Security analysts' reports are frequently merely the conduits of Wall Street's conventional wisdom and just pass along the corporate management's position. This leaves an opening for professional short sellers who delve into the accounting numbers and have the time and the skill to perform the necessary thorough investigations to form their own conclusions on whether to short a stock.

If reviewed at all, 10-K and 10-Q financial statements are read on Wall Street at a very slow pace. This leaves an opening for astute short sellers who know when the reports are scheduled to be issued, can review the key indicators quickly but carefully and can act on the information promptly.

Inefficient Markets

Investment bankers on Wall Street always seem to be pushing the purchase of common stock which makes the stock market inefficient. The investing public's predisposition to always acquire stock on the long side also offers no balance and results in an inefficient market.

An inefficient market gets out of equilibrium, consequently, the stock market typically responds dramatically to one or more of the three reoccurring Wall Street bugaboos: 1) inflation; 2) fraud; and 3) panic. How the news of a company's financial reorganization complicates the short sellers task is discussed next in short-sale trigger points.

Short-Sale Trigger Points

Trigger points help identify when to short a company's stock. A reason that short-sale timing is consistently poor is that Wall Street often continues to back a failing company by arranging for new financing and/or new business partners. This is economically desirable because the additional money allows management to revise the defective business plan for another run at success, but often causes consternation for short sellers already short the company's stock.

Also, the announcement of a corporate merger may spike the stock's price and force short sellers to cover their positions. The political-economic conditions could also change for the better and the half-dead company could return to life, thus, thwarting the short-sellers expected profits. Why timing is so important to short sellers is discussed next.

Timing, The Primary Art Or "Art of Arts"

Timing on Wall Street is the primary art or "art of arts." The major concern for speculators selling stock short is always "when," the "what" to sell short is always of secondary importance and the stock's price or "how much" is received for the shorted shares is only number three in significance. Many speculators have the story right but the timing wrong and, consequently, have lost all.

Timing of the short sale is the chief failing for short sellers. Being years early on a short trade position is common. The reason for this is that shorts see the problems that the longs want to overlook. The investing public, long on the stock, wants to remain forever hopeful even when the foreseen reality for the corporation or the economy is bleak.

The investing public is slow to sell their stock because they hope that things will eventually improve and they can get out even. The stock may stay overvalued for years in the face of no earnings, no markets, no products and no management expertise—until the longs finally have to come to terms with their untenable position and sell out in mass. This is the perception of the trader being at odds with the reality on Wall Street which is presented next.

Perception Vs. Reality

The short seller can identify a myriad of reasons why a stock is overvalued and should be sold short, but may invariably short years too early because the investing public, ever long and optimistic, believes and hopes that things will eventually turn out as advertised by Wall Street. In this case, the investing public's perception becomes stock price reality.

Most investors and speculators value pride of opinion over making money so when optimistic perceptions versus facts differ, facts traditionally get ignored. Setting a premium on always being perfect, vanity and the need of high self regard means that one's ego can never suffer humiliation at the hands of the stock market.

Astute speculators can wait for perceptions to become real and still make money because so many long investors and speculators cling to their illusions even in the face of obstinate, contradictory facts. Incorrect speculators in wrong long positions are reluctant to change their minds and give up hope and only sell at very low panic points after very large losses.

Even if an important event occurs that should change a stock's direction, often the price continues on unabated as before. Just because a speculator sees something real that should change market conditions does not mean that others see it at the same time or in the same way.

Momentum is now in effect, speculators and the investing public continue to buy, regardless of the new event, since that previously was the best course of action. An overvalued stock is only a short-sale candidate, wait for a trigger point to materialize prior to shorting the stock—as discussed next.

Trigger Points

Markets and stock prices can move based on perceptions and expectations for a better tomorrow over a long period of time. In order to make a major change in investor perceptions, a catalyst or trigger point is required.

Knowing the best time to short a stock involves recognizing its trigger point and then acting. Since the majority of the investing public and speculators are optimistic long position players in the market, rosy expectations are the norm which consistently trumps an expected poor reality.

When the economic conditions are positive and the patter from market pundits on Wall Street and on the news is reassuring, longs characteristically cling to their stock positions. It is almost better that the stock has declined from its peak price since the investing public thinks of themselves as investors and will want to hold on until they can get out of their position at least even.

Because there are so few short sellers in the stock market at a long-term market peak or during an intermediate-term bulge, the only way for shorts to win is to have the help of longs who are selling. Therefore, shorts should wait for a vehicle or a trigger point prior to selling stock short which is described next in trigger point reality.

Trigger Point Reality

High expectations for much better times ahead are often held by the investing public and supported by Wall Street when valuing stock shares. Perception of what is hoped for takes on the guise of reality.

It is human nature to desire wealth and in the stock market this occurs when dreaming about the future. A speculator's perception of reality is often better than reality itself and a stock's price reaches its highest level when trader's expectations are at their highest point and not when the reality is ultimately achieved.

Optimism dominates the average person participating in the stock market. At most times, leading business persons, politicians and the average investor all hold exaggerated opinions about the future. There is no need for advanced expertise here, just trade in response to the crowd's optimistic perception—as discussed next.

72

Castle-In-The-Air Theory

John Maynard Keynes (1883-1946) calls this optimistic phenomenon the castle-in-the-air theory of speculation. Regardless of what reality is presently or expected to be twenty years from now, Keynes realizes that a company's stock price can veer very far from its intrinsic, true, or fair value.

Keynes' speculative strategy is sophisticated yet subtle: i.e., think about what the average investor will think about the average investor or crowd's assessment of market or stock expectations and trade along with that determination. Or said in another way, verify what the investing public needs, wants, hopes and desires and then just go along.

Crowds have a conventional means of deduction and arrive at simple conclusions to expected events. Know what the crowds' high or low expectations and standard deductions are and take advantage of them. The trick is to cash in before the crowd cashes in and that is best done when expected reality becomes real, either good or bad, at trigger points—examples follow.

Trigger Point Examples

A short-sale trigger point for an overvalued stock is typically the fulfillment of what is expected. Speculators should delay shorting a weak stock until reality, either good or bad, is confirmed at a trigger point. Expectations then become frustrated and no longer hold their allure when perceived reality becomes real, accomplished or not. When reality and castles-in-the-air collide, reality in the stock market always wins. The following trigger points may be anticipated for companies on a short-sale candidate watch list:

1. Short when the company discontinues all dividend payments.
2. Short when the founder, CEO or president resigns under questionable circumstances.
3. Short just prior to the Food and Drug Administrations (FDA) rendering an opinion on a corporation's first regulatory approval.
4. Short when a major piece is published in an important financial daily newspaper, newsletter, weekly newspaper, or magazine which is very critical of a company.
5. Short after the company splits its stock two, three, or four etc. for one.
6. Short after the first bad break in the stock's price on heavy volume.

7. Short if the accounting firm auditing the company's books resigns for any reason.

8. Short if the 10-K or 10-Q financial report submittal dates are slipped for any reason.

9. Short if the 10-K or 10-Q financial reports are issued with less than an unqualified or clean opinion from the accounting auditors.

Even if no short-sale action is currently feasible, short sellers should place overvalued companies on a watch list to wait for just the right trigger point before shorting.

IPO Trigger Points

The first time a corporation's securities are offered for sale in the primary market, normally with the help of an investment banker, is termed an initial public offering (IPO). IPO's may or may not be good investments, depending on the specific offering.

Prior to shorting an IPO stock: 1) read the prospectus thoroughly to see if the business plan makes sense, analyze the financial data, evaluate the officers of the company and concentrate on the "Investment Considerations" section to learn all the company supplied pitfalls to its success, e.g., a me-too laggard company in a poor industry that has never made profits is a good short sale candidate; 2) any benchmarks given in the prospectus by management should be duly noted—missing benchmarks may be a reason to sell or short the stock; and 3) new cash put into the company or merger talks may only temporarily prop up its stock price, so do not be overly concerned if and when this occurs. All of the above are trigger points indicating when to short an IPO.

When a highly promoted initial public offering (IPO) sinks below its offering price for a few months after it is brought to market, this is an IPO failure and normally a good indication that the market is nearing its long-term peak or the IPO is not viable. When the market fails in some way or something takes place that should not happen, this is usually a signal that the long-term market trend is turning down.

Single-Product Company Trigger Points

High growth single-product companies have a growth cycle that should be monitored to identify the zenith in the stock's price, at which time the stock may be sold short.

The concept is called "pipeline fill" which refers to shipping product through the distribution channel. A hot new single-product company will take awhile in filling the pipeline at all the possible retail outlets and sales growth will look fantastic. Once the pipeline is full and product inventories at the company are growing faster than sales, this is indicative of sales not matching plan and could be the trigger point and a wonderful time to short the stock.

In addition, funding needs during the fast sales growth stage should be reviewed to see if it supports this growth without the need for additional outside financing. A company with a positive free cash flow but a margin-of-safety multiple considerably under one is overvalued and a possible short-sale candidate, at a trigger point.

A fast analysis calculation may also be used, it is the company's return on equity (ROE) multiplied by its retention rate which is the percentage of its net income not paid out in dividends. Since growth companies do not normally pay dividends, their retention rate is usually 100 percent. A single-product company with a ROE percentage lower than its growth rate is a possible short-sale opportunity.

Bank Trigger Points

Banks typically only have equity equal to five percent of assets on their balance sheet which makes them highly leveraged companies. A contracting real estate market is a dead weight on the overall economy because it restricts the commercial banking business and bank loans. Banks take a beating in a contracting real estate market, with their share prices eventually selling at only 40 percent of their book value.

Once the downturn begins in real estate, it lasts a minimum of three-to-four years, to as much as ten years, to work off the buildup in supply that overhangs the market. It is interesting to note, as this is written, that U.S. housing starts are believed to have turned down off a long-term peak during January of 2006. Wait for the banking industry group to enter the lowest 25 percent of six-month industry rankings prior to shorting bank common stock, as explained in chapter 6.

Financial Statements

Not having the necessary information for a thorough analysis leads to incorrect snap judgments. Relying solely on mathematical formulas to do the speculator's thinking is not appropriate, either. Instead, look for information in corporate financial reports, make the necessary calculations and then come to a decision based upon sound speculative judgment.

Short traders should be very adept at reading and understanding corporate financial statements. Finding muddled accounting on a company's 10-K or 10-Q financial report is a red flag that management may be trying to hide something.

Be skeptical, call investor relations at the company for a complete explanation of any troubling points. A less than forthcoming response means that this company's stock may be added to the speculator's watch list as a possible short-sale candidate. The following are financial ratios that should be monitored to help identify short-sale candidates.

Check Financial Ratios

Compare the accounts receivable growth rate to the growth rate in corporate sales revenue. Accounts receivable growing faster than sales may be due to: 1) purchasing subsidiaries; 2) speeding up the booking of revenue; 3) lengthening payment terms; and 4) difficulty in account collections. This is mitigated if a recent acquisition has made these figures difficult to compare. However, each of the last three reasons above for a high account receivable growth rate are cause for concern.

Management may manipulate the income statement by advancing revenues and deferring expenses. The result is that corporate net income growth still looks good but is in reality, weak. A telltale sign that this is occurring is that the prepaid expense account on the balance sheet increases, for no apparent reason. Check with investor relations for a good explanation and if not received, the stock may be added to a short-sale candidate list.

Deferred charges occur when management pushes expenses into later periods. Unexpected large earnings reversals can occur if revenues on the income statement decline, even slightly. Capitalizing ongoing expenses to make it appear that costs have been reduced is a clear indication of earnings manipulation. Also, an inflated goodwill account is a warning that a recent acquisition was made at an extravagant price. Anything out of the ordinary is an indication that management may want to cover-up something.

If the accumulated depreciation account on the balance sheet drops significantly, make sure the reason why is known. It may be due to a subsidiary sale or other asset sale, or because of a revision to the equipment salvage value. If accumulated depreciation on the balance sheet declines while at the same time the property, plant and equipment account increases, the company may have changed the depreciation schedule which inflates total revenue on the income statement.

Check the inventory turnover ratio closely. If the inventory account on the balance sheet is growing much faster than the cost of goods sold account on the income statement—this is a very dependable indicator that a retailer or manufacturer will have serious problems in the future.

On the income statement, change all the numbers to percentages to check any significant proportional changes in successive years. This is an effective way to spot noteworthy growth or decline in relative prices through time.

On the balance sheet under liabilities, check whether the names being used to describe company liabilities are unusual and if approximated values or present value assumptions are used for these account entries. Check the footnotes for explanations, if any seem extraordinary this may be an indication of management trying to hide something that is wrong with the company.

Asset Shuffling, Buyouts And Mergers

Assets that are not easily converted into up-to-date monetary prices, be they real estate, financial derivatives, junk bonds, unusual preferred stock, or bond convertibles all may have hopeful valuations assigned to them by management in an attempt to hoodwink investors. This is called "asset shuffling" and is used by less than scrupulous managers.

When buyouts and mergers are prevalent in the stock market, all a company need do to increase its share price is announce that the sale of certain assets is warranted or even that a suitor is being sought. Ironically, a poor operating company discussing a possible corporate takeover is often a trigger point indicating that the corporation is a good short-sale opportunity.

10-K's, 10-Q's And 8-K's

Not knowing the information in 10-K's, 10-Q's, and 8-K's (report of material corporate events whenever they occur), Form 144 (officers of the company report the sale order of the company's stock prior to execution), Form 4 (officers report the purchase or sale of the company stock), 13-D's (entities purchasing five percent or more of the company's stock report this to the SEC), report footnotes (perhaps the most important information of all) and in proxy statements is evidence that the short seller is not doing his or her job properly.

The 10-Q, a quarterly financial report to the SEC of the corporation's performance, is required reading for short sellers who are interested in a particular company. Since few investors, speculators, or security analysts bother to study the 10-Q report, it gives the conscientious short seller the information needed to determine whether to stay with their position, add to the position, or to cover.

Shorting a wonderful company with a seemingly high stock price or shorting a company that is not half bad is typically the wrong approach. Have more than two good reasons to identify a good short-sale candidate. The following example shows astute investors how to evaluate a possible short-sale candidate and what the indicated trigger points might be.

Short-Sale Example: General Motors Corp.

The following are recommended steps to identify a possible short-sale candidate. This is an example with actual market and company data as of April 30, 2006. The steps proceed from the issues concerning the long-term trend in the stock market, to industry rankings, to analyzing a specific corporation as a short-sale candidate.

Long-Term Trend: Favorable Or Unfavorable?

Step A. Make sure the long-term trend is in the speculator's favor. Astute speculators realize that approximately 50 percent of a stock's price is determined by the overall political-economic conditions that affect all common stock issues, called systematic risk. Astute speculators always what the overall market conditions favorable and will only short a stock if the market is in Stage 4: Distribution - Topping or Rounding Over or Stage 1: Mark-Down – Downtrend.

Graph 2 - 1: Stage 3: S&P 500 Index Market Mark-Up - Uptrend

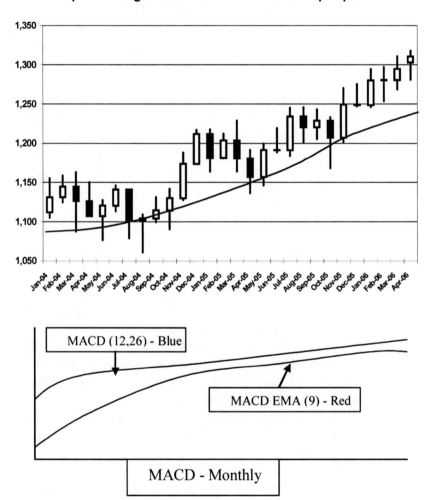

Use only the S&P 500 Index and the proper perspective of monthly data to see the long-term trend in the stock market. Graph 2 – 1: Stage 3:

S&P 500 Index Market Mark-Up - Uptrend shows monthly data from January 1, 2004 to April 30, 2006 and the trend line indicates the trend in the market. Graphs may be drawn using the BigCharts.com website at http://bigcharts.marketwatch.com/.

The S&P 500 Index Nine Month Moving Average (MA) Trend Line is trending upward and signals that the stock market is in Stage 3: Mark-Up – Uptrend. Confirming indicators on the S&P 500 Index monthly chart such as: 1) monthly data higher-highs and higher-lows; 2) two month moving average trend line being above the nine month moving average trend line; and 3) the Moving Average Convergence Divergence (MACD) blue line (12,26) being above the red line EMA (9) all confirm the stock market is in Stage 3: Mark-Up – Uptrend.

As of April 30, 2006, with the S&P 500 Index at approximately 1,311, now is not the correct time to go short on a specific corporate stock, regardless of its merits. However, it should not stop the astute speculator from identifying short-sale candidates to be prepared for stage 4 or 1 market conditions when they occur.

Industry Ranking

Step B. Make sure the industry ranking is weak prior to shorting a stock. When selling short, it is preferable to select the stock from the lowest 25 percent of six-month industry rankings (more on this in chapter 6).

Going to the Dow Jones U.S. (DJ US) Sector and Industry Index rankings at the www.marketwatch.com website identify the ten worst performing industries. Over the prior twelve months from 5/1/05 to 4/30/06, the DJ US Automobile Index is the worst performing industry—down -16.91 percent. Over the past six months, this index is down -9.81 percent and in the lowest 25 percent of industry rankings. An industry that is already trending downward, even though the long-term trend in the stock market is up, is an excellent place to identify short-sale candidates to be shorted when the appropriate time comes.

Draw an industry graph to get a clearer picture of the price action in the industry over the past year. Industry graphs may be found at Standard & Poor's, Yahoo Finance, Dow Jones, Zacks, CNN Money websites as presented in chapter 6. The industry Graph 2 – 2: U.S. Automotive Index shown next is a composite representation.

Graph 2 – 2: U.S. Automotive Index

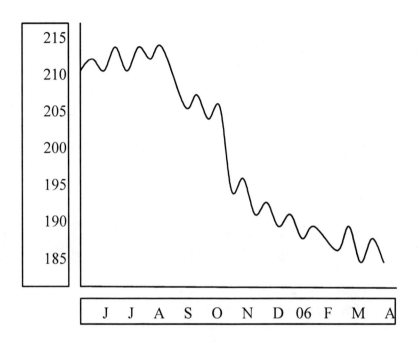

The automotive industry chart clearly shows that this industry is in decline. An industry declining while the overall market is in a long-term uptrend is already a weak industry. When the long-term trend in the overall market turns to Stage 1: Mark-Down – Downtrend, the automotive industry is expected to remain weak and be a good place to find laggard companies to sell short.

The DJ US Automobiles Index over the past six months identifies a list of the worst performing common stock. General Motors Corporation (NYSE: GM) is down approximately -33 percent and did worse than the poor performing automotive industry in which it is included. Consequently, GM is a laggard stock in a weak industry and is selected for further analysis as a possible short-sale candidate—as presented next.

Graph 2 - 3: General Motors

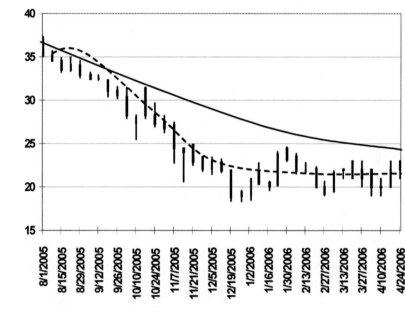

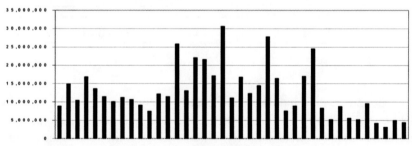

10 Week MA Trend Line (Dashed Line)
40 Week MA Trend Line (Solid Line)

GM: Undervalued Or Overvalued?

Step C. Make sure GM's stock is overvalued when shorting. Approximately
40 percent of the stock price is directly determined by specific factors within

the company, called unsystematic risk. To get a good picture of the historical price movement of GM's stock from August, 2005 to April, 2006, a weekly candlestick chart—Graph 2 – 3: General Motors—shows GM's stock in a downtrend since August of 2005 and in a trading range since December of 2005. Both the 10 week moving average (MA) trend line (dashed line) and the 40 week MA trend line (solid line) depict GM's stock in an intermediate-term downtrend.

Trading volume, represented by the bar chart in the lower half of Graph 2 - 3, is double the normal volume during the precipitous downward fall in GM's stock price during November and December of 2005 and into the beginning of 2006. However, because individual companies have unsystematic risk, the trend shown on a company's chart cannot be counted on to continue. Therefore, GM's chart price trend is not a reason by itself to take action but does give support as a confirming indicator as other data are analyzed, specifically, making the under or overvalued calculation determination using the intrinsic, true, or fair value calculation.

GM: Strategy And Stock Price

Recent record high gasoline prices highlights flaws in GM's product-mix sales strategy with their current dependence on large sport utility vehicles. GM's stock declined and is trading, as of April 30, 2006 at approximately $22.60 per share, down approximately -44 percent from $40.50 at the beginning of 2005.

GM: Delphi Troubles

General Motors Corporation (NYSE: GM) and the automobile industry are in the news due to the recent bankruptcy filing by Delphi Corporation (OTC: DPHIQ), an auto supplier spun off from GM approximately seven years ago.

A major downside for GM in Delphi's troubles is that GM will experience increased retirement liabilities, potential increased costs and supply disruptions for parts, and possible problems during upcoming United Auto Workers (UAW) labor negotiations.

GM: Debt

As of April 30, 2006, Standard & Poor's downgraded further into junk bond status GM's credit rating from BB to BB- on its $286 billion dollars in outstanding debt, thus, significantly increasing GM's borrowing costs.

GM: Float, Short-Interest-to-Float And Short-Interest Ratio

From The Wall Street Journal online at http://online.wsj.com, GM's share float is 425,400,000 shares or 75 percent of GM's total shares outstanding. GM is a large cap stock, with high liquidity and typically trades approximately 50 million shares during a trading week. GM has a large float which insures that buy ins and short squeezes are very unlikely. Institutional ownership for GM is reported at 84 percent.

On March 8, 2006, short interest on GM's stock is 87,525,000 shares sold short. GM's short-interest-to-float is approximately 21 percent with a short-interest ratio of 8.75 days of trading to cover short positions. Both the short-interest-to-float of 21 percent and the short-interest ratio at 8.75 days seems high and not conducive to shorting GM's stock at this time.

GM: Dividends

On the negative side for short-sellers, GM is paying dividends of $1.00 per share resulting in a dividend yield of approximately +4.4 percent as of the April 30 2006 stock price. GM short sellers would have to pay the $1.00 dividends while carrying their short position which would be expensive.

The question for astute speculators is, "Has all the bad news come out on GM, or is there more to come and is GM a good short-sale candidate." This important question is addressed next.

Is GM A Good Short-Sale Candidate?

Astute speculators recognize that they are speculating in the stock first and the company second. GM's board of directors does not set GM's stock price, that can only be determined by the amount traders are willing to pay for GM's shares on the open market.

To properly answer if GM is a good short-sale candidate, astute speculators should separate the company from its stock. GM is a wonderful company making high-quality products; however, industry economics often outweigh an excellent company's specific circumstances to make its stock a poor investment. Financial statements are analyzed to determine GM's intrinsic, true, or fair value as discussed next.

Please go to GM's website for financial information at: http://www.gm.com/company/investor_information/sec/ or Morningstar's website listed below for GM's ten-year income statement:

http://quicktake.morningstar.com/Stock/
income10.asp?Country=USA&Symbol=GM&stocktab=finance

GM: Intrinsic, True, Or Fair Value

Over the past ten years from 1996-2005, GM's sales revenue increases approximately +1.5 percent a year from $164 billion dollars to $193 billion dollars. Net income over this same time period decreases from approximately $5 billion dollars to a negative -$10.6 billion dollars in 2005. Meager top line growth in revenues for GM and negative bottom line net income growth indicates probable operations management problems. See Table 2 – 1: GM Corp. – Sales Revenue & Net Income (in billions of dollars) below for the 2001-2005 summary.

Table 2 - 1: GM Corp - Sales Revenue & Net Income
(in billions of dollars)

Year	2001	2002	2003	2004	2005
Sales Revenue	177	187	186	194	193
Net Income	**0.5**	**1.7**	**3.8**	**2.8**	**(10.6)**

Table 2 - 2: GM Corp. - Cash Flow Statement (billions of dollars)

Year	2001	2002	2003	2004	2005
Cash From Operating Activities	**9.17**	**17.11**	**7.60**	**13.06**	**(16.85)**
Purchase of Property and Equipment	(8.63)	(7.44)	(7.33)	(7.75)	(8.18)
Purchase of Investments*					
Maturities and Sale of Investments*					
Proceeds from Sale of Assets	(12.55)	(3.47)	(47.90)	(17.40)	5.62
Acquisitions, net of cash acquired	0	(0.87)	4.15	(6.63)	0.84
Cash from Investing Activities*					

*Investment accounts not pertinent for the calculation of Total Capital Expenditures and Free Cash Flow (FCF).

Astute speculators, wanting to short stock, look for a negative intrinsic value company that may be headed into bankruptcy during the next economic downturn. Lets look at the all important free cash flow each year that is easily calculated with the help of Zacks' website below:

http://www.zacks.com/research/report.php?type=cfs&t=GM

Free cash flow (FCF) in billions of dollars for each year (YR) from 2001 through 2005 is calculated from the cash flow statement and is defined as cash from operating activities (COA) minus total capital expenditures. The data for the calculations are shown in Table 2 – 2: GM Corp. – Cash Flow Statement (billions of dollars).

Summing the total capital expenditures and subtracting from the cash from operating activities indicates a negative FCF and is shown in Table 2 – 3: GM Corp. – Free Cash Flow (billions of dollars) below:

Table 2 - 3: GM Corp. - Free Cash Flow (billions of dollars)

Year	2001	2002	2003	2004	2005
Cash from Operating Activities	**9.17**	**17.11**	**7.60**	**13.06**	**(16.86)**
Total Capital Expenditures	(21.18)	(11.78)	(51.09)	(31.78)	(1.72)
Free Cash Flow (FCF)	**(12.01)**	**(5.33)**	**(43.49)**	**(18.72)**	**(18.58)**

GM's FCF averages a negative -$20 billion dollars per year from 2001 through 2005. GM is not generating enough money from internal operations to support itself. GM, over the past five years, issues an average of $28 billion dollars of new debt each year as well as paying an average of $1.1

billion dollars per year in dividends, thus, the continued need for outside financing is a long-term detriment for GM's stock price.

Dividend payments going forward have been lowed to approximately $566 million dollars per year, but are still significant. A negative intrinsic value is not an option when FCF is negative; therefore, GM's intrinsic value is zero.

GM: Market Value Capitalization

Market value capitalization includes the total number of GM's diluted shares outstanding, i.e., approximately 569 million shares, multiplied by the April 30, 2006 closing stock price of $22.60 per share, equaling approximately $13 billion dollars. GM's bargain value ($0 - $13) is a negative -$13 billion dollars.

GM: Margin-of-Safety Multiple

The margin-of-safety multiple is the intrinsic value of $0 dollars divided by the market value capitalization of $13 billion dollars, equaling zero which is no where near the 2.0 minimum value required for investment purposes; therefore, by the margin-of-safety multiple method GM's stock is considerably overvalued and is a good short-sale candidate.

GM: Ten Additional Crucial Factors

Ten additional crucial factors for General Motors Corp. are checked next: (from GM's December 31, 2005 financial statement).

1) *Current Ratio: 0.71* — The current ratio is a test for short-term solvency, creditors would like a safety cushion value of 2.00, this measure for GM is poor.

2) *Debt-to-Equity Ratio: 31.54* — GM is using $31.54 dollars of liabilities for every $1.00 dollar of shareholder equity which makes GM a super-hyper-leveraged company. An effective limit for manufacturing companies is often set at a one-to-one debt to equity ratio. GM's debt-to-equity ratio in 2004 was 16.30, meaning that this very important ratio has significantly worsened over the past year. This is a very precarious state of affairs and could seriously affect the viability of GM as a going concern if

U.S. political-economic conditions turn negative and the U.S. goes into a recession.

3) *Return-on-Equity: -72%* — GM lost approximately -$10.6 billion dollars in 2005. Astute speculators prefer to have ROE over 15% for a manufacturing company.

4) *Operating Profit Margin: -0.6%* — GM had a negative -1.2 billion dollar operating profit in 2005. Astute speculators prefer to have operating profit margin in the 15-to-25 percent range. A more experienced operations management team may be required.

5) *Diluted Net Earnings Per Share: -$15.13* — Over the past five years, diluted EPS have averaged $0.64. Diluted EPS turned negative in 2005.

6) *Continued good service is apparent.* GM is one of the leaders in U.S. automotive manufacturing. However, if customers feel that bankruptcy is an option, sales could be seriously effected.

7) *GM's management* is having trouble translating top line sales growth (+1.5 percent per year) into bottom-line net income growth (negative per year). As mentioned, a more experienced operations management team may be required.

8) *GM's marketing/sales/distribution* organization is judged to be acceptable, with sales growing by approximately +1.5 percent per year in a very difficult automotive industry.

9) *GM* is one of the leaders in the automotive manufacturing category in North America: however the U.S. automotive industry is highly competitive.

10) Any interviews with customers, vendors, employees, etc. are reported positive.

GM: More Short-Sale Calculations

Additional important calculations for short-sale candidates are helpful. James S. Chanos explains his return on invested capital indicator calculation that uncovers many companies that are unhealthy. Operating earnings, i.e., earnings before interest and taxes (EBIT) are divided by total liabilities & shareholder equity, minus total current liabilities, plus short term debt. Please see Table 2 – 4: GM Corp. – Invested Capital Indicator, shown on the next page.

Table 2 - 4: GM Corp. – Invested Capital Indicator
(billions of dollars)

Year	2001	2002	2003	2004	2005
EBIT*	10.1	9.8	12.4	13.2	(1.2)
TL&SE – TCL + STD**	262.1	279.5	349.2	366.0	362.1
Return on Invested Capital	**3.85%**	**3.50%**	**3.55%**	**3.60%**	**(0.33%)**

*Earnings before interest and taxes (EBIT)
**Total Liabilities & Shareholder Equity (TL&SE)
**Total Current Liabilities (TCL)
** Short Term Debt (STD)

From 2001 through 2005, the return on invested capital indicator percentage averages a low +2.83 percent and turned a negative -0.33 percent for 2005, operating earnings are approximately minus -$1.2 billion dollars in the last year.

To identify key accounts to watch, the income statement is recalculated as a percentage of sales for 2001 through 2005. Please see Table 2 – 5: GM Corp. – Income Statement (in percentages).

The two accounts to watch the closest are highlighted in bold. The cost of goods sold increased from 81.2 percent in 2001 to 88.8 percent in 2005. Clearly, GM has an inventory control problem. The most important account to watch is the interest expense account. Interest expenses increased approximately +15 percent per year, from 4.9 percent of sales in 2001 to 8.2 percent of sales in 2005. This growth in the interest expense account is not sustainable and should be closely monitored.

Table 2 - 5: GM Corp. - Income Statement (in percentages)

Year	2001	2002	2003	2004	2005
Sales	100%	100%	100%	100%	100%
Cost of Goods	**81.2**	**82.1**	**82.0**	**82.7**	**88.8**
Gross Profit	18.8	17.9	18.1	17.4	11.2
Selling & Admin, Depreciation & Amortization	13.1	12.6	11.3	10.5	11.8
Income After Depreciation & Amortization	5.7	5.2	6.7	6.8	(0.6)
Interest Expense	**4.9**	**4.1**	**5.1**	**6.2**	**8.2**
Net Income	0.3	0.9	2.0	1.4	(5.5)

GM: Short Sale Candidate Analysis

General Motors has a ravenous appetite for outside financing because it is not generating enough free cash flow internally to fund its ongoing operations, resulting in the need for approximately $28 billion dollars more each year in outside financing. GM is at the mercy of Wall Street for new financing going forward and is in a weak financial condition with junk bond status for its debt causing interest expenses to skyrocket.

GM has a fundamental product mix strategy problem as their large truck and car lineup are difficult to sell in a persistently high price gasoline environment. The cost of GM's product line in the U.S. is also increasing.

Labor problems associated with Delphi Corporation (DPH), a GM crucial supplier that is in bankruptcy, is ongoing and could cause part supply problems, in this era of just-in-time inventory supply, causing GM's production to cease operations during a Delphi strike.

GM's margin-of-safety multiple of zero does not approach the margin-of-safety multiple minimum value of 2.0. Additional crucial factors are mostly poor, consequently, astute speculators, at this time, should consider GM an excellent company but with an over valued stock price. Therefore, GM is a short-sale candidate. The all important "when" to short GM's stock has yet to be determined, as discussed next.

GM: When To Short?

Carrying stock too long on the short side ties up money without a sufficient return. The primary speculative art and the "art of arts" is knowing when is the best time to short a short-sale candidate. The important factors should all be favorable for a short position, i.e., the market is down trending long term, the industry is very weak relative to other industries and down trending and the stock is extremely overvalued with other crucial indicators being mostly very poor.

Since the investing public and speculators are almost exclusively optimists and are in long stock positions, a trigger point is needed for the astute speculator to know when to short GM—as presented next.

GM Short-Sale Trigger Points

Two excellent reasons for not shorting GM stock as of April 30, 2006 are: 1) the stock market is in stage 3 with the S&P 500 Index Nine Month MA Trend Line trending upward which is supported by confirming indicators; and 2) GM is paying dividends of $1.00 per share per year which a short seller would have to pay on all shares borrowed. Consequently, these impediments to shorting should be eliminated prior to considering shorting GM stock.

Once the stock market is in stage 4 or 1, the following are possible trigger points that astute speculators may use to determine the correct time to short GM's stock.

Specific Short-Sale Trigger Points

The following trigger points for GM include: 1) if the CEO resigns for any reason; 2) if the independent accounting firm doing the annual audit resigns for any reason; 3) if a sensationally critical article is published in a major business newspaper or magazine on irregularities in management or accounting practices; 4) if GM suspends the $1.00 per share dividend payment; and 5) if the United Auto Workers go on strike at Delphi or at GM.

The astute speculator patiently waits for the fulfillment of what is expected at trigger points which prompts the longs to eventually sell to produce the largest profit for the shorts in the shortest possible period of time. The resulting downward move in the stock price is expected to be rapid and steep rendering the astute short seller a quick position turnaround profit.

Some stock profits may be given up with this strategy because shorting at the very top GM price is not feasible. Nevertheless, it is much better to have a known weak market, weak industry and weak company with a clearly indicated trigger point that tips the stock price over the price edge—i.e., all of these factors being in the speculator's favor help ensure a quick short-sale profit success.

Same Amount of Money Made

It is comforting to note that when using the same amount of capital, by shorting a stock at $20 dollars per share that goes to zero versus $10 dollars per share that goes to zero, nets the speculator the same amount of profits. While the number of shares shorted at $10 dollars per share is double that at $20 dollars per share, the resulting profits to the astute speculator in both cases remain identical.

Summary

"Sell high, buy low" describes the correct procedure when short selling. The same objective as long buyers follow, however, the actions are reversed. The speculator, on the short side, is planning to profit from the drop in the stock's price. An astute short seller is skeptical of conventional wisdom and uses financial statement analysis and good judgment to make timely trades.

It is estimated that 99.8 percent of the investing public trades on the long side of the market when buying and selling common stock. A March, 2006 statement from the NYSE reports only about 2.2 percent of the total number of shares outstanding have been sold short. Accordingly, the vast majority of all investors and speculators trade on the long side of the market.

Speculators who are always long are persistent optimists, those who are always on the short side of the market are eternal pessimists. Astute speculators are willing to trade either long or short, as market conditions dictate. Short selling deflates boom-bubble buying at market tops and buying to cover creates market liquidity at panic-selling market bottoms.

Timing on Wall Street is the primary art or "art of arts." The main concern for speculators selling stock short is always "when," the "what" to sell short is always of secondary importance and the stock's price or "how much" is received for the shorted shares is only number three in significance. Many speculators have the story right but the timing wrong and, consequently, have lost all.

Timing is the chief failing for short-sale traders. Because there are so few short sellers in the stock market at any one time, the only way for shorts to win is to have the help of longs who are selling. Knowing the best time to short a stock involves recognizing its trigger point and then acting accordingly. A short-sale trigger point for a short-sale candidate is typically the fulfillment of what is expected. Speculators should delay shorting a weak stock until reality, either good or bad, is confirmed at a trigger point.

Usually there are three steps in a long-term downward sloping market. The first step is the initial break where prices decline stunningly swiftly but soon recover during the first technical rally. The second step is a steady stock market decline as business conditions and earnings continually weaken. During the third step, terrible business conditions are evident— resulting in suspended dividends, bankruptcies, mass layoffs and talk by politicians about tax cuts.

The first technical rally in a long-term down market is the safest time to go short. As the market rallies back close to its market high, the ability to short common stock at an advantageous price presents itself.

Stock sold short should conform to the following SEC requirements: 1) the exchange handling the trade must be informed that the order is a short sale; 2) the sale execution must be in conformance with the uptick rule; and 3) the broker handling the sale must have borrowed the stock to make delivery at the time of the sale.

A "hard-to-borrow" short condition indicates that this stock has a very limited floating supply. The SEC uptick rule requires the short sale to take place on a plus tick or zero-plus tick from a prior transaction price. Buy ins and short squeezes are downside hazards for short sellers who should know the stock's float, short interest, short-interest-to-float and short-interest ratio prior to taking a short position.

Short sellers use 10-K and 10-Q financial reports which explain the business plan and match the financials to the plan to identify the crucial numbers to monitor. Short sellers have an advantage over security analysts on Wall Street because security analysts seldom bother to closely scrutinize financial statements.

Telltale signs of a short-sale candidate include: 1) accounts receivable growing faster than sales; 2) prepaid expenses increasing for no apparent reason; 3) accumulated depreciation dropping quickly; 4) fast inventory growth; 5) deferred charges; and 6) inflated goodwill.

General Motors Corporation (GM) is analyzed as an example of a possible short sale candidate. Expected trigger points on when to short GM common stock are listed and discussed.

3

Buying Common Stock

Introduction

FOR COMMON STOCK PURCHASES, like selling short, the "when" is most important followed by "what" to buy and only then "how much" to pay. Planning and scheduling are imperative when purchasing common stock which should be corroborated by the market's action. Why the investing public purchases stock at the wrong time as the market comes off a market peak is explained.

Buying is complicated, the eight rules for purchasing common stock are presented based upon knowing the market's technical condition and when stock shares are held in "strong hands." Stock purchase price, stated bid & offer prices and intrinsic, true, or fair value differences are emphasized.

It is best to purchase stock market leaders hitting all-time high prices which are included in the top 25 percent of industry rankings. Learn how to judge halfway price points and what these points mean for a stock or the overall market.

Patiently waiting for the correct time to buy stock is fundamental for astute speculators. When purchasing common stock, the ability to say either "yes or no" is paramount, be patient, look for an appropriate trigger point and then take timely action.

Buying Principles

Buying common stock involves the thrill of the investigation, the persuasiveness of the information, the important judging of conclusions, the excitement of the purchase and the anticipation of future profits. The fascination with the stock market challenge often draws first time speculators into an arena they little understand, instead, it is much better to learn how to speculate prior to beginning the enterprise.

The important concerns for the stock purchase decision are complex and include, in this order of importance: 1) "when," whether to buy now or later on; 2) "what," identifying which stock to purchase; and 3) "how much," what price should be paid for the stock. Additional factors are: 1) knowing the type of speculator you are—e.g., impulsive, nervous, or lethargic (please see chapter 8); and 2) how much risk capital should be committed in each trade (please see chapter 7).

The small speculator with $10,000 dollars has to be as careful with his or her money as the wealthy speculator is with millions of dollars at stake. The stock market is a serious business requiring due diligence, hard work and intellectual effort. The stock market should not be viewed as randomly efficient where buying stock is like making a bet at a casino and blind chance rules. Instead, the stock market is a discounting mechanism where systematic political-economic conditions, industry circumstances and unsystematic risk specific to each corporation determine stock prices.

Risky Stock

Winning in the stock market requires taking an equity position, if all the speculator's money is lost no equity position can be taken, consequently, the minimization of risk and having the probabilities on the speculator's side are necessary for success.

Speculators should not assume that overly risky stock has to be purchased in order to increase profits. The effort to reduce risk involves gaining as much useful knowledge and making the necessary calculations concerning the stock market, industry and stock prior to making the commitment. The goal is to reduce risk as much as possible prior to making the purchase decision.

Speculative victory in the stock market turns on reducing the money lost rather than increasing the money gained (please see chapter 7). Risk is always present in the stock market which is positive because, without risk, the possibility for outsized stock speculation profits would not be possible.

Use Proper Analysis And Good Judgment

The reason that proper analysis and good judgment are emphasized is to give speculators the best opportunity, in an uncertain world, to make money. To increase the probability of speculative success, select the leading most active common stock to purchase that is included in an industry in the top 25 percent ranking of all industries. The test of speculative ability over the intermediate term is to speculate in the new active stock leaders as the current active stock leaders begin to fade.

The typical amateur speculator starts out expecting outsized stock profits but often fixates on another goal, i.e., how to get out of a losing stock position, even. At any point in time there are perhaps many tens of thousands of investors and speculators hoping and vainly imploring stock they purchased to regain the price they previously paid. These unfortunate traders attempt to wait out the decline but most likely sell out at a major loss at a stock market bottom. This all-to-often scenario reverses the proper procedure, as explained next.

Buy Low, Sell High

Speculative success necessitates the minimization of risk, requiring the trader to: 1) "buy low, sell high"; 2) minimize losses; 3) earn substantial profits; and 4) steer clear of chronic trading.

Many stories are told about an important stock find and the enormous gains made as a result. Searching out the best stock buying opportunities has a certain romance to it. Many in the securities industry are willing to help when making the buy decision—e.g., institutional salespeople travel to see mutual fund portfolio managers to pitch common stock purchases with much fanfare.

Buying stock is the first step in the process and its importance for success is often underrated. Buying stock is relatively easy, while selling stock is emotionally difficult, therefore, the salability of all stock positions have to be assessed prior to taking a speculative position (please see chapter 4).

The stock market buying process often requires taking a position while the market's action is ongoing. Now with after hours stock trading the market's action has the potential to be ongoing 24 hours a day, seven days a week (24/7).

Because the stock market has the capability to be in continuous operation 24/7, the need for a continuous decision making capability leading up to the buy decision may frustrate and emotionally drain traders. Speculator's nerves become frazzled, their mind swims and emotions run rampant while they contemplate making a stock purchase, consequently, the speculator's ability to say "yes or no" is paramount, as discussed next.

Ability To Say "Yes or No"

The most desirable quality leading up to a stock purchase decision is that speculators have the ability to say "yes or no." Remaining patiently in a neutral cash position is the most powerful speculative ready-to-buy position, so use it wisely.

Astute speculators always keep some cash available for extraordinarily rare trading opportunities. At these times, all the trading forces come together to present the ultimate juncture to make money (please see chapter 7).

During stock market panics, it should occur to traders to go long and when everyone is the most optimistic at a market top, to then go short. The feeling of power is electric during bubbles or panics when speculators know they have cash waiting to move into the market at just the right time. Tips offered on the stock market or on common stock are illogical and should be avoided, as discussed next.

Stock Market Tips

Stock market tips are illogical for both the giver and the taker, and should always be shunned by astute speculators. As an exercise, envision the difference between true information and stock tips. Information on an expected stock price movement may be investigated by the speculator and is based upon solid objective truths and facts, correct analysis and sound reasoning that is developed using corporate financial statements, technical analysis and economic reports. A stock tip can only be taken at face value, it is just someone else's opinion about a stock price movement who may possess questionable motives, incomplete information, specious reasoning and use incorrect calculations.

What makes stock tips, which are valueless and untraceable, such a potent force is that they are almost always given in a cloak of secrecy, consequently, novice speculators naturally feel important when they receive a stock tip. Since the tyro speculator is often lost in a maze of data and conflicting opinions they are constantly in a state of hesitancy and mental bewilderment, accordingly, the stock tip has mass appeal. The befuddled amateur speculator who desperately wants to be in the market will, incorrectly, act on a stock tip.

What makes the stock tip so insidious is that even if it is started based upon simple guesswork, the probability of success or failure is normally still 50-50. If stock tips constantly failed they would quickly fade away, however, outcomes are acceptable enough to give deceived followers continued confidence. Stories, true or false, based upon stock tips earning millions of dollars are also a distraction. However, it is certain that continued speculative success does not rely on stock tips.

Penny Stock Tips

Stock-tip selling methods by the "pump and dump con men" peddling penny stock are used to cloud and obfuscate the facts and to keep the speculative neophytes from thinking. Once the stock tip is sent out by fax or the Internet, typically on Sunday, the stock price gets pumped up the next business day. Insiders quickly dump their penny stock on the same day, leaving the gullible public holding stock certificates of little value. Always be on the lookout and know the difference between valuable information versus stock-tip propaganda.

Professional Speculators

Professional speculators may help their own success, just prior to selling. Less than scrupulous speculators create a public following in the stock by sending out a positive stock tip to the news media. As expected, the investing public buys on the good news. Because the stock then passes from "strong hands" into "weak hands" as the public buys (discussed later in this chapter), the possibility of precipitous stock decline or even panic increases.

Rather than welcoming public aid, professional speculators quickly liquidate their stock holdings and calmly step aside when a stock tip becomes common knowledge and is published in the media. Therefore, almost invariably, a stock tip received is public property and is too late for speculators to make any real money on the tip.

Buying On The News

The investing public assumes that news rationally moves stock prices, not realizing that the expected news has already been discounted in the market by professional speculators (please see *The Astute Investor*, chapter 8). Instead, stock price movements typically precede the reported news, i.e., actual stock price movements determine which reasons for stock price movements get reported in the media. Prior to taking any action when purchasing common stock, the astute speculator should always ask himself or herself, "Has this news already been discounted in the market?"

The investing public is typically not equipped to exploit the news for market purposes, even when its legitimacy is above reproach. Traders should rather be deaf and blind than willingly conduct their stock market operations based solely upon market pundit comments and opinions presented on business television (TV) programs, heard on radio talk shows, or read in the financial sections of newspapers.

Be wary of companies that are promoted heavily and all over the news. The wise speculator seeks information that can be suitably verified from official corporate sources and spurns the phone call sales pitches and unsolicited fliers touting common stock that come by mail, by fax and over the Internet.

Stock market fluctuations, paradoxically, are not caused by the news itself but by how speculators react to the news that for the most part has already been anticipated, and how millions of speculators believe, rightly or wrongly, the news will influence the market's outlook.

Unexpected News

The unexpected news accident, be it natural, political, economic or legal is more commonly the pretext for, rather than the grounds for, any serious or extensive market decline. If all the unexpected accidents over the past ten years had not occurred, it is sensible to believe that common stock prices would be approximately what they are today.

Excellent stock never go begging for buyers but rather have to be sought out. A wonderful speculative idea is never just delivered from an unknown source, instead, the successful astute speculator has to diligently investigate high potential situations.

Buying At A Market Top

The fear of losing money in the stock market is the reason that the investing public comes in late during stage 3 toward a market top. The investing public watches the market to be sure that prices have advanced prior to investing, but it is too late to make much money when they invest as a result of crowd behavior.

Once the investing public is in the market late in its upward swing, they are slow to react to a severe downward plunge coming after a market peak, called a break, that may last from one to three months. Conditions in the economy still seem good, therefore, the investing public is slow to acknowledge and does not quickly change their opinion about stock prices that, until then, continually advance.

Stock Price Bargains?

At a major long-term price break, the investing public thinks they see stock bargains because these shares have pulled back off market top prices, consequently, the investing public begins to purchase more stock during the break. The investing public attempts to buy low and sell high by purchasing stock only because it has dropped in price. The investing public adores bargains and wants to believe they are scooping up stock at discount prices.

The investing public is aware of the Wall Street adage to "buy low, sell high." Consequently, from the beginning to the middle of the market's stage 1 long-term decline is when the most stock are distributed to the investing public, because, it is human nature for novice investors to see a large price decline and think they are picking up expected stock bargains. Typically, the investing public gives no thought to the intrinsic, true, or fair value of the stock being purchased.

Beware Of Price Bargains

James R. Keene (1838-1913), the legendary stock speculator was hired by J.P. Morgan (1837-1913) to manage the introduction of the U.S. Steel Corporation's stock and operated in the following way. Selling stock to the public is best accomplished by first buying the stock and pushing its price to the maximum price point feasible, to get the public's attention, and only then selling these same stock shares, previously purchased at lower prices, as they decline in price off their high price point. Keene comments that it is unbelievable how much stock can be sold to the public in this manner.

While stock manipulation by a syndicate is no longer legal, human nature has not changed. The investing public loves what they consider a price bargain and buy common stock coming off a market peak based solely on its price, without any thought to its intrinsic, true, or fair value, the stock market stage or expected future market trend.

Previous High Stock Prices

Amateur speculators on Wall Street are always buying when they should be selling and selling when they should be buying. The investing public remembers previous high stock prices which, unfortunately, is their undoing. They hope that these high prices, once a stock market break has occurred, will be quickly surpassed to make them money. This is the reason many slumping stock issues are purchased at the wrong time by amateur speculators.

Purchasing supposedly bargain priced stock, based on price alone, as it declines in price off of its high price point should be avoided; because, that is the time most stock are transferred from "strong hands" to "weak hands."

Amateur speculators purchasing stock near the top price are more likely to get out of their position early than those who get in near the middle of the downward descent. The midlevel price purchasers remain self-assured longer because they remember the much higher market top price and hope prices will quickly regain those levels. Unfortunately, these tyro speculators have now turned themselves into involuntary investors as they hang on to their losing positions in order to save face.

A steep decline in a stock's price, by itself, is no reason to purchase a stock because its price can decline to zero with the company ending up in bankruptcy. Likewise, selling a common stock just because the price has vastly increased is irrational. The investing public purchases stock during a long-term downward movement in stock prices simply because prices are down so much and sell too soon during the long-term upward movement because prices have risen so high. Current market price levels are often less significant, instead, it is the direction of the market trend that should be of major importance to speculators.

Averaging Down

Averaging down, i.e., naively purchasing stock at each step down in price must always be avoided. Averaging down is an impulsive response to a declining stock price without having a plan.

Averaging down is not knowing the market trend or stage, and therefore, merely hoping for a possible price bottom. Astute speculators should never just grope for a bottom stock price and should never average down.

Steady Downward Price Trend

Common stock prices typically, during a long-term market slowdown, fall much further than the investing public initially thinks possible. Common stock prices always seem ridiculously low at a long-term market bottom when measured against their earlier price highs. Buying an undervalued stock at a ridiculously low price requires patience and courage because there is always the feeling of doubt within the speculator that he or she could be wrong.

The speculative strategy of buying while the rest are selling and selling when the rest are buying is certain to make money, at the correct time. The long-term trends in the stock market cast their shadows prior to their arrival.

The world, the nation and individuals all periodically are either flush with money or have trouble keeping up with bills—the astute speculator's job is knowing when these two conditions will most likely occur.

This lingering question at a market-low point is mulled over, "If I see it, why doesn't everyone else see it?" Be satisfied with the knowledge that long-term or intermediate-term stock market bottoms never engender buyer eagerness in the investing public. Instead, fear rules emotions and most traders become notoriously frugal. Ironically, because enthusiastic buyers are effectively eliminated at a climactic long-term or intermediate-term stock market low point, the resulting buying condition is then low risk.

Steady Upward Price Trend

The investing public longs to see a steady upward price trend for a specific common stock prior to purchasing because they feel they are now following the trend and it is now safe to be in the market. They begin to hear the stories of easy profits being made and follow the crowd's stampede into this stock, normally close to the stock's top price.

Positive stock market action is the most persuasive way to entice the investing public into the market. Likewise, at a long-term market low, the investing public is now ready to sell out or even go short. Astute speculators do not allow themselves to be lost in crowd behavior, but instead, benefit from it by doing the opposite of the crowd at the correct time.

When a stock or the overall stock market does not advance or decline, but moves in a tight trading range, either accumulation or distribution is ongoing. It is only a matter of time before a breakout to the upside or a reaction to the downside occurs. The market rarely stands still or is in equilibrium for long.

Planning And Scheduling The Stock Purchase

Astute speculators should focus on creating the best speculative plan and schedule possible and then have the discipline to follow it consistently. The money earned is secondary and should not be obsessed upon as the plan plays out. Realize that the money takes care of itself when the planning and scheduling are performed properly.

Speculators should know what is happening in the stock market, i.e., the objective truths of "what, who, where and when." Additionally, reasoned inference and judgment requires knowing the subjective "how and why" of stock price movements (please see chapter 12 in *The Astute Investor* for more on this). Analyze the market facts objectively and then let the market help in confirming the speculator's subjective assessment.

Plan and Schedule Creation

The investing public seems to be either unknowing, uncertain or lazy concerning their significant stock market investments versus any other purchase. Spend at least as much time planning and scheduling a stock market speculative enterprise as would be spent determining which car or washing machine to buy.

For a plan and schedule to work successfully in the stock market, it must be based upon your own trading strategy for only you know what will work best for you. Tailoring your speculative strategy to your character, personality and lifestyle is explained in chapter 9.

Commit to making the required examination of the company's intrinsic, true or fair (ITF) value, market value capitalization, bargain value and margin-of-safety multiple prior to purchase, rather than afterwards. Stock market buying is best accomplished according to an intelligent, unambiguous, speculative plan and schedule with exact buying rules (discussed later in this chapter).

Planning and scheduling is used to protect risk capital. Planning requires risk management by planning for both the best and worst case scenarios. Plan the proper buy price point and stick to this figure.

Prior to entering a stock position, the mind should be clear and judgment sound. This allows for effective speculative planning and scheduling. Prior to purchasing stock, have an explicit plan that is written down in a journal. Determine the price to be purchased, what you plan to do if the stock advances or declines, then do it.

Once a stock position is entered into, it is impossible to remain completely objective because judgment becomes biased due to the very human need of self-justifying the stock commitment. Pride-of-opinion is a human weakness that needs to be guarded against. Remain committed in the face of competing opinions, but be willing to change promptly when new compelling objective truths become known.

Plans and schedules created with complete sincerity are meticulously followed for awhile but typically end with a crash owing to impulsive actions caused by fright, panic or perplexity during a market loss, or speculative excitement resulting whenever a trade is profitable. Emotional and impulsive traders who daily modify their plan and schedule are certain of failure in the stock market, as explained next.

Planning And Scheduling Implementation

Knowing what to do is one thing but having the courage to carry through and actually do it is quite another. Have a strategy based upon your character, personality and lifestyle. Create a speculative plan and schedule based upon objective and subjective truths, logical reasoning and then implement it with discipline. Stick to the speculative plan and schedule, do not be knocked off course because of emotions.

Develop and follow a speculative plan and schedule but let the market action, including trading volume, turning points and tape reading (discussed in chapter 5), tell you if the plan is correct. If the market is not acting as it should, go to, or stay in a neutral cash position. Once in a neutral cash position construct a new plan and schedule, never act impulsively when participating in the stock market.

Never try to dictate to the stock market what it should be doing. A stock is only worth what a speculator can get for it in the marketplace. Try to enter stock positions as close as possible to turning points and use stop-loss orders (discussed in chapter 4) as an insurance policy if your judgment proves incorrect. Remember, the market is always right so do not argue with it.

Some apprehension goes along with buying even good common stock. Whatever strategy, analysis, trigger point and final judgment are used to determine when to buy, the execution always elicits nervousness. Patience in waiting for the correct buying opportunity is crucial, as discussed next

Patience When Buying

Patience is key to making money in the stock market and is required to identify the appropriate occasion to purchase common stock. Sitting and waiting for the correct time to purchase stock is the most difficult yet the most financially rewarding facet of speculation.

Do not try too hard. Trying too hard means expecting too much from the markets when the market or stock is not ready for a high probability trade. Have patience, when there is nothing to do, do nothing. The novice speculator often attempts too much too quickly, but soon realizes the markets cannot be controlled or directed and certainly cannot be rushed to meet their own timetable or need for money.

Those who understand the stock market realize that money made in the market comes about relatively slowly. If a semi-investor, it may be required to keep money in a money market account earning a lowly two percent interest per year while waiting two years for just the right opportunity to present itself to purchase stock. If the speculator cannot control the need to always be playing the market, the market cannot be beaten.

Do not get caught up in the excitement and the need to play the stock market just because it is there. Mental depression can develop by being out of the market because the speculator wants to feel part of the action and the need to be gloriously correct. This is called having an "itchy wallet" leading to chronic trading which should be strenuously resisted. Instead, be patient, act according to plan and take action only when there is a high probability of making money.

It seems to be a speculative decree that the largest losses come after the largest gains, therefore, be patient when reentering the market after a big gain. Before getting back into trading after consistently poor trading results, have patience by taking a break, think hard about trading and focus on constructing a new speculative plan and schedule. After a losing streak in trading, beginning confidently with a small monetary position win is crucial.

Waiting for the proper time to purchase stock is most difficult. The only sound reason to purchase a stock is because the timing is right and the stock it is undervalued. During a long-term stage 1 market downturn, common stock may appear cheap even though they have further to fall—ending in a crash during panic selling at a market bottom. Be patient, wait for the right reward-to-risk entry point (discussed in chapter 4).

Time To Purchase Stock

A good time to purchase a leading company's stock is in the latter part of stage 2 or early days of stage 3 when the market begins its long-term uptrend. Semi-investors may purchase a leading, high-quality stock for the "long pull" that coincides with long-term swings in the stock market. The objective is to buy a stock at a low price during stage 2 or 3 and hold throughout the major swing in the market and only sell when profits are considerable.

Short-term fluctuations in the stock's price are expected over the "long pull" but may be safely ignored by the "panic or contrarian specialist" (further discussed in chapter 9). Novice traders have difficulty buying at a long-term market low because courage is lacking and they feel more comfortable trading with the crowd.

Knowledgeable speculators are prepared to make low-risk trades in the stock market. Purchase a company's stock when it is ignored and not in the news, when trading volume is heavy during a stock price advance, or the stock price looks weak but refuses to decline in the face of persistent selling at a market low point. Halfway points are a good way to judge stock strength or weakness, as discussed next.

Halfway Points

The stock market's strength or weakness is often determined by judging halfway points. As the stock price advances or declines, the tendency of the market is indicated.

A way to judge how a stock is reacting during a long-term or intermediate-term upward trending market is by halfway points. If a stock price advances two points and then a pullback of one point occurs, this is a normal reaction and the stock is expected to resume its upward trend. If the pullback is less than a point, this is a strong stock that should quickly resume its advance. If the pullback is greater than half, in this case larger than one point, this signifies stock weakness and a possible poor performer.

In a downward trending market, the halfway points are two down and one back. Less than a one point rally signifies a stock that should continue its decline.

Buy-Limit Order

Attempt to trade at support turning points using a buy-limit order (discussed later in this chapter) so that the stop-loss order (more on stop-loss orders in chapter 4) may be placed one-quarter to one-half point beneath the price entered. The resulting risk is now significantly reduced, and when the stock price advances move the stop-loss order up quickly to ensure that no loss is sustained on the position.

Once a significant profit is assured, move up the stop-loss order price point in progressive steps to trail the continued upward progress in the stock's price. The technical position of the market and identifying stock in "strong hands" are important to know prior to purchasing stock, as explained next.

Technical Position

Technical position refers to the internal state of the stock market which is very different from superficial market appearances that have no lasting influence. Overbought and oversold circumstances describe the technical condition of the stock market. The stock market hardly ever makes three or four days of consecutive gains or losses without an opposing pullback or rally. Overbought and oversold conditions occur in the short term, intermediate term and the long term in the stock market.

The technical position of the stock market balances buying with selling, it is the equilibrium supply and demand balance. The observer of a stock market technical position does not care about why an imbalance in supply and demand is occurring, only that it is happening. He or she only cares about not arguing with the market and staying on the correct side of the market's trend.

Strong Technical Condition

It happens that a commodity or stock market is in a strong technical condition, i.e., going up, and all the published market reports and conventional wisdom say that it should not be happening for a plethora of seemingly convincing reasons. For example, valuation is poor, new competition is imminent, political factors are deteriorating, etc. The question for the speculator is, "What should he or she believe, the strong technical condition or the reasoned analysis?"

The astute speculator will always believe the technical condition and the long-term and intermediate-term trends in the stock market at that time. The subjective whys are always more difficult to understand than the objective fact of what is transpiring on the tape and reflected on the chart.

An unexplained stock price improvement, followed by price support and then an additional price advance is normally the consequence of yet unpublished developments that are of an auspicious nature. The market by itself ascertains how significant known and unknown factors are more precisely than any speculator possibly can.

Strong Hands

Whether the stock is in "strong hands" or "weak hands" is determined by knowing the technical position or the internal state of the market. At each overbought or oversold stock market condition, stock is held either by speculators with "strong hands" or "weak hands" and it is essential for astute speculators to identify which is the case. Overbought and oversold circumstances continually occur, consequently, only purchase common stock held in "strong hands."

Following an economic expansion, reduced employment and a recessionary economic contraction lowers inflation but is detrimental for the stock market. At a stage 2 market bottom—during gradual accumulation over many months by institutions, corporate insiders and professional speculators—the market is in a strong technical position and stock ownership is in "strong hands."

A strong technical position is in effect at a market bottom because professionals have gradually purchased common stock at low prices and now stock is in "strong hands" rather than being held in "weak hands" by the investing public, as discussed next.

Weak Hands

A market in a weak technical position has stock ownership in "weak hands." For example, at a market top during stage 4 when stock is being gradually distributed over many months to the investing public—employment is good and people have money to spend. During times of high inflation, too much money is chasing too few goods which contributes to surface prosperity; but technically, the stock market is in "weak hands."

The technical position is at its weakest at a long-term market top because the investing public only seems to get interested in the stock market late in the upswing during price inflation and therefore carries the stock during the long-term downward trend in the market. A stock may be in a weak technical position in the intermediate term when many outside speculators have purchased shares and are now contemplating taking profits.

Coming off of a market bottom during the long-term uptrend during stage 3, the technical position starts strong, however, it weakens as the stock market enters distribution during stage 4. When further buying cannot be encouraged and buying power is worn-out, stock prices will decline, regardless of how good the corporation's management, cash flow, or earnings are currently.

Rules When Purchasing Common Stock

As Justin Mamis makes clear, buying a weak stock just because it is way down in price is simply an act of foolishness. Guessing that the stock's price will not go any lower just because it is low already is fighting the stock's trend and the tape.

Since the interest is in buying stock that will increase in price, do not buy poor companies in weak industries that are going down in price. Buying stock as a result of price weakness should be a warning, do not attempt to be a contrarian simply because a stock's price seems cheap.

Leading Companies

Common stock in a leading company from a highly ranked industry (please see chapter 6) that is just coming off a long-term market bottom may have already increased significantly in price. Purchasing common stock that have already proven that they can go up in price is advantageous.

Leading stock in highly ranked industries that have recently doubled in price are very likely to double again, so take advantage of active stock that are strong movers. In this case, speculators want difficult to buy stock that they have to bid higher and higher to purchase.

Watch for stock that do not decline as much relative to the overall market during a long-term market decline. This is a strong acting stock in the face of a market downtrend. Monitor the stock and add it to your buy candidates list, do all the analysis and be ready when the overall market long term hits a double bottom or head and shoulders bottom and the stock's price has an upside breakout over the 40 week MA trend line on confirming heavy trading volume (more on volume in chapter 5).

A successful upside breakout through resistance on much higher than normal volume distinguishes a price bottom and a new support level. Speculators with money are buying which pushes the stock price up and astute speculators should participate along with them. If the analysis looks good and the probabilities are in the speculator's favor, now is the time to purchase this strong stock already going up in price. A stock's price and trading volume strength corroborate each other, as discussed in chapter 5.

A company with strong fundamentals, such as a high margin-of-safety multiple and launching important new products, is mandatory when buying stock. However, bad fundamental news may only come to light six-to-twelve months after a stock tops out in price. This is because the market is a discounting mechanism and traders use their foresight to predict forthcoming events. Perfection here is not assumed, only having the probability on the speculator's side is expected.

Purchase Price, Bids & Offers And Intrinsic Value

A stock's purchase price, stated bid & offer prices and intrinsic, true, or fair value are different stock market concepts. Stated bid & offer prices frame a possible stock exchange purchase, however, only the purchase price designates a concluded exchange. The stock's purchase price may not be equal to the stated bid & offer prices or intrinsic, true, or fair (ITF) value. Additionally, the stated bid & offer prices and the ITF value of the stock being purchased do not have to be equal.

Stock shares may seem low-priced or expensively priced and a large amount of money has been lost based on this speculative determination; however, common stock are by no means ever too dear to purchase or too cheap to sell. It should be understood that a cheap stock price is not a reason for buying. The temptation to buy a stock solely because the stated price appears cheap causes even experienced speculator to lose money.

Perceptions

Perceptions are the reason for almost all human behavior. What we believe, rightly or wrongly, objectively and/or subjectively, forms our decisions and guides our actions (please see the life and happiness model in chapter 12 of *The Astute Investor*). Traders' perceptions, correct or not, move stock market prices.

Common stock prices move to their highest point at the very time when the largest number of investors and speculators believe the most optimistic story about a company or the overall stock market. This high price stock point is normally attained long before the overall stock market or a company's highest earnings are actually achieved.

Market prices are determined, over the long, intermediate and short-term, by the emotional behavioral characteristics of speculative fear and greed. Emotional traders, especially, place a higher value on their subjective perceptions or expectations than on objective reality and trade accordingly.

Speculators should continually question their perceptions. Getting the objective truths correct prior to reaching a final judgment is paramount when speculating. One can withstand many negative opinions from market pundits quoted in the media when speculators have their facts straight. A vital speculative fact is to know the company's intrinsic, true, or fair value, as discussed next.

Intrinsic True, Or Fair Value

The cardinal principle when speculating in a corporation's common stock, upon which the entire effort depends, is knowing and recognizing stock value. No continued long-term speculative success is feasible without knowing a corporation's intrinsic, true or fair (ITF) value, and nearly all stock market failures are manifest because the speculator is ignorant of this objective fact. Astute speculators compare ITF value with market value capitalization to calculate the stock's bargain value and margin-of-safety multiple prior to purchasing.

The ITF value of a common stock is the price that should be paid at a specific time as determined by experts who know best and understand the circumstances of the corporation being evaluated. Both the stated share price and ITF value vary through time because trader perceptions change though time.

The ITF value of a stock can never be known for certain nor remain fixed for all time and is continuously changing relative to other assets. As an example, increasing stock market prices reduce the dollar's purchasing power because the market is now more expensive. During a recession, when inflationary expectations fall, fewer high-value dollars now purchase more low-priced stock.

It is impossible to know, beforehand, the exact best time to purchase stock. But being in a common stock investment of the highest ITF value and margin-of-safety multiple is similar to an individual with scrupulous integrity, i.e., they both come through the adverse times and prevail over misfortune more easily. Staying vigilant while in a speculative position requires continually updating these facts and judgments and acting promptly as events demand.

Knowing a stock's ITF value and margin-of-safety multiple is the astute speculator's job. Examples of corporate ITF value and margin-of-safety multiple calculations are presented in chapter 2 for General Motors Corporation and chapter 9 for Intel Corporation. Correct timing is paramount for successful speculators and may be aided by recognizing and acting upon buying trigger points, as presented next.

Buying Trigger Points

Timing is the primary speculative art or "art of arts" and is a major challenge for buyers. Being years early when purchasing a stock position is not unprecedented for speculators. When it comes to scheduled buying, the vast majority of amateur and many professional speculators are fooled. Speculators should take their time, be patient, look for trigger points and then act accordingly.

Trigger Points

When an active stock reaches an all-time high price, not just a fifty-two week price high, this is a good indication that things are going well at the company and an indicator that the company should be further investigated. Active common stock hitting new all-time high prices as the market comes out of the accumulation stage 2 are typically hot prospects worth analyzing further and represents a good potential trigger point for purchase.

The investing public rarely, as high as 98 percent, purchases high priced stock that are hitting an all-time high in price. Therefore, a high priced stock (over $100 dollars) hitting a new all-time price high is typically held in "strong hands."

For high priced stock hitting an all-time price high, calculate the margin-of-safety multiple to see if it is undervalued and investigate the ten additional crucial factors. Select leading companies to purchase from the top 25 percent of ranked industries. If the long-term trend of the stock market starts upward, a position in the stock may be initiated during a short-term reaction.

The strategy is to purchase leading companies in top ranked industries held in "strong hands," because, they are high-priced stock hitting an all-time price high that looks too high in price to the investing public, hold until it moves still higher in price and then sell to the investing public—who now think it looks appealing because it has moved up so far in price—when the good corporate news is reported in the media. This stock market philosophy is to "buy high and to sell still higher."

Buy-Limit Orders

Speculators typically pay too high a price to buy stock. Purchasing stock at too high a price creates, in the vernacular of Wall Street, a "poor market position." To guard against this, use a buy-limit order to purchase stock at a support level (discussed in chapters 4 and 5) rather than reaching up for a price using a market order. The adage on Wall Street is, "well bought is half sold."

To ensure getting the price the speculator wants on a stock, place a buy-limit order with the added instructions "immediate or cancel." Only the current shares available to buy at the limit price are filled, the remainder of the order is then cancelled automatically. This approach also prevents paying too much for stock increasing rapidly in price.

Scale-In, Buy-Limit Orders

A straight buy-limit order remains on the books and requires further instructions to be canceled. The buy-limit order is particularly effective on scale-in orders. The plan on the scale-in, buy-limit order could be to purchase a specified number of shares at half-point price intervals down. Additionally, the number of shares specified may increase as the price declines.

Scale-Out, Sell-Limit Orders

The scale-out, sell-limit order may be used to exit a position at half-point price intervals up with varying amounts of stock sold at each point. Scale in-or-out orders plan to buy or sell the most shares at the best average price. Adding the instructions on the scale order, "good till cancelled," maintains its priority position on the books.

Scale in-or-out orders should only be used in conjunction with knowing the intermediate and long-term turning points, as discussed in chapter 5. The scale-in buy-limit and scale-out sell-limit orders are useful because the markets do not have to be monitored all day while the orders are in effect.

Not-Held Order

Buying shares "at the market" means immediately buying all the shares at the best execution possible. NYSE and AMEX floor brokers may use their discretion if they receive a "not-held order." The floor broker is permitted to wait when purchasing stock on the speculator's not-held order, as the stock's trading situation warrants.

Professional speculators use the "not-held order" in an attempt to get better price fills on large share orders by having the floor broker work for them. A simple not-held order tells the floor broker to use his or her best judgment. Adding the instructions of a buy-limit price to the not-held buy order tells the floor broker not to run the price up when filling the order. Further directions may specify, "time is not important," or "buy prior to the close."

The not-held order should only be used with very large volume share orders. If the floor broker does a good job, make sure he or she is complimented and the brokerage company that he or she works for knows about the wonderful service.

Stock Purchasing Rules

The following eight rules should be followed when purchasing common stock:

1. Buy common stock when the S&P 500 Index long-term market trend is making a transition during stage 2 or is trending upward in stage 3.
2. Buy common stock in leading companies that are included in the top 25 percent of industry rankings.
3. At turning points, purchase common stock in leading companies that you know about and understand.
4. At a buying trigger point, purchase only listed common stock on the major exchanges, e.g., NYSE, NASDAQ, or AMEX.
5. Purchase undervalued common stock with a margin-of-safety multiple above 2.0 with good ten additional crucial factors.

6. Purchase high-priced common stock hitting an all-time high price for the first time, the higher the stock's price the better, of at least $10 dollars per share.

7. Purchase high potential companies that Philip Fisher says are either, "prosperous and gifted," or "prosperous because they are gifted."

8. Determine the long-term and intermediate-term technical condition of the market and whether the stock is in "strong hands" or "weak hands"— only purchase common stock held in "strong hands."

Summary

The important concerns for the stock purchase decision are complex and include, in this order of importance: 1) "when," whether to buy now or later on; 2) "what," identifying which stock to purchase; and 3) "how much," what price should be paid for the stock. Additional factors are: 1) knowing the type of speculator you are—e.g., impulsive, nervous, or lethargic; and 2) how much risk capital should be committed in each trade.

The keys to speculative success are: 1) "buy low, sell high"; 2) minimize losses; 3) earn substantial profits; and 4) steer clear of chronic trading. Stock market buying is best accomplished according to an intelligent, unambiguous, speculative plan and schedule based on the speculator's personal strategy.

It is human nature for novice investors to see a large stock price decline and to think that now the stock is at a bargain price and begin to purchase this stock. The investing public gives no thought to the intrinsic, true, or fair (ITF) value of the stock being purchased or the overall market's trend.

Once a position is entered into, it is impossible to remain completely objective because the speculator's judgment becomes biased due to the very human need of self-justifying the prior stock commitment. Keep a journal and follow a speculative plan and schedule but let the market action, including trading volume, turning points and price, tell you if the plan is correct.

The stock market's strength or weakness is often determined by judging halfway points. When buying, the ability to say "yes or no" is paramount. Always keep some cash in reserve for those extraordinarily rare trading opportunities.

A stock's purchase price, stated bid & offer prices and intrinsic, true, or fair value are different stock market concepts. Stated bid & offer prices frame a possible stock exchange purchase, however, only the purchase price designates a concluded exchange. The stock's purchase price may not be equal to the stated bid & offer prices or intrinsic, true, or fair (ITF) value. Additionally, the stated bid & offer prices and the ITF value of the stock being purchased do not have to be equal.

Perceptions move stock market prices. Common stock prices move to their highest point at the very time when the largest number of investors and speculators believe the most optimistic story about a company or the overall market, not when corporate earnings are at their highest.

Patience is key to making money in the stock market. When purchasing stock, be patient, look for trigger points and then be timely when implementing the plan. When an active stock reaches an all-time high price, not just a fifty-two week price high, this is a good indication that things are going well at the company and a good indicator that the company should be further investigated.

Purchase stock in leading companies in the top 25 percent of industry rankings when the overall stock market is in stage 2 or 3. Commit to making the required examination of the company's intrinsic, true or fair (ITF) value, market value capitalization, bargain value and margin-of-safety multiple prior to purchase, rather than afterwards.

Determine the price to be purchased and what you plan to do if the stock advances or declines in price, write it in your journal, then do it. Follow the eight rules for purchasing common stock when the market's technical condition is positive and the stock is held in "strong hands."

4

Selling Or Covering Stock

Introduction

THE SECOND ART OF SPECULATION, after correct timing, is knowing how to sell stock or cover a short position once attained. Selling or covering stock is a stressful act, psychologically difficult for traders to conclude and often a solitary enterprise. Astute speculators learn to like the act of trading and monetary success more than they fear criticism and/or small failures.

The number of traders and investors made rich by the stock market are many, the number able to keep their profits are few. Stock profits on paper are not real until collected and turned into cash. Greed and guilt prevent speculators from selling their large winning positions.

While it is impossible to know when the absolute right time to sell or cover is, the goal is to prevent selling or covering at the much easier to know "wrong time." Selling or covering is prevented at the wrong time, defined as having huge unsustainable losses, by using stop-loss orders.

Stop-loss orders are used to compensate for a trader's inability to sell or cover stock. Selling is properly accomplished by performing risk-reduction calculations to ensure that the planned profit is at least an advantageous four-to-one in proportion to the possible loss. Capital is the lifeblood of stock trading, learn how to use progressive stop-loss orders and time stops.

Selling Or Covering Principles

Stock market speculators normally have ability and are good buyers, but have the fatal character flaw of overreaching or overplaying their hand which manifests itself in not knowing how best to exit their stock positions. Knowing when to stay out of a stock position, when to buy and the ability to stay in a winning position are all crucial; however, how to sell or cover stock is the second art of speculation, after timing, that requires mastering.

The financial and emotional sting of settling up always comes with the stock's sale or short covering, never during the stock's purchase or short sale. Making a stock purchase or a short sale commitment is complicated but relatively straightforward, the much more emotionally difficult task is closing out the stock position once attained. Traders, especially in the beginning, are often terrible sellers which results in speculative failure. Why stock selling is so difficult is discussed next.

Stock Selling Difficulty

The difficulty of the sale decision becomes evident after a stock is purchased. The price paid to purchase common stock is often utterly beside the point when determining a stock sale. The probability that the stock sale is correctly performed is much less assured than the buy decision. Speculators recognize that increased errors associated with closing out a sale versus buying a stock are inevitable, consequently, traders plan for that eventuality.

Buying stock is a prestigious act while selling stock is often treated like an orphan. Buying requires confronting many choices that may seem bewildering but many organizations are willing to help traders with the buy decision. As an example, institutional salespeople have many purchase oriented meetings with mutual fund portfolio managers but have very few meetings with these same managers about when to sell common stock once purchased.

Selling common stock is difficult, even for professional money managers. Mutual fund portfolio managers normally remain close to fully invested, irrespective of the stock market's stage. If a mutual fund manager were told that the market is in a long-term downtrend, he or she would probably just purchase stock on a more moderate pace rather than sell their currently held shares.

Speculators are typically left to their own devices when selling. Speculators experience anxiety and stress based on the necessity of using incomplete information, become emotional at times with non-rational hope, fear, or greed and may display the irrational need to save face, the need to make a perfect trade and stock market addiction (for more on this please see chapter 5 in *The Astute Investor*). The trouble that amateur speculators have when selling their stock is discussed next.

Amateur Speculators

Amateur speculators, especially, have trouble selling stock correctly. The investing public purchases stock but do not sell if it declines slightly in price. Losing $200 dollars on paper is preferable to the emotional setback of an admission of failure, no matter how small. Instead the stock is held, often with their small loss turning into a major loss. At a long-term panic-selling market bottom, amateur speculators and the investing public finally sell their long-held stock at a considerable loss and try never to think of this painful experience again.

Amateur speculators sit calmly with paper losses. Because the investing public refuses to entertain the idea of selling stock at a loss, the struggle to make the decision to sell is blocked out of their mind. The investing public is resigned to the paper loss and remains optimistic that tomorrow will be a better day.

Excuses not to sell are legion for amateur speculators. Irrelevant or specious reasoning helps to bandage the bruised speculative egos associated with paper losses. Subconsciously, if speculators do not want to sell, rationalizing non-action is easy to do.

The investing public and amateur speculators typically become nervous, fidgety and anxious when they have a profit and are now required to think about selling. Stress produced during the selling or covering act becomes intense. To counteract this human feeling, speculators should not berate themselves if the stock races upward in price after they sell.

The stock market is a never ending auction supplying unlimited anticipation for the future. Paper losses are often overlooked and self regard is maintained by holding losing stock positions and hoping for future favorable prospects. Often the goal for amateur speculators is to eventually get out their losing positions, even.

A major difference between amateur speculators and professional speculators is that when conditions are right to sell, professional speculators act while amateurs waver. Speculators should resolve to see the looked for signals, act in a timely fashion and feel good about the eventual result regardless of the trade's outcome. Why selling or covering stock is always a mistake in one way or another is discussed next.

Selling Or Covering Mistakes

Speculators must realize that any stock sale or short covering is in some way a mistake and fully acknowledge that errors are part of what the act of selling or covering is all about. The question is always, how do speculator's separate the emotional influences that subvert intelligent speculating from the "stock selling or covering facts of life."

The reason that every stock sale is somehow a mistake is even if speculators perform market timing to perfection, which is impossible, by getting in at the exact bottom and selling at the exact top price—winning speculators would then believe they should have purchased more shares of stock.

Do not look back with regret concerning a stock market sale, either when an actual loss occurs or when missing out on earning additional money as the stock races up in price after the sale. Remember Lott's wife who turned into a pillar of salt when she looked back with regret. Do not look back with regret on any stock sale or short covering; because, all sales or short coverings are always less than perfect, as discussed next.

Selling Or Covering Perfection Is Impossible

Ironically, making money in the stock market is a secondary priority for almost all traders, instead, the most valuable speculative possession is saving face and maintaining a high self regard—even when the speculator is the only one who knows about the outcome of the trade. Consequently, both profits and losses in the stock market are agonizing if speculators hold themselves to a standard of perfection.

Speculators become anxious to sell as the stock advances in price because the ego cannot stand to see a stock continue to increase in price once it is sold. The speculator castigates himself or herself for selling too early or too late rather that complimenting himself or herself on having made an acceptable profit. This is human nature playing itself out in the stock market.

Everything in the stock market is relative, so looking for absolutes or trying to be perfect is self defeating. Imperfection is a fact of life on Wall Street, speculators should be resigned to it and use it to their advantage when they recognize the irrational perfection impulse in others.

Speculators should not criticize themselves for not getting out at the very top of the market, instead, be satisfied with capturing the middle two thirds of a price move. The courage not to be perfect and the will power to sell stock at less than the highest price or to cover at less than the lowest price is encouraged.

The best time to sell or cover stock is impossible to know, upfront. To control risk, the stock must be sold or covered according to set procedures that are presented later in this chapter. Do not obsess on any past errors, instead, speculators should prepare themselves for what is coming next. Speculators should adopt the following attitude, "What happens in the stock market stays in the stock market."

The Fundamental Stock Selling Or Covering Rule

Failure is not the opposite of success in the stock market, when the resulting loss does not knock the speculator out of the game. Some failure is required for speculative success and since selling or covering mistakes are inevitable, resolve to discipline your ego by admitting the mistake freely and exiting the position without delay. Learn from the mistakes to become a progressively better trader. The fundamental stock selling or covering rule is, "Astute speculators learn to like the act of trading and monetary success more than they fear criticism and/or small failures."

Misfortune enters all our lives and to preserve our own self-esteem, we incorrectly prefer to blame others for our troubles. Instead, speculators should always take full responsibility for all their speculative losses. No excuses are allowed, going into denial to save face is not acting like an astute speculator.

Speculators have to deal with inadequate information, therefore, feel comfortable with essential and satisfactory information leading to less than perfect results. Thinking that things out of your control caused a loss is counterproductive to being an astute speculator. The best way to conquer the pitfalls of selling is to understand the psychology of selling or covering a short stock position, as explained next.

Psychology Of Selling Or Covering Stock

The stock market may be thought of as a dream factory and is entertainment for many. The investing public incorrectly believes that participating in the stock market is like gambling on American roulette, they place their money down and vainly cheer their stock selection on to victory. Even if their trade does not work out at first, tomorrow could be a better day, consequently, they sit and hope. Watching as the stock market fluctuates, speculators fear completing the trade because that would remove it from a dream state to one of reality.

Making a purchase commitment is more complicated but much less emotional than concluding it. Psychologically, selling stock or covering a short position is an infinitely more difficult act than buying or shorting the stock.

Once having bought or sold short, it is emotionally difficult even for professionals to sell or cover their position. Immediately, as the stock is purchased or sold short, the right to evade a decision is lost. Upon the completion of the buy or sell short order, the speculator is forced to contemplate many more decisions concerning this stock—i.e., each day the question is either, "hold, sell or cover."

Speculators have an inordinate fear of selling or covering stock, the fear is not rational, but nonetheless, real to them. Typically, the decision to sell or cover is agonized over to the point of complete paralysis. Pride of opinion plays an important part in why speculators find selling or covering difficult, as explained next.

Pride of Opinion

Pride of opinion or the need to save face is the number one priority for most investors and speculators in the stock market and even overcomes their need to make money. This is why investors and speculators typically are risk adverse in the face of stock profits and risk seeking when stock positions show a loss.

Law of Compensation

Those who make sudden stock market fortunes have another pitfall, overextension. As wealth builds, their judgment declines. Larger monetary gains change a speculator's attitude, perspective and typically cause ego problems. The explosive growth in paper profits convinces the now egotistical speculator that he or she has finally arrived and anything is now possible. The Law of Compensation is at work here, i.e., every advantage is offset by a disadvantage.

As the now arrogant speculator's bank account increases, their thinking ability declines. The need to feed the constant endorphin rush of earning more and more money becomes insatiable. Forgotten is the fact that the market fluctuates and the stock price can easily move in the opposite direction. Instead of lightening up on the stock position, the tendency is to feel secure by following the crowd and adding to the position—leading to an eventual reversal in fortune.

Greed & Guilt

Greed prevents speculators from cashing in their huge winning positions. Larger monetary gains change a speculator's attitude, perspective and may cause ego problems. Avarice makes speculators believe that they are earning the outsized profits rather than the result of the stock market's advance. Overly optimistic speculators assume that after doubling or quadrupling their money, they can earn more simply with their will to believe. More often than not this is a losing strategy, dictated by greed.

Psychological issues such as guilt, the need to fail because speculators feel comfortable losing, sexual frustration, the secret desire to be punished, thinking like a victim and social aggression may play a part in the speculator subconsciously seeking chastisement for doing wrong—real or imagined—manifesting itself by losing money in the stock market.

Some of the above issues may be the speculators' psychological reasons for not being able to properly sell or cover their stock positions. The concluding insight is, "Everyone gets what they want out of the stock market whether they recognize it or not." Paper profits are never real until they are turned into cash by selling or covering, as discussed next.

Real Profits Vs. Paper Profits

Most speculators never get an opportunity to spend their paper profits because they are reluctant to sell or cover their positions. Selling, if done too early, takes them out of their position and stops the intoxicating endorphin rush they feel when earning money on paper as their stock advances in price. This wonderful feeling clouds the speculator's mind, even as the market turns negative, all the while the speculator remains optimistic about tomorrow.

What is lost in this speculative emotion and market swirl is that owning common stock is not the goal—cash is! Profits are only real after a stock sale or a purchase to cover occurs. The following example explains the importance of real profits versus paper profits.

Real Profits Vs. Paper Profits Example

Daniel Drew (1797-1879), Jay Gould (1836-1892) and James Fisk (1834-1872) fought Cornelius Vanderbilt (1794-1877), who initially began business in shipping, for control of the Erie Railroad, in the Erie War of 1866-1868, by using newly printed Erie Railroad convertible bonds to immensely increase the number of common shares outstanding. Eventually buying Vanderbilt's shares at an inflated price, Daniel Drew and company force the Erie Railroad into bankruptcy—a procedure they pioneered—and then reorganize the railroad under their control at a immense profit to themselves.

Later in 1870, Gould and Fisk double-cross Drew by manipulating the Erie Railroad stock and cause Drew to lose heavily. Fisk is shot dead during a dispute over money and a Broadway showgirl. Drew files for bankruptcy and dies a pauper. Vanderbilt at the time of his death is the richest man in

America valued at more than $100 million dollars and Gould's fortune, at his death, is estimated at $72 million dollars.

Four legendary stock traders become multimillionaires, but only two are able to hold on to their money and their lives. How to hold on to paper profits is paramount in speculation and is discussed next.

Hold On To Paper Profits

Speculators should realize that the alleged easy money on Wall Street is mostly loaned as paper profits, never given away and rarely ever kept as cash. Paper profits are all show and eventually immaterial, it is the cash that one keeps that matters. Jay Gould, called the Mephistopheles of Wall Street, intimately understood stock trading and relates the following story of what it means to be a successful speculator.

If the names of persons first made rich by the stock market and then subsequently made poor were written down in books, these books would fill an entire library. If the names of persons who are able to keep the riches that Wall Street provides were written down in books, they would fill only a few volumes. The moral of the story is, "speculators cannot spend paper profits." Living in a fool's paradise with illusory riches is irresponsible. Paper profits are by no means tangible, a profit is only a profit when money is in the speculator's account.

Bernard M. Baruch (1870-1965)—called The Lone Wolf on Wall Street—also believes that making paper profits on Wall Street is easier then being able to keep the money once earned. As a result, Baruch sells stock early prior to it reaching a top price and feels this is the key to retaining his fortune. Perhaps Baruch could be richer by holding longer but he avoids a stock price collapse and the possibility of losing all which he sees happen quite often to many other Wall Street traders.

Stock profits on paper are not real until collected and turned into cash. A paper profit, regardless of the amount, can quickly become a loss due to a mental lapse or the inability to act. Techniques to help speculators become successful sellers by properly turning paper profits into real profits are presented next.

Second Art Of Speculation

The second art of speculation, after correct timing, is knowing how to sell stock or cover a short position once attained. Speculators seem to get the "buy low" portion of the famous Wall Street adage correct, make sizeable paper profits, but completely miss out on the "sell high" part.

When an inevitable buying or short-selling mistake is made and a loss is inescapable, the secret to selling or covering the short position is to lose the least amount possible over the shortest period of time. To win requires knowing that speculators will make mistakes and in those instances, speculators should sell or cover quickly without wavering in order to minimize losses.

Sell Losers Quickly And Let Winners Run

Knowing how to win in the stock market is understanding how to benefit the most from trading successes and how to quickly limit trading failures. The investing public and amateur speculators turn this correct procedure on its head, as explained next.

The investing public and amateur speculators, at the first sign of stock market trouble, will sell shares in their portfolio that are slightly profitable and keep those that have experienced a decline in price. This is a naïve attempt to be contrarian. Typically, the kept weak stock tend to break down quickly and the investing public or amateur speculators are reluctant to sell any stock with a paper loss. The hope is the stock price will quickly turn around and they can get out even. The correct procedure is just the opposite, instead, astute speculators should sell the losers quickly and keep the winners and let them run up in profits.

The courage necessary to sell a stock at a high price cannot be underestimated. Be unafraid to sell common stock that have advanced substantially in price, let the next person who purchases this stock have an opportunity to make money. If having difficulty, reduce the position by half and move the profits from the brokerage account to a bank account. And once sold out, do not rush back into the market again, instead, speculators should patiently plan and schedule their next stock operation.

Using market orders to sell stock when getting out of a large winning position is a good idea. It is not worth hoping for an extra quarter or half point when the next day could be disastrous for one's holdings. Have an opinion on the underlying forces in the stock market, but wait until the market confirms these opinions with market price movement prior to taking action—as explained next.

Selling Do's

If a stock does not participate in an overall stock market advance this is a significant failure and should be heeded, consequently, sell the stock at the market price. The stock is being distributed underneath the cover of an increasing average such as the Dow Jones Industrial Average (DJIA). Once the stock failure is recognized, do not freeze on the sale—make the sale and feel good about the result, regardless of the stock's future action.

Sell Stock At The Open

Leave orders with your broker to sell stock at the market's open. The specialists on the NYSE and AMEX, at the market's open, decide a fair, objective price to balance supply and demand for outside orders and their own accounts. Consequently, the daily open price is probably the most noteworthy price to know for a specific stock. At the open, buyers generally outnumber sellers and selling at the open takes away the emotional stress of the continued stock market action occurring during the trading day.

When speculators judge it is time to sell, go ahead and sell. The timing of that sale may be done best at the opening the next day. If the stock closes up for the day, it is probable that placing an order to sell at the market during the opening the next business day will return a higher price. Strength in a stock at the market close normally engenders strength at the open the next trading day. Additionally, making the decision to sell while the market is closed is easier to accomplish because it minimizes the speculator's emotional stress.

Obviously, if the expectations for political-economic conditions are poor and the market is entering stage 1—the entire portfolio should be sold at the market and plans made for going short at a trigger point.

Stock Brokers

Stock brokers never seem to be treated fairly. Full-service brokers get blamed by their clients for any poor positions that are enter into, but rarely are asked about when to sell or cover a winning position. This is the human ego at work. Losses are someone else's mistakes, winnings, it seems, are believed to be due to the trader's own sagacity and wisdom and not because of the market itself.

A cardinal rule in the brokerage business is not to tell a client when to sell a winning stock position unless it can be done exactly at the very top price. At less than the top price, the client feels duped into selling too early and the broker is blamed even though their account is showing a large profit. So while the client may be put into a profitable stock position, almost invariably, the client has to get himself or herself out.

When using a full-service broker, make certain to ask him or her to pass along sell or cover recommendations. Listen to the broker's advice and then act accordingly, because, that is why the speculator is paying for the full-service broker.

Cash Positions

Periodically changing all stock market positions into cash to keep the speculator's mind clear is a good strategy, especially in a trading-range bound market. Also, not speculating with all the cash in the speculator's account at any one time allows for a cash reserve that is particularly beneficial when something exceptional comes along in the stock market that is too good to pass up (more on this in chapter 7).

Stop-Loss Orders

Emotions can overwhelm a speculator at the time the decision to sell or cover stock is being made, resulting in impulsive selling or covering mistakes. Because selling or covering a stock position is a stressful act, the need for the stop-loss order to automatically make the transaction for the speculator is required. By using a stop-loss order, the selling or covering action is effectively removed from the speculator and transferred to the marketplace.

The elimination of mistakes is impossible when speculating, consequently, the way to minimize a selling or covering misstep is through the use of stop-loss orders. The stop-loss order is a safeguard throughout he trading day. Once set, the stop-loss order requires no ongoing assessment of current market conditions.

Human emotional vulnerability is trumped by using the stop-loss order which dependably closes the stock position according to a plan. Stop-loss orders help maintain confidence and keep the mind clear. A small loss that turns into a major loss, as a result of not using stop-loss orders and not being able to sell or cover a position, shakes the speculator's composure, the courage to make decisions and the ability to take proper action.

Risk Reduction

Risk reduction is the reason that stop-loss orders are used. In this way the planned possible profit is in advantageous proportion to the planned possible loss. Edward H. Harriman (1848-1909), who left an estate estimated at $400 million dollars, as well as James R. Keene and Jesse Livermore emphasize that the way to reduce risk when speculating in the stock market is to always use stop-loss orders.

While it is impossible to know when the absolute right time to sell or cover is, the goal is to prevent selling or covering at the much easier to know "wrong time." Selling or covering is prevented at the wrong time, defined as having huge unsustainable losses, by using stop-loss orders.

The stop-loss order saves speculators from becoming involuntary investors. Being locked into a stock with considerable paper losses results in "dead risk capital," possibly for an extended period of time. Not having these funds available for more productive uses is an opportunity cost of capital loss.

Stop-Loss Orders Are Insurance

The stop-loss order is a programmed safeguard to protect against large losses. The stop-loss order is certain protection against a speculator's human limitations.

Traders often lose a great deal of money when stop-loss orders are not used. Stop-loss orders act like insurance policies for speculators and should always be in place the moment after a stock is purchased or sold short. The adage on Wall Street is, "The first loss is the smallest loss and the best loss."

The stop-loss order safeguards risk capital. Lets assume the speculator plays American roulette and has a guarantee that all that is forfeited when losing is $5 dollars on a $100 dollar bet, this is considered great odds and would be readily accepted. This is similar to how the stop-loss order operates in the astute speculator's account.

The stop-loss order is the insurance protection that the astute speculator should never forego. Astute speculators, regardless of the number of times their positions are stopped out for small losses, will eventually make more money by letting winning positions run for large gains. No one is always correct in the stock market, consequently, the ability to take a small loss is fundamental for success when speculating in this volatile arena.

Protect Profits

The effective elimination of a possible loss when a stock is showing a profit is perhaps the most significant means of achieving speculative success. Never let a winning trade turn into a loss. Place the stop-loss order at the purchase price or short-sale price at the first opportunity. Failing to protect paper profits will allow many of them to slip away which will trouble the speculator's mind and not permit clear thinking for the subsequent trade.

A stock often sells off quickly and returns to its breakout point just above its resistance level. Such a pullback is troubling, but should not cause the speculator to act impulsively. Let the stop-loss order work as it should. The stop-loss order price points may be calculated when being set, as presented next.

Calculating Stop-Loss Orders

Speculating on the intermediate-term swings in the market requires stop-loss orders to shield against major losses. Think about potential stock losses rather than just possible profits when planning market operations. It is preferable to lose two points when the stop is caught rather than lose fifteen or twenty points when no stop-loss order is in place.

The stop-loss order to sell stock held in a long position or when buying to cover a short position, turns into a "market order" the instant the stock sells 100 shares "at or above" the buy to cover stop-loss price and sells 100 shares "at or below" the sell stop-loss price. How to set a stop-loss order price point is discussed next.

Setting Stop-Loss Order Price Points

Speculators lose money in the stock market as a direct result of not using stop-loss orders. Buy stock only when a stop-loss order can be prudently placed, e.g., just below the support level when long and just above the resistance level when short.

One winning speculator has a strict policy to ensure that losses are cut short. A two-point stop-loss order for the average stock is always attached to every order. When in doubt, a maximum two point stop-loss order should be used.

The stop-loss order, both on the long and short side, averts common mistakes from turning into financial calamities. Use intraday prices, rather than closing prices, to set stop-loss order price points. At support and resistance levels, use intraday prices and then set the stop-loss order price points.

The stop-loss order price point, on a long position medium priced stock, should be placed from one to two points under the low intraday price touched by the stock the day the stock reached a turning point (please see chapter 5). Limit losses when shorting stock by setting stops from one to two points above the stock intraday price resistance level.

The stop-loss order price point should be set between one and two points away from the intraday support or resistance level for the average priced stock. Stock stop-loss order price points should never be set at more than 10 percent away from the purchase or short-sale price. Find a good entry point to acquire the stock position. When setting the stop-loss order price point below support or above resistance, but more than 10 percent away from the expected purchase or short-sale price, make this a reason not to take the position.

Also, never assume that a mental stop-loss order price point will be honored. When using a mental stop the trader promises himself or herself to exit a position at a certain price. Mental stops put too much responsibility on the trader and should not be trusted.

The stop-loss order price point on a stock is never to be lowered in price if long or increased in price if short. The stop-loss order price point is always to be moved to decrease risk, never to increase the risk on a trade, i.e., speculators should not second guess themselves.

Whole Or Half-Numbered Interval Strategy

Human nature contributes to stop-loss orders being placed mostly at whole or half-numbered intervals. This is especially true at round dollar numbers like $10, $20, or $30 dollars etc.

Speculators should use this to their advantage by setting stop-loss order price points just above whole or half numbers when in a long position and just below whole or half numbers when in a short position. Placing stop-loss order price points in this way ensures better execution. The whole or half-numbered interval strategy should also be incorporated for buy-limit orders.

Stop-Loss Order Price Point Calculation

Careful observation may allow the setting of calculated stop-loss order price points. The use of the stop-loss order to limit the loss to a set number of points or percentage loss can be improved upon through calculation. A stock in a trading range indicating intraday support at $50 dollars per share and resistance at $55 dollars per share should have the stop-loss price point set, if long at $49 and if short at $56, regardless of the price the stock is purchased or sold short.

Buy stock only when it can be determined, before the purchase, that a reasonable stop-loss order price point is indicated. Do not be premature in setting a stop-loss. If no reasonable stop-loss price point presents itself, monitor the stock until one develops. On the other hand, do not purchase stock just because a calculated stop-loss order price point can be determined.

To purchase the stock close to the support price, use the buy-limit order. Placing the calculated stop-loss order price point based solely on the price action and not on the purchase price is required. Not observing this rule is the reason that approximately 70 percent of stop-loss orders are unexpectedly filled, to the detriment of the speculator.

Reward-to-Risk Ratio

If the stop-loss order price point is set two points below an average priced stock, as this is written that is $37.55 on the NYSE, the expected profits need to be at least eight points for this to be considered a good purchase. This sets the minimum reward-to-risk ratio of four-to-one. To recap:

purchase at $37.55, stop-loss at 35.55, with an expected target price of $45.55.

Assuming the a speculator wins +60 percent of the time on the above trade and loses -40 percent of the time. Over the positive sixty percent of the time, 10 percent of the time an increase of $37.55 or +100 percent return is expected, 20 percent of the time a $22.53 increase or a positive +60 percent return is expected and 30 percent of the time a positive $8.00 increase or a positive +21 percent return is expected. Forty percent of the time a negative -$2.00 point loss is expected or minus -5.3 percent. Table 4 – 1: Reward-To-Risk Expected Payoff presents that amount of expected returned with this approach.

Table 4 – 1: Reward-To-Risk Expected Payoff

One Chance In Ten To Make 37.55 points	.1 x 100% = .10
Two Chances In Ten To Make 22.53 Points	.2 x 60% = .12
Three Chances In Ten To Make 8 Points	.3 x 21% = .06
Four Chances In Ten To Lose 2 Points	.4 x -5% = -.02
	Total = +30%

The probabilities are now in the speculator's favor, total returns for the ten trades are expected to be a positive +30 percent on the risk capital prior to transaction costs. This minimum reward-to-risk ratio of four-to-one is applicable when shorting weak stock, as well.

Speculators should feel confident that outsized returns are probable when the proper knowledge, foresight, patience, iron nerve, discipline, judgment and proper timing are used effectively in the stock market. The setting of stop-loss order price points and calculating reward-to-risk ratios are further discussed in Chapter 7: Money Management.

Progressive Stop-Loss Orders

As soon as a stock shows a profit, regardless of its size, progressive stop-loss orders are set during the stock's rise when long and during the stock's fall when short. However, the progressive stop-loss price should be increased slower than the stock's price rise; because, downward reactions at higher price levels tend to be more pronounced. Also, the progressive stop-loss order price point should be reduced slower than the stock's price fall when short; because, upward bulges at lower price levels tend to be more pronounced.

More money is normally made by following the market as it advances toward a top and selling only after the market turns down. The best way to accomplish this is to use a progressive stop-loss order, once it hits a target sale price. Raise the progressive stop-loss order price as the market advances. When a third move up on a stock's weekly chart appears, i.e., higher highs and higher lows, move the progressive stop loss within a point of the stock's price to lock in profits.

Time Stops

Jesse Livermore explains the importance of time stops. Because risk capital is the lifeblood of trading, it is imperative that this capital always be in effective circulation. If a stock does not perform as expected, Livermore would close out the position after only a few weeks.

If a position is entered into because the market is expected to breakdown and it does not happen when anticipated, the position is closed out even if no money is lost. It is better to be out of the market and patiently waiting in cash for the next superb trading opportunity than to have cash locked in a listless drifter going nowhere.

Hold the major movers, those earning over +20 percent in a month, for six-to-twelve months, depending on how they act. Those that are not very strong but have earned up to +20 percent in three months are sold. Listless drifters that have not done much in a few weeks are sold. A trade showing a loss after a week or two is a good indication that the timing is wrong and it should be closed out so the money is available for a truly extraordinary upcoming speculative situation.

It is best to have profits in a stock the first day the shares are purchased or sold short. A leading indicator that the overall trade will be successful is an immediate profit on the position. However, if no profits result within a few weeks, close out the position using a time stop and go to a neutral cash position and plan later to purchase or sell short an active stock.

Stop-Loss Orders In Practice

Initially, speculators have to take the stop-loss order rule on faith until they get experience using it. If not convinced, use simulator or paper trading (please see chapter 8) to test the strategy over a period of time. Keep a journal with the reasons for purchasing or shorting the stock, the reward-to-risk ratio, the open, high, low, closing prices and daily trading volume figures so that the accumulation or distribution explanations for gains and losses may be determined at the conclusion of the test.

Stop-loss orders, especially, come into play during intermediate-term swings. During steep declines, layer after layer of sell stop-loss orders are uncovered propelling the market downward. Similarly, during stock market rallies, layer after layer of buy to cover stop-loss orders are reached forcing the market upward.

Gap Opens

A problem with carrying stock overnight or over the weekend, even when using stop-loss orders, is the gap open. This is a stock price range where no shares are traded which can result in significant losses beyond the price set by the stop-loss order. The NASDAQ seems to have wider gap opens than the NYSE or AMEX, because, the latter two exchanges use specialists to set open prices.

Canceling Stop-Loss Orders And Limit Orders

Speculators may decide, incorrectly, to cancel their stop-loss order at the sign of danger. This strategy is foolish, rather, the stop-loss order is in place to protect the speculator from danger.

Making the stop-loss order "good till cancelled (GTC)," which keeps the order in force now and into the future, sets a priority for sale on the specialist's book or in the computer system. Professional off-floor traders use GTC sell-limit orders to sell a stock automatically at a profit when the purchased stock attains its expected limit price.

Speculators may decide to sell at a set price but when that price is close to being reached, everything seems so wonderful they elect to raise the sell-limit price. Professionals try not to reach for too much and feel it is bad strategy to ever raise the sell-limit order once set because that would be acting like a hog which has a tendency to get slaughtered in the market.

Stop-Loss Orders And Sell Decisions

Stop-loss orders are wonderful defense and offer protection against emotional non-action. However, stop-loss orders should not take precedence over thinking. An over reliance on stop-loss orders blinds speculators to making more up-to-date judgments based upon current objective truths concerning their stock positions.

Has the stock failed in some way? If a stock is not doing what is expected of it, e.g., going sideways or even declining while the overall averages are advancing strongly, this may be the indication to sell "at the market" and quickly get out of the position. Always ask yourself, "is now the right time to sell at the market."

Selling Signs

Whenever a particular stock or the overall stock market generates so much general public interest that an article on a fantastic happening is published on the front page of a major daily newspaper, astute speculators realize the time to sell is coming.

Typically, the common stock that are the first to hit all-time high prices off a market low in stage 2 are also the leaders to first turn down prior to a general market downturn during stage 1. When the majority of the initial price leaders on the way up begin to top out and then turn down, the rest of the market will not be far behind.

Speculators who take a long position watch the 10-Q quarterly reports from these corporations. If two quarters experience an earnings momentum slowdown from the past year's quarters, for example from 40 percent growth to 20 percent growth, this is reason to sell. The company's growth has probably topped out and rather than be caught in a period of price consolidation, it is time to sell. However, even the best companies can experience one disappointing quarter which is the reason two poor quarters are required prior to a sale.

Stock splits are normally a reason to sell stock, not, as the investing public thinks, a reason to purchase stock. Professional speculators often use the good news generated in the media by the stock-split to sell their stock positions to novice speculators.

Nervousness, based on the stock's price, leading to premature sales should be guarded against. A good reason is required to sell or cover a stock, especially one that is solidly in the speculator's plus column. If the stock is acting the way it should and doing nothing wrong, do not sell or cover.

Summary

The second art of speculation, after correct timing, is knowing how to sell stock or cover a short position once attained. Failure is not the opposite of success in the stock market, when the resulting loss does not knock the speculator out of the game. The fundamental stock selling or covering rule is, "Astute speculators learn to like the act of trading and monetary success more than they fear criticism and/or small failures."

Watching as the stock market fluctuates, the amateur speculator fears completing the trade because that would remove it from the dream state to one of reality. Once having purchased or sold stock short, it is emotionally difficult to sell or cover the position—even for professionals. A major difference between amateur and professional speculators is that when conditions are right to sell or cover, professionals act while amateurs waver.

Those who make stock market fortunes often fall into the pitfall of overreaching. As wealth builds, judgment declines. Larger monetary gains change a speculator's attitude, perspective and typically cause ego problems. Most speculators never get an opportunity to spend their paper profits because they are emotionally reluctant to sell. Stock profits on paper are not real until collected and turned into cash.

Greed and guilt prevent speculators from cashing in their huge winning position. The courage not to be perfect and the will power to sell stock at less than the highest price or to cover at less than the lowest price is encouraged. When speculators judge it is time to sell, sell "at the market." Selling at the open takes away the emotional stress of continued stock market action during the trading day.

While it is impossible to know when the absolute right time to sell or cover is, the goal is to prevent selling or covering at the much easier to know "wrong time." Selling or covering is prevented at the wrong time, defined as having huge unsustainable losses, by using stop-loss orders.

Because selling or covering is an emotional act, the need for the stop-loss order to automatically make the transaction is required. The stop-loss order is protection against becoming an involuntary investor and guarding against the speculator's limitations. Risk-to-reward calculations ensure that the planned profit is at least an advantageous four-to-one proportion to the planned possible loss. Use intraday prices, rather than closing stock prices, to set stop-loss orders no more than a few points or 10 percent away from the transaction price at support or resistance levels.

Once set, the stop-loss order price point requires no ongoing assessment of current conditions and should not be lowered if long or raised if short. Progressive stop-loss orders should be continually raised if long or lowered if short as the stock position becomes more and more profitable, to ensure that increased earnings are captured.

Stop-loss orders are wonderful defense and offer protection against emotional non-action. When long, being locked into a declining stock with considerable paper losses results in "dead risk capital," possibly for an extensive period of time. Because risk capital is the lifeblood of trading, it is imperative that this capital always be in effective circulation; therefore, use time stops to sell listless stock drifters.

5

Volume And Turning Points

Introduction

TAPE READING HELPS speculators determine whether buying or selling power is moving the stock market. Price action indicates but is secondary in importance to trading volume which validates the market's buy-side advancement or sell-side decline.

Money, represented by trading volume, designates the importance of a stock's supply and demand disequilibrium. The current and potential supply and demand characteristics are crucial to understanding why trading volume is so important in determining whether accumulation or distribution is ongoing in the stock market.

How to recognize a stock turning point is presented. Volume activity patterns at long-term and intermediate-term turning points reveal where common stock price advances or declines lose momentum. New 52 week high & low price lists, most active lists and selling climax days assist when determining turning points.

Trading along with the investing public at stock turning points is to be avoided. Instead, develop the judgment and the iron nerve necessary to act properly at stock turning points by having confidence in the information presented.

Tape Reading Basics

Speculation necessitates judging what other traders are doing which is represented on the stock market tape (also called electronic tape). Successful tape reading is a study in determining whether the buy-side or the sell-side has the most forceful power in the stock market and then having the courage to participate on that side of the market.

Tape reading occurs in real time and presents purchase price and the quantity of shares traded information and, as importantly, the tape does not lie. Consequently, it is possible to spot the active stock leaders versus the weak or laggard stock issues by reading the stock market tape.

The supply and demand battle goes on between buyers and sellers during the trading day and is recorded in real time on the tape. Being able to tell whether a stock or the stock market acts favorably or disappointingly, based on tape reading principles, is an indispensable asset for the astute speculator.

Tape reading is an exercise in anticipating stock price changes based upon the stock's purchase price and volume transactions that are reported live on the tape. This requires forecasting stock trends and turning points by understanding the consequences of how past price and volume transactions affect future stock price movements.

The tape is both a compass and a truthful friend that may be counted upon to point the speculative way. The tape gives traders ample opportunity to make timely trades. The astute tape reader may think of themselves as transaction analysts. A brief tape reading history is presented next.

Tape Reading History

Tape reading is an art and science practiced by some of the speculative legends on Wall Street. Jesse Livermore (1877-1940)—called the Great Bear of Wall Street—is an active devotee of tape reading and earns $3 million dollars in the market panic of 1907 and $100 million dollars in the market crash of 1929 by correctly shorting stock designated by the action on the tape.

Tape reading today can no longer be practiced in exactly the same manner used by Jesse Livermore; because, the volume of stock market trading today is too large and the market is too broad to predict what a company's share price will do simply by the action on the tape. Nonetheless, certain aspects of tape reading remains informative and worthy of study—as explained next.

The Composite Mind On The Tape

Millions of traders' minds are represented with buy and sell price and trading volume figures on the tape. Amateur speculators overlook the importance of the tape and see it as a hodgepodge of unconnected data. However, the story of the stock market is played out in real time on the tape, so take the time to appreciate the chronicle of transactions recorder on the tape by each trader.

An astute speculator judges the tape as the composite or single mind of all traders participating in the stock market. The single speculative mind is exposed for any person who cares to observe the action on the tape. Astute speculators understand the truth of what is being explained for all to see on the tape.

The composite mind represented on the tape is always superior to the mind of an individual speculator, consequently, professional traders use the tape to their advantage. Realize that "pride of opinion" causes as many mishaps in the stock market as the non-rational emotions of fear and greed. Speculators should keep their ego in check and merely carry out the tape's instructions.

What To Look For On The Tape

Everything on the tape has significance. Observe and study closely the advances or bulges and the downturns or reactions that are shown on the tape. The astute speculator focuses on trading volume action and can explain when volume is light, average, or heavy in relation to price advancements or declines and to market momentum.

Competent tape readers understand how the investing public translates breaking news and expectations into buying or selling and can read the tape as confirmation of the investing public's buying and selling actions. It is the astute speculator's job to know the single market mind and judge what the investing public and amateur speculators will do with their money before they do it.

Some speculators find it beneficial to spend time watching the tape throughout the trading day to compare stock price and volume transactions to breaking news stories. A feel for the market is developed and in this way the tape reader judges whether the market is acting normally.

Tape Confirmation Required

The tape is always reliable. Judgment becomes suspect the instant a speculator makes up his or her mind that they know more about the stock market than what is represented on the tape. Once a speculator starts overriding or ignoring what is happening on the tape is the exact moment when his or her trading results become subpar.

It is instructive to know that approximately 99 percent of those who trade on Wall Street believe, incorrectly, that they are right and the tape is wrong. Astute speculators should know how to read the tape, and more importantly, believe the tape. When the importance of tape reading is accepted and tape reading can be performed correctly, the tumult of the stock market becomes much more understandable—with outsized trading profits the result.

Continuous daily surveillance of the tape, as practiced by Jesse Livermore, is less beneficial today. However, if stock quotations on the tape are studied over a period of time they do reveal price movements in relation to the volume of shares being transacted during each trade. Combining price and trading volume information in relation to asymmetrical bids and offers on the tape gives a sense of what is occurring real time in the stock market, as explained next.

Tape Reading Analysis

Balanced or symmetrical bid and offer quotations, i.e., 200 shares bid and 200 shares offered, on each side of the stock's price, is a good sign that interest in this stock is minimal.

When bids and offers become asymmetrical or unbalanced, lets assume to the upside, buyers reach up to the "offer to sell price" on larger than normal share transaction volume. In this case, eager buyers are identified on the tape with asymmetrical or unbalanced quotations to the upside on larger than the customary sized volume transactions. The following asymmetrical example proves helpful to understanding how this takes place.

Asymmetrical Example

In this example, a stock is purchased for $45.50 and the trading volume bid and offers now become asymmetrical. The price quote and shares to be traded become $45.40 bid for 10,000 shares and 200 shares offered at $45.60. If buyers immediately reach up to the offer price with an order to buy at the market, demand is higher than supply and the stock price will advance. However, if the stock becomes dormant and no transactions take place for awhile, the tenor of the market changes and the market price for the stock will likely drift downward.

Amateur speculators think the asymmetrical bid of 10,000 shares at $45.40 is a positive for the stock price, however, just the opposite is true because it is now easier for sale transactions to take place at the lower bid price of $45.40. When markets are drifting close to equilibrium, price movement goes toward the larger sized bid or offer share quantity, in this case, the share transaction price is expected to drop down to $45.40.

Watching the tape all day every day is not considered the best use of the astute speculator's time when speculating over the intermediate term, however, valuable lessons are learned from tape reading. The major lesson is the importance of trading volume when analyzing stock price movements which is discussed next.

Tape Reading And Trading Volume Analysis

Tape reading is analyzing the dominant direction the stock price is moving, irrespective of momentary price reversals. The crucial factor for analysis is the amount of trading volume coinciding with each trade. Price action is of secondary importance, what enlightens is the amount of money going into either the buying or the selling of a particular stock.

Stock supply and demand are normally unbalanced which results in trends where the market moves along a line of least resistance. Determining either an up or down movement is based solely upon the volume of shares or the amount of money being traded on either the buy-side or sell-side. The stock price continues in the direction indicated by volume until some new cause changes the advance or decline.

Identifying Active Stock

Knowledgeable and practiced tape readers can identify and sort out active stock leaders from listless drifters. When watching an intermediate-term downtrend, occurring during a stage 3 long-term uptrend, some common stock are very weak while others only grudgingly decline in price. The reluctant decliners are monitored for possible purchase when the overall market turns and begins to rally back.

The company's stock that is the most active, with the largest percent increase in shares traded and the first to rebound off the market low point, is determined to be a market leader. Astute speculators select the market leader to speculate in for this new intermediate-term movement. Lesser leaders and market dawdlers are relegated to the not interested file.

Supply And Demand

Buyers or sellers, which dominant? Determining whether stock accumulation or distribution is ongoing in the stock market is always the central question. Justin Mamis explains that supply and demand is an economic law in the stock market that cannot be rescinded.

The following two chief supply and demand characteristics are crucial to understanding why trading volume is so important in determining whether accumulation or distribution is ongoing.

1) *Current Supply And Demand.* Stock price purchase and trading volume figures are reported in real time on the tape and indicate what the supply and demand conditions are in the stock market. Newspapers and the nightly business news give daily stock market transaction figures and the purported reasons for the day's stock market action. Day-to-day, stock price movements look tumultuous and chaotic but the asymmetrical trading volume transactions revealed on the tape indicates buy-side or sell-side interest.

2) *Potential Supply And Demand.* Stock prices over the intermediate and long-term move in trends or with recurring patterns. Potential supply

and demand points on a graph or chart are indicated at support and resistance levels. A support level is the price where sizeable new buying demand materializes and keeps the price from falling below this level. A resistance level is the price where substantial new selling supply comes in that keeps the price from rising above this level.

Look for long and intermediate-term turning points (discussed later in this chapter) to identify when the preponderance of trades change from buying to selling and back again at potential supply and demand resistance and support levels. Trading volume is the fundamental indicator of the current and potential supply and demand level determination, as discussed next.

Trading Volume Activity

Interpreting what is happening in the stock market is best done by considering trading volume behavior, not solely on price behavior. It is the amount of money going into the move that chronicles the importance of a stock's supply and demand disequilibrium.

Trading volume is the preeminent indicator of speculative power. The quintessential promotion available to a stock is a strong advance in price on heavy volume. Knowing what to look for on the tape is important and explained next.

Volume On The Tape

Search for and recognize unusual trading volume activity on the tape. If an inactive stock all of a sudden becomes active for approximately four weeks and the number of shares traded goes up by at least four times normal volume each week—the higher the percentage increase in volume the better—this is an indication of abnormal positive interest in this stock.

The stated bid to buy and offer to sell prices bracket the purchase price of the stock. The purchase price is the pivot point on an imaginary scale. The volume of transactions, either reached down to on the sell-side or reached up to on the buy-side, indicate current supply and demand and the direction of prices.

The size of the individual trades, especially, are significant. Many 30,000-share trades are more important than numerous small 300 share trades and is normally a good indication that either accumulation or distribution is ongoing—depending on whether the large volume trades are on the buy-side or the sell-side of the price movement.

Whenever the number of shares traded over approximately four weeks shows an unqualified increase from the average number of shares traded each week, there is something momentous taking place in this particular stock. It is the astute speculator's job to determine what it is and how to take advantage of the situation.

How To Use Trading Volume

Astute speculators are conscientious trading volume pupils. Watch how buying moves prices and how selling is absorbed, especially at potential support and resistance levels. Speculators should check volume numbers at the end of the trading day and post important market index and stock trading volume figures in their journal.

Trading volume in a particular stock must be judged in relation to the overall market. High volume market days should be factored into the significance of high volume figures for a specific common stock of interest.

Trading Volume Activity At A Market Top

At Stage 4: Distribution - Topping or Rounding Over the market is going through a transition from stage 3 to 1. Usually this is a drifting traders market where the S&P 500 Index is putting in a double top or a head and shoulders top reversal pattern while common stock are being distributed by market professionals to the investing public.

Confirming indicators include having an inverted yield curve (please see chapter 7 in *The Astute Investor*) and having the Dow Jones Utilities Average (DJUA) in sync with the overall stock market. The following trading volume is typically observed at a long-term market top.

Trading volume at a long–term top turning point increases but now common stock prices make no headway, prices seem stuck in place because distribution is ongoing. This is especially true at the long-term blow off market top where buying is reckless and trading volume explodes with little stock price movement.

The absolute number of buyers in the market at a market top may surpass the number of sellers, however, the quality of the two groups are important. The buying group is expected to be uninformed, i.e., the investing public and amateur speculators, while the selling group are speculative professionals selling a vast quantity of their stock, normally by using scale-out limit orders.

At a long-term market top, a stock that previously lagged or even an index like the Dow Jones Industrial Average (DJIA) may be pushed up to an all-time high price on heavy volume. These higher prices get reported in the business news and mask what is actually happening to many other common stock companies which experience decided price weakness. Second-tier common stock and the DJIA spike in price to permit the distribution of many other stock issues to the investing public.

At a market peak, the technical condition of the market is considered weak as a result. As share prices sag off the market's top price, trading volume typically is much lighter than normal. If the market's price now breaks support and the volume surges as the share prices drop further, the long-term trend has changed course and is now downward.

Trading Volume Activity During A Downtrend

When the overall market is in Stage 1: Mark-Down – Downtrend, as determined by the S&P 500 Index Nine Month Moving Average (MA) Trend Line and lower-highs and lower-lows are in evidence on the monthly graphs, and intermediate and short-term trends are also downward, then the following three types of trading volume activity may be observed.

1) Higher volumes being traded on the declines with any rallies or short-term upturns occurring on light volume. This volume-to-price relationship arises in a market where the seller's supply of common stock exceeds the buyer's demand and a continuation of the stock's decline is expected. Higher share volumes pick up again on the next leg down in prices and signifies that more stock is for sale than buyers want, except at disturbingly lower and lower prices.

2) Heavy volume at the bottom of a long-term decline for some period of time with a stalling of the price decline, the market seems active but stock prices churn in place. While transactions are heavy, the telltale sign of a long, or intermediate-term turning point is that no progress is made toward lower prices.

3) An exhausted or beleaguered decline where stock prices drift downward on light volume and then completely stall at the bottom. This situation is typical of a reduced buyer's demand and reduced seller's supply

of stock. This normally indicates a turning point where volume picks up on the upward slope as buyers realize that prices are not going lower and this may be the low of the move and now is a good time to buy. The exhausted decline, especially after occurring for a few days, is prone to explosive upside rallies.

Trading Volume Activity At A Market Bottom

At Stage 2: Accumulation - Bottoming the market is going through a transition from stage 1 to 3. Typically this is a traders market where the S&P 500 Index is putting in a double bottom or a head and shoulders bottom reversal pattern while common stock are being accumulated by market professionals. Confirming indicators include having a steep yield curve and having the Dow Jones Utilities Average (DJUA) in sync with the overall stock market. The following types of volume are observed at a long-term market low.

1) Volume at a long-term stage 2 bottom is normally sluggish, dull, listless and stagnant. The investing public is now little interested in common stock. There are many pathetic rallies that are followed by quick dips in price; but, with the saving grace that the low price point is in place and that future dips hold at low-price support levels.

The investing public sells during stage 2 because they are tired of the long drawn-out decline in the market and/or need the money for personal use. Typically, professional speculators at this time do not reach or bid up for any stock by purchasing at the market. The professionals slowly accumulate stock during stage 2 using scale-in limit orders. This is an exceedingly slow process, the tape is dull and the low volume gives the impression of a motionless market.

2) Volume at a long-term stage 2 bottom may also be a dramatic, furious, shattering catharsis of selling, over approximately three to five days, in which all the common stock issues seem to crash together. This engenders universal concern and stimulates additional stock liquidation and panic selling by the investing public.

Market hysteria is at a peak here, with mob psychology prompting novice speculators to dump common stock for whatever price is available. Also, markets during stage 2, may experience a combination of a sluggish market with light volume interrupted by a crashing panic-driven market on huge volume.

At a long-term market bottom, the volume and price movement relationship is not as obvious as it is at a long-term market top. Typically, after repeated attempts to drive prices to new all-time lows have failed, prices stubbornly begin to rise to upper levels of the trading range in spite of the bad news. As prices break through resistance levels, that now become support levels, the propensity for prices to increase on higher volume becomes evident. It is now probable that a long-term market low has been set and a long-term advance is now in place.

Increasing volume during a price decline indicates that sellers dominate buyers. The technical condition of the market is weak and the weak situation will continue as long as the volume stays strong. Once trading volume subsides and is lower than the long-term volume average, the stock market's technical position normalizes and a turning point is expected.

If however, the volume on the rally is low and dullness is experienced on the upside, continued liquidation is anticipated as the overbought condition quickly passes. The light share trading volume shows that buyers and sellers are few and that a rounding over in stock prices is likely. Selling pressure is sure to begin again as the stock's price resumes plummeting on heavy volume. Struggling rally reversals should continue as the market lurches ever downward in price.

Off a long-term market bottom, stock moving upward in price on high volume is an excellent indication of positive things to come in the stock market, as discussed next.

Trading Volume Activity During An Uptrend

When the overall market is in Stage 3: Mark-Up – Uptrend, as determined by the S&P 500 Index Nine Month MA Trend Line and higher-highs and higher-lows are in evidence on monthly graphs, and intermediate and short-term trends are also upward, then the following three types of volume activity may be observed.

1) Higher volumes being traded on the advances with any reactions or short-term downturns occurring on light volume. This volume-to-price relationship arises in a market where the buyer's demand for common stock exceeds the seller's supply and a continuation of the advance is expected. Higher share volumes pick up again on the next leg upward and signifies that more stock is wanted for purchase than sellers want to sell, except at distinctly higher prices.

2) Heavy volume at the top of a long-term advance for some period of time with a stalling of the price advance, the market seems active but stock prices churn in place. While transactions are heavy, the telltale sign of a long, or intermediate-term turning point is that no progress is made toward higher share prices.

3) An exhausted or beleaguered advance when stock prices struggle to inch ahead on light volume and then completely come to a halt at the top. This situation is typical of a reduced buyer's demand and reduced seller's supply of stock. This normally indicates a turning point where volume picks up on the downward slope as sellers realize that prices are not going higher and this may be the high of the move and now is a good time to sell. The exhausted advance, especially after occurring for a few days, is prone to abrupt downside reversals.

During stage 3, the stock market rallies on increasing volume which is expected. As stock advances slow down, watch volume figures carefully. If volume decreases along with the restrained stock advance, this is an encouraging situation because buy-orders and sell-orders are both reduced and are now in balance or equilibrium. Likewise, if prices fall slightly on light volume this also bodes well for a continued price advance in the not too distant future.

Intermediate-Term Trading Volume Activity

Trading volume determinations are more difficult to read during intermediate-term counter swings within the long-term trend but are very important to speculators. Some special conditions are explained next.

Intermediate-Term Upward Market

Trading volume in a intermediate-term upward market for a stock, regardless of the long-term trend in the market, should increase during the price advance and diminish during the reactionary decline in price.

Volume at intermediate–term top turning points also increases but now the stock price makes no headway, it seems stuck in place because distribution is ongoing by speculators. As the price sags off the top price, trading volume typically is much lighter than normal. If the price now breaks support and the volume surges as the share price drops further, the trend is now changed course and is downward for possibly an intermediate term correction. If the volume is heavy when the stock price reaches its price support level, it is expected that this is a turning point and the stock should rally back in price.

Intermediate-Term Downward Market

Trading volume in a intermediate-term downward market for a stock, regardless of the direction of the long-term trend in the market, should increase during the price decline and diminish during the counter rally price rebound. Volume at intermediate–term bottom turning points also increases but now the stock price makes no headway, it seems stuck in place because accumulation is ongoing by speculators. As the price rebounds upward off the bottom price, trading volume typically is much lighter than normal.

If the stock price now breaks through resistance and the volume surges as the share price increases further, the trend is now changed course and is upward for possibly an intermediate term. However, if the volume is heavy when the stock price reaches its price resistance level, it is expected that this is a turning point and the stock will fall back in price again.

Higher than normal trading volume at the beginning of a trend, either upward or downward, after a long or intermediate-term turning point bodes well for a continuation of the trend. However, higher than normal volume after a relatively long or sustained intermediate-term movement is a good indicator of a trend reversal. During the next intermediate-term rally, if the volume is much heavier than normal then that is the new stock price trend.

At intermediate-term lows where trading volume is very high, price volatility is high but there is little price change at the market close—an intermediate-term low point is expected.

Short-Covering Trading Volume

A rally during stage 1, in a long-term downturn, may simply be due to short covering. In this instance the rally is short lived and an extension of the downward price movement is anticipated. To find out if this is the case, watch trading volume.

If the volume is light on the advance and volume picks up on the decline, this is a stage 1 rally and should be discounted. On the other hand, volume dullness following the rally signifies a further advance.

Heavy volume on a stock price advance, up to a point, indicates a further advance. Light volume on a rally indicates a halting advance, but in both instances, just up to a point. Volume determinations require close observation, are conditional and are only thoroughly understood with trading experience. Stock turning points are a change from accumulation to distribution, or vice versa, as explained next.

Turning Points

The investing public and speculators cannot all be right at the same time. The astute speculator makes the most money by being contrarian, at turning points. Turning points may be thought of as the market losing momentum over the long-term or intermediate-term trend, either up or down. The goal is to make the trade close to the exact turning point when the market or stock then starts going the opposite direction. Turning points typically occur on heavy share trading volume but with no headway in price.

The long-term turning points at a market top or bottom are dynamic because the market is now reacting to the long-term action. The intermediate term action-reaction turning points are more frequent but do not have the same forceful magnitude. In fact, intermediate-term turning points are often difficult to detect in real time. Astute speculators need to stay especially focused on stock price and trading volume interaction to spot intermediate-term turning points, the following explains how this is accomplished.

Reading The Trends

The investing public and amateur speculators invariably misread market trends, and consequently, buy when they should be selling and sell when they should be buying. Instead, to catch turning points correctly requires disagreeing with the opinion of the average trader who is using what he or she considers to be logical reasoning.

The ability for an overbought market or stock, i.e., one that has quickly moved upward on high volume, to make significantly more progress is improbable. The market or stock price is due for a intermediate or short-term reaction.

Similarly for an oversold market or stock, i.e., one that has quickly moved downward on high volume, the ability to make significantly more downward price progress is considered unlikely. The market or stock eventually becomes due for an intermediate or short-term rally.

The exact long-term peak of a market is defined as that instant where professional traders act in almost complete unity to unload stock while, concurrently, the investing public attains a zenith of enthusiasm in their purchases. The intermediate-term tops are similar but this time the distinction in players is between professional speculators and amateur speculators.

Intermediate term turning points match at long-term stock market tops and bottoms. By studying intermediate-term moves the astute speculator becomes better at identifying long-term turning points which are so important to successful speculating and investing. A good way to identify turning points is to study new 52 week high & low price lists, as explained next.

New 52 Week High & Low Price Lists

A turning point during stage 4 market top is denoted when volume increases appreciably but the number of companies with new 52 week high prices do not increase. This is the failure of many companies to reach new 52 week high prices after frequent and persistent attempts have been made. The number of companies with new 52 week high prices decline along with an increase in the number of companies with new 52 week low prices. Subsequent rallies all are a little weaker and lower in price than the one before and each new reaction or dip in price goes successively lower in price.

Whenever subsequent rallies fall short on light volume with fewer number of companies with new 52 week high prices and more new 52 week low prices, and reactions lurch downward on heavy volume, this is an excellent indication that stock is being liquidated. The correct policy here is to sell all long positions and consider taking up short stock positions.

At a long-term market high, some second-tier stock hit new 52 week highs while the majority of stock churn in place on heavy volume. Stock hitting new 52 week highs while the market is turning over is normally the result of professionals pushing up high visibility stock or the DJIA so that most of the remaining stock issues can be distributed out of sight from the investing public.

Study the new high and new low figures to see if a deterioration is ongoing and review how the second and third echelon stock are performing. This is early verification of a market reversal at a turning point.

Names On The New 52 Week High & Low Lists

A good indicator for changing leadership is to monitor which common stock companies are hitting new 52 week high and low prices.

Monitor common stock on the NYSE, AMEX and NASDAQ hitting new 52 week highs and new lows on the following website http:// dynamic.nasdaq.com/asp/52weekshilow.asp?exchange=NYSE&status=HI.

During a stage 4 market top, the previous stock leaders are superseded by second or third-tier ersatz stock leaders which provide the unsuspecting speculator with the incorrect belief that the long-term upward trend remains intact. Typically, this is not the case and masks what is actually occurring in the stock market.

Most Active Lists

Stock names on the most active list, those companies trading the most shares daily, should also be monitored. When the market leaders on the most active list are replaced by low-priced speculative issues, a major top turning point is forecast. The long-term upward trend is now looking tired and the stock market is in danger of turning lower.

Changing leadership from stock leaders to second or third-tier stock signifies that distribution is ongoing in a market trading range and the stock market is marking time near the top of its long-term move.

The investing public observes many reactions in which there is a stock market decline and see no difference as prices retreat off of a stock market top. Orders are placed by amateur speculators or investing public a few points from the previous top price in active issues. Professional speculators satisfy this demand by selling, as explained next.

Supply And Demand At Turning Points

Supply and demand are momentarily in balance at long and intermediate-term turning points. However, markets do not stay in equilibrium for long. A sideways trading market is always experiencing one of two things, accumulation or distribution, and it is the astute speculator's job to determine which is in effect.

At a long or intermediate-term market top or bottom there is a tug of war occurring in the minds of buyers and sellers. The job of speculators at turning points is to judge supply and demand discrepancies. If stock demand dominates supply, prices advance. If stock supply dominates demand, prices decline. Supply and demand imbalances are identified using the number of shares being traded, and in conjunction with stock prices they indicate the monetary value of that volume.

Turning points typically occur on heavy volume but no headway in price. Heavy trading volume is normally in evidence at the end of a trend reversal. At a long or intermediate-term stock market top, volume becomes very heavy while prices do not budge. Buyers want more stock while professional sellers, who are use to sitting on their stock and not selling during the stock advance, now offer an enormous quantity of stock for sale.

At an intermediate-term bottom, share prices remain stable and volume is exceedingly heavy. This time sellers want to sell more stock while professional buyers, who are use to sitting on their hands and not buying during a price decline, offer to buy larger quantities of stock.

Accumulation And Distribution

A stock experiencing accumulation imperceptibly inches up over a period of weeks as stock operators use scale-in orders to build stock positions. Eventually an upward trend develops as stock demand dominates supply. The high and low daily prices tend to work their way consistently higher, irrespective of the fluctuations in the stock's closing prices.

For a stock encountering distribution, typically the stock has had a considerable run up in price and now has trouble making price advances coincident with heavy trading volume. The stock price no longer reaches new highs. Scale-out selling by large professional interests may be ongoing. Corporate earnings reports, as a rule, continue to be good but the market is discounting trouble ahead.

The length of the accumulation or distribution phase in the stock market depends upon the importance of the turn. Long-term turning points take longer to develop than intermediate-term turning points. Active stock market churning is more pronounced at major turns. At a long-term market low, some stock hit new lows while most just churn in place on heavy volume.

Human nature is at play here. At turning points, the decisions of all the active buyers and sellers are evenly split based on their weight in the market and supply matches demand. The goal of astute speculators is to recognize the timing of the turn, then to be on the side of the large stock market professionals and not on the side of the investing public or amateur speculators.

Because the investing public and amateur speculators only concern themselves with price changes, they miss valid stock trends that are confirmed by a significant increase trading volume. So after analyzing volume, feel good about being on the correct side of any long, or intermediate-term turning point.

Selling Climax Day

An example of intermediate or long-term support at a turning point is the selling climax day. A selling climax signifies a market capitulation. The market opens weak and plunges straight down on very heavy volume. Selling climax volume is normally one-and-a half times average NYSE volume during a day where stock prices drop precipitously for the S&P 500 Index in a broad market decline.

The precipitous break tries the patience of investors and speculators alike and cleans up overhead supply as those who want to sell throw their stock on the market to obtain whatever price they can get. This is also called the "clean out day."

The market eventually reaches an intraday equilibrium point, churns for awhile and then shoots straight upward, retracing the prior plunge in prices. What makes the selling climax day unusual, for the S&P 500 Index, is that the market rallies intraday to close at a higher price than the previous day's closing price on heavy volume.

The selling climax day normally coincides with very bad news that causes the investing public and amateur speculators to dump their stock holdings at distressed prices while more knowledgeable buyers, who have already discounted the news, now buy the excess supply resulting in higher closing stock prices.

A selling climax day turns around the technical condition of the market which changes it from being long or intermediate-term weak to now being a strong market. An eventual upturn in stock prices is now expected.

The selling climax day is not as strong a signal as the outside reversal day, consequently, it may take a while for a base to develop and for prices to advance during the next long or intermediate-term upward rally. A selling climax at a long-term bottom may require several months for an adequate base to develop and a long-term upturn to begin in earnest. An intermediate-term base may take several weeks to develop.

A selling climax day occurring at an intermediate term turning point support level during a long-term downward trending market is followed by a rally, however, an eventual new lower price is expected after the rally peaks. The selling climax intermediate-term rally should take approximately twice the time it took for the intermediate-term decline.

An intermediate-term selling climax day involves high volume, therefore, the resulting intermediate-term rally occurs on diminished volume. This is one instance where lower volume on an advance is expected. The intermediate-term rally should eventually retrace 50 percent of the prior intermediate-term plunge and crest at its top price turning point on very low volume. Once the intermediate-term rally peaks, the long-term downward trend resumes with increased volume as prices break through prior support levels.

Turning Point Force

Studying the stock market requires assessing the forces that are in place above and below the current price point. Each trend in the market, whether long, intermediate, or short-term, has a foundation phase, an implementation phase and a finishing phase. The foundation phase is the assembly of the force needed to propel the stock either upward or downward. The longer the foundation phase takes to develop, the more sustained the probable price swing will be.

Judge stock turning points as an exercise in force and have the courage to go with the side that has the newfound volume strength. Each swing, either long, intermediate, or short, teeters on a balance scale and heavy volume tips the scales in the direction of the next trend. Learning to spot turning points gives astute speculators a good method for winning in the stock market.

Make the trade, either long-term or intermediate-term, close to the turning point, elect the side based on judging trading volume and set a stop-loss order price point based on support or resistance levels. In this case, "The speculator's losses are cut short and their profits are allowed to run." Speculators now have the probabilities on their side leading to stock market success. Turning point speculative issues to work on to be a better trader are discussed next.

Turning Points: Speculative Issues

An event that happens continually in the same way is presumed to repeat itself. Consequently, a stock that has been rising in price is expected to keep rising in price. A stock increasing three or four days in a row will attract buyers at this higher price. A stock declining three or four days in a row will produce sellers at this lower price.

Speculators may think it strange that whenever a snap-judgment stock purchase is made at the top of a bulge during a short-term rally or short sale at the bottom of a short-term reaction, the stock quickly turns around and they are sitting with a loss on their new position. Human nature can bear only so much strain and this is the case where trading tension produces an impulsive act that is detrimental to a trader's pocketbook. Instead, it is better to sell on the short-term bulges and buy on the reactions.

Learn to be contrarian. Strong hands like to sell after the first reaction has had a chance to rally back to resistance because the second reaction will most likely be much more severe. Liquidation—i.e., an extended downward price movement on increasing volume—is usually in evidence at this time. Liquidation is high volume selling by important interests that is accomplished by reaching down to the bid price.

Assumed Price Bargains

During stage 1 when the market is in a log-term downtrend, recognizing selling is easy because the professionals are in charge. Trading volume is very heavy while prices continue to decline. The investing public continues to buy on the way down because, as previously discussed, they like buying assumed price bargains. A signal of a turn at a market bottom is that stock market pundits, incorrectly, start predicting much lower prices for stock market averages.

162

The turning point arrives in stage 2 when leading company stock advance significantly higher in price on high volume while the overall averages remain listless and make no headway. These are the demonstrably strong stock to speculate in as the market begins its transition into stage 3.

Speculation And The News

Who is selling and the size of the trading volume of the market orders establish the nature of the liquidation. At some point, a disturbing news story is fixated upon to supply the required excuse, not the cause, the market needs for the major downward slide occurring during stage 1 on heavy volume. Typically, unexpected accidents are the purported reasons that cave in an already weak market.

Normally, an amateur speculator shorting a stock continues to sell more shares as the price drops on bad news in an attempt to drive the price down further, regardless of turning points. Bernard M. Baruch found it is often more profitable to purchase stock in a weak market during reactions and sell stock in a strong market during bulges.

Iron Nerve At Turning Points

John W. Gates (1855-1911), is known as "bet-a-million" Gates. His manners are rough but he had an intrepid demeanor and a confident incisive intelligence. Gates had high-stakes speculative success in steel, oil and railroads. Reportedly, Gates had "iron nerve but no nerves." Gates understood human nature and had the nerve necessary to act at turning points, in order to make money.

Successful speculation requires going counter to, at turning points, what the investing public and amateur speculators are doing. This requires the ability for speculators to think for themselves as well as possessing self control, iron nerve, a clear mind and having the requisite information and the courage to act properly at the correct time.

Summary

Tape reading is an exercise in anticipating price changes based upon the price and volume transactions represented on the tape. The tape is the composite mind of all traders participating in the stock market. The astute speculator focuses on volume action and can explain when volume is light, average, or heavy in relation to price advancements or declines, market momentum and with regard to breaking news.

Successful tape reading is a study in determining whether the buy-side or the sell-side has the most forceful market power and then having the judgment and the iron nerve to participate in the market at turning points. Interpreting what is happening in the stock market is best accomplished by considering trading volume behavior, not simply price behavior.

Price action indicates but is secondary in importance to trading volume which validates the stock market's buy-side advance or sell-side decline. The current and potential supply and demand characteristics are crucial to understanding why trading volume is so important in determining whether accumulation or distribution is ongoing in the stock market. Money, represented by trading volume, designates the importance of a stock's supply and demand disequilibrium.

Search for and recognize unusual trading volume activity on the tape. If an inactive stock all of a sudden becomes active for approximately four weeks and the number of shares traded goes up by at least four times normal weekly volume—the higher the percentage increase in volume the better— this is an indication of abnormal positive interest in this stock.

The investing public and amateur speculators only concern themselves with share price changes and overlook trading volume, consequently, they miss stock turning points. Turning points typically occur on heavy volume but no headway in price. The length of the accumulation or distribution phase in the stock market depends upon the importance of the turning point. Long-term turning points take a longer period of time to form a foundation than intermediate-term turning points.

Trading volume activity patterns at long-term and intermediate-term turning points indicate where common stock price advances or declines lose momentum. New 52 week high & low price lists, the most active list and selling climax days assist when determining turning points.

The goal of astute speculators is to recognize the timing of the turn and then trade when the market begins going the opposite direction. Be on the side of the large stock market professionals and not on the side of the investing public or amateur speculators.

6

Momentum Speculating

Introduction

CORPORATIONS WITH SHARED BUSINESS characteristics are sorted into twelve stock market sectors. Cyclical sectors either lead, are coincident with, or lag the long-term trend in the overall stock market. Companies within sectors are further sorted into smaller groups called industries which display market momentum.

Industry momentum is the propensity for prices or earnings of companies within an industry, once in an upward or downward trend for six months, to continue to increase or decrease over the next twelve months. How momentum speculating is used for the speculator's benefit and how it differs from momentum investing is explained.

Nine momentum speculating fundamentals are presented. Momentum speculating requires identifying a leading company within the top 25 percent of industry rankings to purchase while laggard second and third-tier companies in the 25 percent of the lowest ranked industries should be sold short, at the correct time.

In general, during a long-term upward trend in the stock market, buy the wonderfully managed quickly growing company with sound fundamentals in an exciting new industry and, during a long-term downtrend, sell short mediocre companies with poor fundamentals in distressed industries.

Sectors

Stock market sectors are major groupings of corporations classified by similar business characteristics. Companies on the NYSE, AMEX and the NASDAQ exchanges are sorted here into twelve different sectors. Sectors are subdivided into smaller groups within each sector, called industries, which are discussed in detail later in this chapter.

Sectors do not have market diversification but companies within each sector are business related and display comparable stock price performance, because, they participate in the same regulatory environment and experience related vendor supply and customer demand conditions. Consequently, stock prices for companies included in each sector are expected to move together over the long and intermediate term relative to the long-term trend for the overall stock market.

The rationale for grouping companies by sector is straightforward. For example, the basic materials sector includes companies that make products that go into the production of other goods, e.g., forestry & paper products, chemicals and metals. Sector groups tend to move together relative to the overall stock market, as explained next.

Sectors: Lead, Coincident Or Lag

Sectors which typically move in advance of the long-term stock market trend are the technology, basic materials, industrials and consumer cyclical sectors—in this specific order. These sectors tend to lead the long-term trend in the overall market on the way up and also lead the market's long-term trend on the way down.

Sectors which normally closely track and tend to be coincident with the long-term stock market trend are, in order, the telecommunications, retail, transportation and utility sectors. Sectors which are likely to lag the stock market's long-term trend on the way up and turn down only after the overall stock market turns down are, in order, the energy, financial and health-care sectors.

The consumer staples sector, listed last, is a defensive sector that is less cyclical and more steady in its advance because consumers consistently purchase consumer products both in good times and in bad. The sector list follows and includes explanations of what and why industries are included in each sector and how industries interact within sectors.

Sector List

Twelve stock market sectors are presented and a short list of the representative industries that are included within each sector are listed below the sector's name. Each cyclical sector either leads, is coincident with, or lags the long-term trend in the overall stock market. How each sector normally relates to the long-term stock market trend is listed in order and specified in the parenthesize.

1) Technology (Lead 1)
   - Computer Hardware
   - Computer Software
   - Semiconductors
   - Internet

2) Basic Materials (Lead 2)
   - Forestry & Paper Products
   - Chemicals
   - Metals

3) Industrials (Lead 3)
   - Heavy Construction
   - Aerospace & Defense
   - Factory Equipment
   - Containers & Packaging
   - Waste & Disposal Services

4) Consumer Cyclical (Lead 4)
   - Appliances
   - Automotive
   - Home Construction
   - Clothing Manufacturing
   - Restaurants

Hotels

Media

5) Telecommunications (Coincident 1)

Land Line

Wireless

Phone Equipment

6) Retail (Coincident 2)

Department Stores

Apparel Retailers

Specialty Retailers

7) Transportation (Coincident 3)

Airlines

Railroads

Trucking

Shipping

8) Utility (Coincident 4)

Electric

Gas

Water

9) Energy (Lag 1)

Oil

Natural Gas

Coal

Ethanol

Hydro, Wind & Solar

10) Financial (Lag 2)

Banking

Insurance

Real Estate Investment Trusts

Investment Brokers

11) Health Care (Lag 3)

Pharmaceuticals

Medical Equipment

Medical Services

Biotechnology

12) Consumer Staples (Defensive)
   Beverages
   Food
   Tobacco
   Household Products
   Cosmetics and Personal Care

The first eleven sectors in the above list are cyclical and are expected to either lead, be coincident with, or lag the long-term trend in the stock market. For example, as the stock market begins its long-term rise from Stage 2: Accumulation - Bottoming, typically the first sector to rise and lead all the other eleven cyclical sectors is technology. Technology also tends to peak and start down prior to the long-term peaking of the overall stock market and the other three leading sectors.

Presumably, the technology sector leads all the other sectors because the other sector companies purchase leading edge technology to make themselves more efficient corporate competitors prior to the beginning of a long-term stock market uptrend and terminate technology purchases long before their own business cycle peaks.

How industries within different sectors interact is important. As an example, home construction is grouped within the consumer cyclical sector. During an active housing market, lumber from the basic materials sector is used during construction. Higher interest rates, occurring late in a long-term market expansion during Stage 4: Distribution - Topping or Rounding Over, are good for the financial sector but depress home construction and the lumber business.

Consumer Staples Sector

The consumer staples sector is defensive because the companies included here do not closely follow the long-term trends in the overall stock market. Products and services provided by companies in the consumer staples sector include food, beverages, tobacco, household products, cosmetics and personal care.

Speculators look to consumer staple companies as a defensive stock position as the market enters a long-term downturn during stage 1. The strategy is tied to the realization that people need to eat, drink and take care of personal hygiene at all times. Consequently, final demand for consumer staples gradually increases during the good times and remains relatively stable during bad economic times.

During a long-term upturn during stage 3, common stock within the consumer staples sector do not rise as fast as the overall stock market because consumers do not use these products and services significantly more during this period, instead, overall consumer staple demand tends to track overall population growth rather than long-term stock market trends. Wall Street further divides sectors into smaller industry groups, as presented next.

Industry Groups

Companies assigned to sectors are further sorted into smaller groups called industries. The primary business pursuit of the corporation determines how companies are classify by industry groups. Companies are organized here into twelve sectors and further sorted into anywhere from approximately 100-225 industry groups, depending on which organization is making the determination.

The following websites list specific industries and the specific companies that are part of an industry: Standard & Poor's at their website: http://www2.standardandpoors.com, Smart Money Sector Tracker at their website www.smartmoney.com, Yahoo Finance at their website http://biz.yahoo.com/ic/, Dow Jones at their website www.marketwatch.com, CNN Money.com at their website http://money.cnn.com and Zacks at their website www.zacks.com all are examples of financial organizations that classify and report on industry groups by sector.

Affect On Stock Prices By Industry Groups

Astute speculators recognize that roughly 50 percent of a stock's price is determined by the systematic risk of overall political-economic conditions that affect all common stock alike. Industry groups by sector account for about 10 percent of a stock's price as determined by industry trends that affect all common stock issues in that industry group alike. The remaining 40 percent of the stock's price is usually conditional upon unsystematic risk due to the internal circumstances associated with each corporation.

Astute speculators require overall political-economic conditions and industry trends to be in their favor prior to speculating in a specific company. Consequently, speculators should only buy a leading company if it is in a high ranking industry group during market stages 2 or 3 and only short a laggard second or third-tier company's stock if it is in a very weak industry experiencing poor performance during market stages 4 or 1.

Industry Groups Vs. Specific Companies

It is possible for the stock price of a specific company to go either up or down at any time, i.e., past company price trends by themselves are irrelevant in predicting future company price trends due to the company's unsystematic risk and intermediate-term trends moving counter to long-term trends.

A leading corporation should first be included in a high ranking industry group in a stock market that is experiencing a long-term uptrend, prior to purchasing its stock. In this way, it is assured that at least 60 percent of the stock's move is positive due to industry and market trend conditions. The remaining 40 percent upward trend due to the specific company's circumstances is now more assured.

The specific company's stock should be moving together with other companies within its industry to give the speculator confidence that its price trend will continue over the intermediate term. When industry news in the media is all positive, all the companies in the industry tend to move together regardless of how an individual company's corporate management is performing and what the corporate financials look like.

New IPO corporations must be part of an industry, one company alone is an oddity while two like companies constitute an industry group. Industries are followed by Wall Street analysts. Industry conferences can take place with multiple companies within an industry and the media feels comfortable creating a positive buzz about an industry.

Astute speculators should study the market's stage, industry group and in addition know as much as possible about the company prior to purchasing its stock. This includes making the required corporate financial calculations and having an understanding of industry pricing patterns. Taking a stock position without first investigating the market stage and the company's industry and financial information is gambling—not speculating.

Industry Subgroups

A large industry group may include as many as 100 companies. Subgroups may be identified that represent a niche within its industry. Looking at industry subgroups improves analysis. Industry groups with "miscellaneous" in their title are typically good candidates to be further broken down into industry subgroups.

Companies that are part of an industry subgroup can be identified by reading the company's description available on many of the financial websites listed previously. Annual reports and the 10-K filing with the SEC often list the major competitors of the each firm to help in subgroup determination. The dominate or leading industries have changed throughout history, as explained next.

Outstanding Industries By Decade

The following are dominate and typically new infant growth industries representing outstanding stock groups that have led past stock market advances throughout history by decade:

1830's – Canal and Turnpike
1840's – Railroad
1850's – Telegraph
1860's – Trans-Atlantic Cable
1870's – Oil
1880's – Telephone
1890's – Electric Utility
1900's – Steel
1910's – Automobile
1920's – Radio
1930's – Chain Stores
1940's – Chemicals
1950's – Airlines
1960's – Computer Hardware
1970's – Computer Software
1980's – Biotechnology
1990's – Wireless Telecommunications
2000's – Internet

2010's – ?

Throughout history, dominate fast growing infant industries have first come in and then gone out of favor on Wall Street. The stock market discounts the future, fast growing exciting speculative issues of yesteryear can and often times do turn into the slow growing mature industries and companies of tomorrow.

Dominate Infant Industries Come And Go

The stock market fluctuates and is never in equilibrium for long, because, the market reflects what Joseph A. Schumpeter (1883-1950) describes as "creative destruction," i.e., when innovative entrepreneurs create new companies which force out existing businesses and, thus, long-term economic progress is sustained. Consequently, speculators should treat equities associated with dominate infant industries as fluctuating inventories that first come in and then, eventually, go out of favor on Wall Street.

Individual company stock should not be purchased and then considered a permanent possession. Gilt-edged investments of twenty-five years ago may not retain their luster today because dominate infant industries grow up and mature. For speculators to consistently make money, eternal alertness is the watchword in the stock market.

For the trader, the most active leading corporation in the current dominant new industry is typically the safest and most rewarding stock to select for speculative purchase. When the overall political-economic conditions are favorable, and therefore, almost all common stock shares increase in price, the leading company within the dominate infant industry group will have the most excellent prospects for advancement.

Foresight when predicting industry and stock movements is necessary for successful speculation. Foreshadowing is present in life and in the stock market if speculators are mindful of where to look. The Wall Street saying is, "Coming events make themselves known before they appear." Speculators should always look for the next new dominant fast growing industry and then purchase the leading stock in that industry, at the proper time.

Common Stock Are Created To Sell

A stock market adage is, "Common stock are created to sell." Selling is the reason why common stock are brought to market, first sold in the primary market by investment banking underwriters to professional speculators, and later sold in the secondary market by professional speculators to the investing public and/or to amateur speculators.

To attract stock buyers in the primary market, a considerable amount of underwriter publicity, promotion and selling are required to achieve a profitable turnover of the underwriter's capital. To attract stock buyers in the secondary market, the news in the media typically has to be positive to give the investing public and amateur speculators a reason to buy.

Paper Profits

As explained in chapter 4, investors may earn a vast amount of money on the overall market upswing, but often do not turn profits on paper into cash. Investors do a poor job of selling and lose their profits when the stock bubble bursts and they are forced out at a low point during stock market panic selling.

Paper profits are immaterial to astute speculators, instead, learn to keep cash rather than stock. For the end game, cash is what is wanted and not common stock. In the stock market, it is more difficult to preserve cash than accumulate profits and being able to keep the money earned is ultimately the most impressive accomplishment. The astute speculator is vitally concerned with the best time to turn paper profits into cash by selling their stock position in industries losing momentum.

Why Industries Are Studied

The reason that industries are studied is because once momentum begins in an industry it tends to continue over the intermediate term, consequently, profits can be made by speculating along with industry trends.

Looking at the S&P 500 Index Nine Month MA Trend Line along with confirming indicators is the best way to determine which stage the stock market is in and the long-term trend in the market. However, intermediate-term trends can move counter to the long-term trend in the overall market. Consequently, intermediate-term trends are best identified by looking at how industries are performing and then trading along by purchasing leading company stock in the highest ranking industries or by selling short laggard companies in the lowest ranked industries.

A comparison of common stock movements within industries should produce like results. If the industry as a whole is up ten percent and a particular stock included in the industry is down five percent, this is a telltale sign that this stock is lagging the industry's advance and it should not be purchased. Empirical study results of how and why industry momentum occurs over the intermediate-term are presented next.

Industry Momentum

Momentum is the propensity for common stock earnings or prices, once going in a particular direction either up or down, to continue in that direction. Momentum is based on the rate of change of prices or earnings rather than on actual price or earning levels.

Supply and demand imbalances over a period of time create both long and intermediate-term market momentum. Outsized asymmetrical market orders to purchase stock that greatly outweigh sell orders produce positive momentum. Traders prefer to purchase rapidly rising active stock with positive momentum, and therefore, become attracted to industry momentum.

Industry Momentum: Empirical Study

The persistence of industry group profit return momentum for companies included in an industry is empirically studied by Moskowitz and Grinblatt and found to be significant. Industries have momentum and identifiable intermediate-term trends can be successfully exploited by speculators who earn approximately twelve percent higher profit returns than a buy and hold strategy, exclusive of trading costs.

The past six months of industry returns are rank ordered from the best performing industries to the worst performing industries. All high industry group stock positions are held for one month, three months, six months, twelve months and two years. The industry momentum returns are positive and strongest over one month and continue positive over three-to-twelve months. After twelve months, positive industry momentum returns tend to dissipate. At two years in duration, industry momentum returns become negative.

Small common stock companies contribute less than one percent of the profits while the large capitalization common stock companies contribute 75 percent of the overall profit returns. The largest companies have the most liquid stock for trading and typically have the most professional management. Consequently, the leading common stock companies tend to be large capitalization companies within the industry where most of the momentum profits reside which is a good reason to speculate only in industry leaders.

Industry returns are conditional and once they are established, based on price returns over the prior six months, an intermediate-term industry trend tends to stay in place for the next twelve months. This is important for speculators because prior six month industry returns, relative to the overall market, are easy to identify and give an intermediate-term planning horizon target when profits should be taken to lock in the largest speculative gains.

Industry momentum, conditional on the past six months of price data, outperforms a buy and hold strategy and contributes considerably to the profitability and stock price advance of individual companies included in high ranking momentum industries. Conditional momentum strategies confirm that intermediate-term profits are not diversified across all companies but are concentrated in high ranking industries.

Industry Momentum Conclusions

Positive industry return momentum occurs when common stock included in a high ranking industry outperforms the average stock price in the prior six months and then outperforms the average stock price in the succeeding twelve months. It is shown that higher industry momentum returns directly translate into higher stock prices and lower industry momentum returns predict lower stock prices.

Momentum of a stock price on its own, without the benefit of a industry moving either up or down, is not significant. Momentum of an individual common stock on its own is not consistent enough to make money because the individual stock's price trend may quickly change direction due to the company's unsystematic risk, industry momentum or long-term stock market trend. Industry momentum always dominates individual stock price momentum, meaning that high ranking industries should always be analyzed prior to selecting a stock for purchase.

Once price momentum in a specific high ranking industry is identified, industry momentum for all included stock in the industry are expected to earn outsized returns. The important point addressed in the scientific study is to use high ranking industry price momentum, not only individual stock price momentum, when selecting active common stock for speculation. Momentum investing, as a strategy for stock speculation, has long been practiced on Wall Street and is explained next.

Momentum Investing

Momentum investing is popular during the technology stock market boom between 1995 to 2000. However, selecting common stock to purchase based on momentum investing did poorly during the long-term stock market downturn from 2000 to 2003. While momentum investing went out of favor during the stock market's 2000 to 2003 long-term decline, since then it has made a comeback. Presumably, this is because speculators are learning better how to use momentum investing in practice.

The foundation of momentum investing is that proven stock winners continue to win while stock losers continue to lose. Momentum investing may be called growth investing where media and investor attention feed on itself. Valuations are much less important than other factors such as price movement, i.e., it should not be assumed that a high price-to-earnings (P/E) stock with momentum will not go even higher in price.

Momentum investing focuses on the momentum of either relative price strength or relative earnings strength. Momentum investing is explained here so that astute speculators understand what the similarities are and how it differs with the recommended technique, "momentum speculating," presented later in this chapter. The following issues are important when implementing momentum investing.

Media Attention

Companies that have positive price momentum often receive outsized media attention which in turn creates more stock buying demand by the investing public. High expectations produce what John Maynard Keynes calls the castle-in-the-air theory of speculation, previously discussed in chapter 2.

Positive news and advancing prices reinforce amateur speculators' perceptions that easy money can be made by purchasing highly active castle-in-the-air stock early and then getting out of their position just as speculative buying peaks. Consequently, momentum investors depend upon positive media attention to propel stock price advances.

Wall Street Analysts

Analysts on Wall Street do not focus on stock momentum because they typically report on earnings and sales revenue, and develop future earnings and sales estimates. Discussing momentum seems too emotional and not objective enough for financially oriented analysts, therefore, momentum investors often have this field to themselves.

Crowd Psychology

Momentum investing is investing along with the crowd and depends upon human behavior and investor psychology. Momentum investing works particularly well during a long-term stock market upward trend leading to a bubble-buying top when investors are overly optimistic and display a heard mentality by purchasing highly visible advancing stock. Please see chapters 5 & 9 in *The Astute Investor* for more on this topic.

Clearly, to be successful using momentum investing, more than just the "greater fool theory of investing" should be utilized, i.e., where the speculative purchase, regardless of valuation or price, is a good one as long as the stock can be sold later on to a bigger fool at a higher price. However, astute speculators should recognize that perception, trading psychology and greed does play a part in what is occurring during momentum investing.

The speculator's perception and imagination are stimulated when a momentum stock becomes active and is always in the news. Investors like winners and want to be invested in and associated with winners. Relative price or earnings strength is a measure of momentum, as described next.

Relative Price Or Earnings Strength

Relative price strength or relative earnings strength is calculated over a period of time based on how the stock's price or earnings performance compares to an overall stock market benchmark such as the S&P 500 Index.

Relative price or earnings strength is the persistence of the stock once in motion to continue the move, either up or down.

The relative price or earnings strength is determined by calculating the stock's price or earnings percentage change and comparing it to the benchmark's price or earnings percentage change. A stock ranking on a scale of 1 to 100 is the result, with 1 being the worst while 100 represents the best momentum. This scale is typically called the relative strength rating for either price or earnings.

A stock with a relative strength rating for either price or earnings of 90 means that this stock has experienced a larger price or earnings increase over a set period of time than 90 percent of all common stock in the market benchmark.

A stock identified as performing much better than the overall market, as ranked by the relative strength rating, is considered a good indicator and excellent reason for purchasing a stock displaying a high positive price or earnings momentum.

The conclusions as to why relative price or earnings strength works in practice is that money flows determine stock prices, therefore, it is expected that money typically flows to the best stock with the strongest momentum.

Momentum Investing And The EMH

Momentum investing strategy results directly refute the efficient market hypothesis (EMH), i.e., the thinking that investing in the stock market is like making a bet at a large casino where stock prices are independent random variables and all trades are a zero net present value transaction, meaning neither the buyer or the seller has an advantage over one another.

Momentum investing does not support the efficient market hypothesis (EMH). Instead, the stock price movements do not follow a random walk but make advances based upon tested strategies using calculations that help reduce investor risk as much as possible.

Momentum investors want to put their money in common stock that is advancing faster than the overall market. The practice requires first identifying which stock to buy, then buying, holding on and selling at the correct time.

Fundamentals Of Momentum Investing

Momentum investors have to prove to themselves that a stock's fundamentals are strong prior to purchase. Stock price activity merely signals a heads up to know what stock to analyze next. Positive momentum investing companies ready for purchase have the following attributes:

1) A wonderful story of how the company's product or service will change the world that can be succinctly explained by the media and understood by the investing public.

2) The company should be relatively new, focused in a new technology area. The investing public prefers the new and exciting companies in comparison to the old stodgy slow growers. Typically the type of companies which fit this category are cutting edge companies in either the high tech or biotechnology groups. However, traditional companies with a good story may be included here, e.g., energy exploration or gold mining companies.

3) Small capitalization (cap) companies, with fewer shares outstanding are easier to put up in price and often have the most explosive price advances. Small cap common stock companies tend to have no security analysts covering the company, or have many fewer analysts than the highly visible large cap stock companies. Therefore, it takes longer for the good news to get out to the investing public on small cap companies, giving speculators ample time for momentum investors to get into the stock position early.

4) A positive earnings surprise where actual earnings for the quarter beat the earnings estimate is indicative of an active share price. The central tenet in momentum investing is that companies which beat earnings estimates will continue to do so and companies which miss their earnings estimate will probably do so again. A stock's fair value is proportionally linked to its earnings, so earnings surpassing estimates typically lead to increased earnings estimates and higher market values.

5) Stock analysts increasing earnings per share estimates for the company is a positive sign. A stock's fair value is proportionally linked to its earnings, so upward earnings estimates tend to increase security analyst share target prices.

6) The stock is close to or at a new 52 week high price. This reduces the overhang of common stock shares ready to be sold by investors so they can get out of their stock positions even.

7) Sales growth, operating profit margin and return on equity (ROE) are fundamental indicators that are used to help rank and compare stock for eventual purchase.

8) Significantly increased trading volume indicates money flowing to an active stock and is required for momentum investing.

9) A liquid stock trading at least one million shares per week.

Once a high momentum investing stock is purchased, knowing how and when to sell becomes the number one priority which is explained next.

When To Sell

Momentum investors, once in a winning position, often have a difficult time changing their mind and selling their stock, even when conditions have obviously changed.

When a momentum stock begins to lose its relative price strength or relative earnings strength, momentum investors should quickly sell. Other indicators, such as breaking its 10 week moving average trend line or missing quarterly earnings estimates are also typically good enough reasons for selling a momentum investing stock.

Companies that lower earnings guidance or expected growth rates may also be summarily sold. Momentum companies are usually high expectation growth companies and when investors experience disillusioned perceptions the stock price also quickly disappoints. Research studies show that momentum investing is profitable, as presented next.

Momentum Investing Study

James P. O'Shaughnessy studies momentum investing strategies and reports that the fifty highest relative strength common stock companies during the previous year, from 1951 to 1994, produce a compound return of +14.45 percent per year, exclusive of trading commissions and taxes, which compares favorably to the S&P 500 Index returns averaging +11 percent a year over the super-long term of twenty years or more.

Momentum investing strategies include fundamental factors to enhance the performance on the relative price or earnings strength approach. Multifactor models are tested which include the following fundamental factors: price-to-earnings ratio, price-to-sales ratio, price-to-book ratio, past one year high relative earnings strength, highest dividend yields and return on equity. Along with these fundamental factors, additional issues such as the company's credit rating, dividend yield, operating earnings and the twelve month target price for the stock are analyzed.

Momentum investing strategies are ranked with relative price strength momentum in conjunction with fundamental factors. Based on how the factors are used and in what combinations, the super-long-term returns are again increased for the fifty highest relative price strength momentum companies over the past year. The Cornerstone Growth strategy is determined best of those studied, as presented next.

Cornerstone Growth Strategy

The premier approach in the momentum investing study is the Cornerstone Growth strategy which requires purchasing common stock with consistent earnings gains, a low price-to-sales ratio and strong relative price strength momentum.

The high volatility Cornerstone Growth portfolio strategy returns +18.22 percent per year which handily beats the approximate +11 percent per year returns for the S&P 500 Index over the same 44 year period. The following momentum investing limitations make this approach less useful to astute investors, however.

Momentum Investing Limitations

The momentum investing strategies studied by O'Shaughnessy have the following limitations for astute speculators: 1) the studies reported are over the super-long term of twenty years or more rather than over the intermediate term of 1, 2, 3, 4, 5 months or more which is the focus of this book; 2) the difference in gains between a buy and hold strategy versus the best high volatility momentum investing strategy, Cornerstone Growth, equals +18.22 percent per year which is a respectable long-term return but is not sufficient for our targeted intermediate speculative return goal of +33 percent per year; 3) momentum investing disregards industry ranking information when determining which common stock to select for purchase; 4) a margin-of-safety multiple calculation for stock under consideration is not made; and 5) momentum investing concerns itself only with being in long stock positions.

It is explained that the momentum of individual common stock by itself cannot be counted upon for outsized profits, and instead, is dominated by overall market and industry group effects. Also, based on the empirical study previously presented, momentum for an industry is better used over the intermediate term of twelve months rather than a duration of 44 years as tested for the Cornerstone Growth portfolio strategy. The use of market stages, industries and what is known about intermediate-term momentum is combined to develop the recommended technique for astute speculators, called "momentum speculating," as presented next.

Momentum Speculating

There are five major differences between momentum investing and momentum speculating: 1) momentum investing does not concern itself with first identifying the long-term trend in the market which typically leads to disastrous momentum portfolio results once the overall market reverses and goes into a long-term downtrend; 2) momentum investing does not focus on the intermediate term; 3) nor does momentum investing first identify the highest ranking industries prior to investing in a high momentum stock; 4) momentum investing does not calculate a margin-of-safety multiple for each stock under investigation; and 5) momentum investing does not consider taking short-sale positions.

Momentum Speculating Attributes

Momentum speculating is better used to identify intermediate-term industry trends for speculative success by looking at market stages, industry rankings and by calculating a corporation's margin-of-safety multiple. When explaining momentum speculating, positive momentum is discussed first and negative momentum is presented in brackets. Positive (negative) momentum speculating stock companies ready for purchase (short sale) have the following nine attributes necessary for consideration:

1) The overall stock market's long-term trend is first identified. Purchase common stock only when the S&P 500 Index Nine Month MA Trend Line and confirming indicators show that the market is in accumulation or a long-term uptrend, i.e., the stock market is in Stage 2: Accumulation - Bottoming or Stage 3: Mark-Up – Uptrend.

Sell short common stock only when the S&P 500 Index Nine Month MA Trend Line and confirming indicators show that the market is in distribution or a long-term downtrend, i.e., the stock market the is in Stage 4: Distribution - Topping or Stage 1: Mark-Down – Downtrend.

2) The relative price strength of the industry group over the past six months should be in the top 25 percent (bottom 25%) of all industry rankings. Look at the shorter duration three-month industry rankings to get a heads up to changing six-month rankings. A new industry group moving into the top 25 percent six-month industry ranking list should be identified for possible speculation in the industry leader. An industry group moving into the bottom 25 percent six-month industry price ranking list should be identified for possible short-sale speculation in the industry laggard.

3) Do the required company specific fundamental analysis. Calculate the company's intrinsic, true, or fair value, market value capitalization, bargain value and margin-of-safety multiple. In addition, investigate the ten additional crucial factors.

A corporate stock with a margin-of-safety multiple over two and ten good additional crucial factors is an excellent candidate for purchase while a company with a margin-of-safety multiple at zero and poor additional crucial factors is a candidate to sell short. The stock's price should eventually follow fundamentals, the only question is when.

4) Look for common stock hitting an all-time high in price for the first time on significantly increased trading volume. When shorting company laggards look for stock priced at an all-time low for the first time on significantly increased volume. A laggard large cap company with poor fundamentals and priced between five and ten dollars per share is particularly good to short, with the expectation that the company is falling into bankruptcy.

5) A liquid stock trading at least two million shares per week. It is necessary to be able to buy and sell close to the market price without unduly affecting the stock's price.

6) A wonderful (sad) story of how the company's product or service will change the world (is obsolete due to creative destruction) that can be succinctly explained by the media and understood by the investing public.

7) The company should be an IPO or relatively new (old), focused in an infant (outdated) industry. The investing public prefers the new and exciting companies to purchase stock in rather than the old and stodgy.

Typically the type of leading companies which fit this category are cutting edge technology companies in new high growth industries. However, traditional leading companies in standard industries with a good story may be included here, e.g., energy or gold companies.

8) A positive (negative) earnings surprise where actual earnings for the quarter beat (come under) the earnings estimate is informative. Companies which beat (miss) earnings estimates will most likely continue to do so. A stock's fair value is proportionally linked to its earnings, so earnings surpassing (lower than) estimates typically leads to increased (decreased) earnings estimates and higher (lower) fair market values.

9) Security analysts increasing (decreasing) earnings per share estimates for the company. A stock's fair value is proportionally linked to its earnings, so increased (decreased) earnings estimates tend to increase (decrease) security analyst share target prices.

Momentum Speculating Conclusions

Having both the long-term overall stock market trend and the intermediate-term momentum trend of an exciting new (old or stodgy) industry group of a fundamentally sound (weak) industry leader (laggard) hitting an all-time price high (low) for the first time on notably increased trading volume prior to a purchase (short sale) significantly increases the probability of success when using momentum speculating.

Speculating, either long or short, in the most active stock issues is a good way to improve timing and staying away from listless drifters which tie-up speculative risk capital. Knowledge and making informed calculations reduce stock market risk and increase speculative confidence. An intermediate-term stock price move for a specific company lasts approximately one year after it is first recognized in high or low six-month industry rankings and is the means to accomplishing outsized astute speculative profits.

In general, during a long-term upward trend in the stock market, buy the wonderfully managed quickly growing company with sound fundamentals in an exciting new industry and, during a long-term downtrend, sell short mediocre companies with poor fundamentals in distressed industries.

Summary

Stock market sectors categorize corporations with shared characteristics into groups. Sectors do not have market diversification but companies within each sector tend to be correlated with one another and display comparable stock price performance.

Twelve stock market sectors are presented where eleven sectors are cyclical and one sector is defensive. The lead, coincident and lag identifications explain how each cyclical sector typically relates to the long-term stock market trend. Companies within sectors are further sorted into anywhere from 100-225 industry groups which display market momentum.

Momentum is based on the rate of change of prices or earnings rather than on actual price or earning levels. Momentum investing requires putting money in high relative price or earnings strength common stock that are advancing faster than the overall market. The foundation of momentum investing is that proven stock winners continue to win while stock losers continue to lose.

Momentum of an individual common stock on its own, without the benefit of other companies in a particular industry, is not consistent enough to make a significant amount of money because the individual stock's trend may quickly change direction due to the company's unsystematic risk, industry momentum or long-term stock market trend.

Momentum investing has the following five limitations: 1) the studies reported are over the super-long term of twenty years or more rather than over the intermediate term of 1, 2, 3, 4, 5 months or more which is the focus of this book; 2) the difference in gains between a buy and hold strategy versus the best high volatility momentum investing strategy, Cornerstone Growth, equals +18.22 percent per year which is a respectable long-term return but is not sufficient for our targeted intermediate speculative return goal of +33 percent per year; 3) momentum investing disregards industry ranking information when determining which common stock to select for purchase; 4) a margin-of-safety multiple calculation for stock under consideration is not made; and 5) momentum investing concerns itself only with being in long stock positions.

Nine momentum speculating fundamentals for evaluation are presented, beginning with first knowing the long-term trend in the stock market. Once positive momentum in a high (low) ranked industry is demonstrated over the prior six months, the industry trend is positive (negative) and is expected to continue over the next twelve months.

Momentum speculating is used to recognize long-term stock market trends and intermediate-term industry trends for speculative success. Momentum speculating requires identifying a leading company within the top 25 percent of industry rankings to purchase while laggard second and third-tier companies in the 25 percent of the lowest ranked industries should be sold short, at the correct time.

Momentum speculators should treat equities as fluctuating inventories that first come in and then go out of favor on Wall Street and realize the real end game is to eventually hold cash and not own stock.

In general, during a long-term upward trend in the stock market, buy the wonderfully managed quickly growing company with sound fundamentals in an exciting new industry and, during a long-term downtrend, sell short mediocre companies with poor fundamentals in distressed industries.

7

Money Management

Introduction

MONEY MANAGEMENT FOCUSES upon position size, or how many stock shares should be acquired in relation to the total amount of risk capital available to the speculator, and upon the downside risk of stock trading where speculators plan for the possibility of trading losses by using risk-reduction strategies. The three goals of money management are: 1) never put one's way of life at risk; 2) only risk as much money on one trade that will keep the mind clear; and 3) be able to keep the money once earned.

Money management rules are emphasized because it is not how much money speculators earn that is most important, instead, it is how much traders do not lose that determines speculative success. The five money management rules are: 1) save half the profits; 2) learn to "say no" and keep a cash reserve; 3) protect capital; 4) use focus speculating; and 5) stay with stock winners.

Focus speculating involves trading in three companies at any one time, each representing 25 percent of total risk capital. This leaves 25 percent of total risk capital as a cash reserve. Approximately 15 targeted trades are required to earn the astute speculative goal of +33 percent per year. Reward-to-risk ratio calculations, drawdown and speculators' emotional trading zones are explained.

Program trading represents approximately 59 percent of the trading on Wall Street and uses computer algorithms to implement the following strategies: 1) a specific portfolio investment objective; 2) duration averaging; 3) portfolio insurance; and most importantly 4) index arbitrage which is a price divergent equalizer between the cash or spot equity markets and the futures & options derivative markets.

Money Management Rules

The speculative decisions, until now, concern: 1) when to buy or sell short; 2) what to purchase or sell short; 3) at what price; and 4) setting stop-loss order price points. Speculators prefer to concentrate on the upside to trading, however, money management issues force traders to prepare for the possible downside losses of stock market trading. Money management concentrates upon position size, or how many stock shares should be acquired in relation to the total amount of risk capital available to the speculator.

Traders who cannot speculate in the stock market cannot earn outsized returns. Speculators who lose all their money trading cannot speculate which is similar to a store without any merchandise to sell, both the store and the speculator are out of business. Therefore, it is imperative that speculators never lose all their money and never risk all of their money on any one trade.

The focus in money management is drawn away from just earning spectacular profits to also controlling the risk of possible speculative losses. Extraordinarily bad events can happen at any time in the stock market which should be planned for in advance. The goal is to protect the speculator's total risk capital so that they are not wiped out as a result of extraordinary events. Speculators with no money are out of business and no longer be able to speculate.

Money management answers the question, "How much of the speculator's total risk capital should be put into any one stock position?" This translates into how many shares of the stock in question should be purchased or sold short. Money management determines the risk of the trade based upon the percentage of the speculator's total risk capital committed.

Money Management Goals

There are three main goals in money management: 1) never put one's way of life at risk by betting it all on one trade—absent this, nothing really catastrophic will ever happen to you; 2) only risk as much money on one trade as will keep the mind clear; and 3) making money in the stock market is difficult, but the real goal is to keep the money once earned—i.e., the end game is to have money available when ending your trading career for a new life interest, leisure, or for a comfortable retirement.

The following are five speculative money or risk management rules that every astute speculator should incorporate into their trading regimen. The significance of patience, having the ability to "say no," having a cash reserve, staying with winners to protect capital, using focus speculating, calculating drawdown, reward-to-risk ratios, specifying the number of targeted trades necessary to attain the speculative goals of earning +33 percent per year and saving profits are all emphasized. The foremost money management rule and real end game, i.e., what to do with trading profits once earned, is answered next.

I. Save Half The Profits

The most important money management rule is to always put half the speculative trading profits, once earned when trading, safely away in a separate bank account. The money in this safe account may eventually be used to purchase a bond annuity when the astute speculator stops trading or goes into retirement. Continuous payments throughout life from the bond annuity may be used for new personal interests, leisure, or for a comfortable retirement (please see Chapter 11: At Retirement in *The Astute Investor* for a complete review of bond annuities). It is imperative that this first money management rule be faithfully implemented—with no exceptions!

Trading in the stock market can be a very humbling experience, therefore, learn not to make it a catastrophic experience by explicitly following the "save half the profits" money management rule. After all profitable trades and especially after big wins, cut the profits earned in half and put them in a safe bank account separate from the risk capital used for speculation. In this way a nest egg is automatically built-up for later use.

The Real End Game

Having money available when the speculator's trading career ends is the real end game and what speculation is all about. The large bank account available at the end of the astute speculator's trading career is the proof of exemplary learning, sound judgment, iron nerve in the face of stressful situations, correct action and the ability to beat the market. Being well-off at the end of trading also gives speculators the flexibility to purse other avenues of interest that may become more important later on in life.

The "save half the profits" rule of money management is to ensure that speculators keep the end game in sight and actually save money while speculating. Speculators alone are responsible for what comes after their speculating career ends, when they no longer have the nerve or stomach for trading and/or want to take up a different pursuit.

As Bernard M. Baruch instructs: making money in the stock market is relatively easy, it is keeping the money once earned that is difficult. Those who have a stellar reputation for making a fortune speculating in the stock market also seem to regularly get themselves in financial trouble, including such trading legends as James R. Keene, John W. Gates, Daniel Drew and Jesse Livermore.

The legendary stock trader Jesse Livermore mentions the "save half the profits" rule as the number one money management rule above all others that should be faithfully followed. The most significant regret Livermore had, when looking back over his spectacular speculative stock market trading career, is that he should have followed the "save half the profits" money management rule to the letter.

II. Learn To "Say No" And Keep A Cash Reserve

The second rule of money management is to learn the power of "saying no" and keeping money in a cash reserve. There are three main types of speculators operating at any one time in the stock market, as explained next.

Three Types Of Speculators

The first speculative category of trader is an agent employed by a company who has superior commodity, product and industry knowledge. Typically the company representative trades in the futures & options markets (please see chapter 10) to lay off some of the risk associated with procuring the company's raw materials or in selling the company's products. The futures & options markets and cash or spot markets are normally used in tandem for an expected advantage by the company trader. Astute speculators should not directly compete with the company agent on their raw material, product, or industry knowledge.

The second speculative category of trader is the floor trader on the NYSE or AMEX exchanges who has the overwhelming advantage of no transaction costs and in making speedy trades. Being faster or trading at a lower cost than the floor trader is impossible, so speculators should not compete with floor traders on this basis.

The third category of trader has neither the superior product or industry knowledge of the company trader or the low transaction cost and speed of the floor trader, but has one overwhelming advantage, he or she does not have to speculate unless all the probabilities are in his or her favor. Astute speculators fall into this third category and have the power to "say no" which is an invaluable asset.

Power To "Say No"

The freedom to wait for just the right moment when all the probabilities are with the speculator is the chief advantage over either the company representative or floor trader. Astute speculators keep time on their side, have patience, make the required calculations, trade at trigger points and use intelligent judgment.

Astute speculators do not do anything except when the opportunity is so compelling that it seemingly cannot miss. The power to "say no" is the most important advantage that an speculator has over the other major players in the market. Prior to beginning a trade always review all the risks and ask yourself, "Is this the best use of my money?" If the answer to this question is "yes," then forget the inevitable lingering doubts and take timely action with courage and confidence.

Patience

Patience, i.e., not expecting to get rich quickly, is a virtue in the stock market. Waiting in a neutral cash position for just the right moment to enter a trade is the mark of a winning trader. If a wonderful trading opportunity is overlooked, which happens from time to time, do not fret, be patient, another good speculative situation is sure to appear. Do not reach for a stock market position, be circumspect in making all purchase commitments.

Patience is much more important than speculative quickness when making a stock purchase. Rather than thinking in terms of time pressure, learn to think of the availability of time as the speculator's best friend.

Do not agree to any trading situation that artificially limits the timing of trading. Arbitrary or fixed time limits on account positions tend to cloud the mind. Fixed time cutoffs associated with futures and options contracts fall under this caveat as well as being pressured to trade a certain number of times a month to satisfy brokerage maintenance fee agreements. The stock market can never be pushed or rushed, so do not try.

Chronic Trading

A chronic stock market trader is typically a speculative loser since no speculator can beat the market if he or she is always trading. Cash just sitting in a trading account has the potential for extraordinary profits because the best situation may be found at the correct time. In the stock market, time is not money, timing is money and the primary speculative art or "art of arts." To guard against chronic trading, it is a good idea to periodically turn all stock positions into cash.

After making a profitable trade, which may have stretched over an intermediate-term of three to six months, speculators should give themselves a week off as a reward. Trading is a mental game and looking to trade all the time without a letup leads to mental exhaustion which then leads to foolish mistakes and correspondingly, big losses.

Keep A Cash Reserve

Speculators should never risk all their money on any one trade. It is always best to keep a cash reserve for truly extraordinary situations that the market periodically presents to speculators.

The investing public has difficulty "saying no" and consequently is often in a fully invested position at all times and, therefore, cannot take advantage of newly breaking stock market opportunities.

Patience is required to be a stellar speculator, not speed. Time should be on the side of the speculator waiting patiently in a neutral cash position. The power to "say no," having patience, not participating in chronic trading and keeping a cash reserve defines the second most important money management rule. Quantifying the amount of the cash reserve is presented later in this chapter in IV. Focus Speculating.

III. Protect Risk Capital

Speculators should not focus simply on making money but also focus on not losing money. Success in the stock market is dependent upon, "not losing a great deal rather than on winning a great deal." Superb defense is what separates successful speculators from stock market losers, not celebrated offence. The two most important secrets to successful stock trading are, "*cut losses short*, and repeated again, *cut losses short*."

Four Trading Categories

Larry Hite, during an interview with Jack D. Schwager, separates trading into the following four categories: 1) good trades; 2) bad trades; 3) winning trades; and 4) losing trades. The crucial point is that a losing trade is not necessarily a bad trade.

A good trade, regardless whether it wins or loses, has the probabilities and potential rewards in the speculator's favor. A higher potential payoff, lets say $8 dollars per share with a probability of success of 60 percent, versus a lower potential loss of $2 dollars per share with a probability 40 percent is a good trade regardless of the trade's eventual outcome. The expected value of the trade is: $8 x 0.6 - $2 x 0.4 = $4 dollars per share.

Make only high expected value trades and stock market winning takes care of itself. Hite goes on to say: 1) without trading, winning is impossible; and 2) losing all one's money negates the ability to trade. Therefore, protect risk capital, do not lose all your money because then speculation becomes impossible.

Stock speculators without money are akin to store owners without inventory, i.e., they are no longer in business. Play defense, defend what you have, never risk your lifestyle or family's security while trading and nothing overly bad will ever happen to you in the stock market. Preserve risk capital by never taking a position or performing an action that has the potential to lose it all. If you never risk it all you will always be secure in your speculative profession.

Zero-Risk Money Management

Zero-risk money management is a good strategy to protect capital. Zero-risk requires cashing in half the stock position the moment the trade account doubles in value. Of course, progressive stop-loss orders are used as the stock price moves in the speculator's favor.

The nice thing about exiting half the stock position once the account doubles in value is that the entire initial risk capital is recovered and now only money earned in the market is at risk. This is zero-risk because traders are now speculating with the "house's money." On the remaining at risk capital, place a close progressive stop-loss order and continue to let the profits run.

Calculate Reward-to-Risk Ratios

Money management relies heavily on risk management. Always calculate the most that can be lost on each trade using the stop-loss order based on a calculated reward-to-risk ratio. While the reward cannot be known with any certainty, the risk can and should always be quantified.

Never sustain a loss of more than ten percent of capital on any one trade. Losing -30 percent on any trade is very difficult to recover since the speculator has to earn +43 percent on a future trade just to get even. Preferably, with good entry points using a buy-limit order, closer stop-loss order price points may be set that significantly reduces the -10 percent limit loss restriction. Try to enter positions close to long and intermediate-term turning points.

The reward-to-risk ratio should be at least four-to-one, i.e., expect to make at least four times what is being risked on the stock position based on its stop-loss order price point. The expected value probabilities are now in the speculator's favor and trading perfection is not required.

This should give confidence to speculators that outsized returns are probable when the proper knowledge, foresight, patience, character, judgment and timing are used effectively in the stock market. An entry point, upside price target, total share position and stop-loss order price point are established in the planning and scheduling step.

Total Risk Capital

The initial size of the total risk capital is immaterial, speculators can begin with $10,000 dollars. Committing 25 percent to a stock trade results in $2,500 dollar position (more on this in the focus speculating section next). With Internet trading at discount brokers there is often a flat trading fee regardless of the number of shares purchased or sold.

Take a stock position of fifty shares if necessary to remain below the $2,500 dollar trading limit. All of the remaining reward-to-risk ratio calculations and stop-loss determinations remain the same is if speculators had $1 million dollars with which to speculate.

The third rule of money management requires speculators to protect their risk capital, make reward-to-risk ratio calculations that are at least four-to-one and always use stop-loss orders.

IV. Focus Speculating

Not every stock market trade makes money. The stop-loss order limits the loss to no more than -10 percent on any one trade, but losing trades may come together in bunches. Drawdown is the term used to describe the probable amount of money lost during a succession of trades as a percentage of the speculator's total risk capital. If all trades showed a profit, drawdown would be zero.

Drawdown is not a portfolio achievement measure of success or failure. Drawdown increases as the percentage amount of capital committed to any one trade is increased. The computation starts at a losing trade and keeps going as total risk capital continues to be lost.

Drawdown

Speculators should have a keen appreciation of how difficult it is to recover from a large drawdown. As the percentage lost in a drawdown increases, the amount of money necessary to recover from the loss grows geometrically. If speculators lose -50 percent of their risk capital it takes a +100 percent gain just to get back to even and an -80 percent loss requires a +400 percent gain which is very difficult to achieve. The risk of a high drawdown based on the percentage of the total risk capital committed to each trade needs to be recognized, controlled for and properly managed.

Strive to keep the drawdown to no more than -20 percent which means that astute speculators have to earn +25 percent to break even. Using the reward-to-risk ratio example presented in chapter 4, the stop-loss order is two points on an averaged priced stock of $37.55 and the expected profits are eight points. This sets the minimum reward-to-risk ratio of four-to-one. To recap: purchase at $37.55, stop-loss order price point at $35.55, with an expected target price of $45.55 resulting in a +21.3 percent expected gain. The stop-loss order price point is set at -5.3 percent ($2.00 divided by $37.55).

If the stop-loss order price point is set at -5.3 percent for each trade and committing 25 percent of the risk capital per trade allows for 15 losses in a row before the -20 percent drawdown limit is reached (0.25 x 0.053 x 15 losses = 0.20 drawdown). This seems very realistic to remain within 15 consecutive trading losses when using a focus speculating approach to selecting stock positions.

If an astute speculator ever has 15 consecutive trading losses in a row, he or she should stop trading and review the speculative methodology being used for a possible change. The market is telling the speculator that he or she is in a losing intellectual rut with so many consecutive losses and it is best to remain inactive until revisions to beliefs and a new trading methodology can be devised. When a revised trading strategy is implemented, begin trading with small amounts of money until confidence in the new trading strategy is achieved.

Determine Your Emotional Trading Zone

Each speculator has a definite emotional trading zone where the size of the trade, in relation to the overall size of his or her risk capital, can be made with a clear mind. A trader with $50 million dollars is not going to be bothered with one thousand dollar trades. The small trader just starting out, on the other hand, may have ten thousand dollars of total risk capital and only feel comfortable trading $1,000 dollars on any one position.

Each trader's emotional trading zone is unique. The individual's emotional trading zone determination should be part of the strategy that the speculator selects for himself or herself (please see chapter 10 for more on this). Risking 25 percent of one's risk capital on a single trade may emotionally overwhelm a speculator while risking only two percent on one trade may not seem worthwhile based on the amount of time required to identify the speculative situation.

The psychological effect of losing money requires speculators to analyze who they are and how they react under pressure. Each speculator has to determine their own emotional trading zone. What is looked for is the emotional trading zone that each speculator can live with in relation to the expected drawdown. The astute speculator wants to be able to endure an acceptable drawdown while preserving risk capital.

The total amount of money committed to each trade is determined by the individual speculator based upon his or her emotional makeup and financial situation. Prior to entering a position, determine the amount of money that will be put at risk in the reward-to-risk ratio and respect it by setting a stop-loss order price point based on this calculation. Each speculator should know how much mental aguish they can stand, plan for it and when it happens make sure they are automatically taken out of the stock position with a properly set stop-loss order.

Stay In Your Emotional Trading Zone

Speculators should determine their emotional trading zone level and stick with it for a period of time until confidence builds. A good recommendation is to begin trading at 15 percent of one's total risk capital on any single trade situation. Perhaps three stock positions of 15 percent each, totaling 45 percent of the total bankroll should be the initial upper limit which allows for a clear mind and a cash reserve.

Initially, it is better to under trade rather than overtrade, so if not confident, the beginning 15 percent position could be cut in half. As trading experience increases and confidence is gained, the percentage of the bankroll risked on each trade will likely increase until it reaches the 25 percent maximum recommended on each trade.

Monitor trading profits in relation to one's emotional trading limit and change the total risk capital percentage on each trade as necessary. As personal conditions and one's lifestyle changes, such as new family additions or purchasing a new house, this may alter the speculator's emotional trading zone. The total risk capital or percent committed on each trade may be reduced.

Countless lifestyle changes shape a speculator's emotional trading zone risk level, consequently, each trader has to judge his or her appropriate trading percentage amount. After all, you know your own personal state of affairs and trading psychology better than anyone else.

Focus Investing

Warren Buffett relies on the quantitative application of the margin-of-safety multiple and intrinsic, true, or fair value calculation championed by Benjamin Graham. Thoroughly knowing and understanding the few companies that are being invested in is called "focus investing" and is Buffett's investment style of choice.

Because the efficient market hypothesis (EMH) is rejected in this book, a statistical diversification approach to speculation is also rejected. Astute speculators should not use a random walk, statistically based gambling strategy as the basis for speculating in the stock market.

Some professional money management companies select stock based on the EMH, representing perhaps hundreds of different companies residing in their portfolio. The astute speculator, instead, rejects the EMH in favor of having in-depth knowledge about the companies being selected, called focus speculating which is presented next.

Focus Speculating

It is assumed here that the astute speculator is an individual acting alone for his or her own account. The speculator is trying to balance the risk of the trade with the costs of evaluating the potential trade and the share transaction costs. Consequently, the percentage of the total risk capital increases on any one trade for the astute speculator.

A "focus speculating" approach based on focus investing is adopted that relies on sound fundamental analysis for selecting undervalued stock to purchase or overvalued stock to sell short using a margin-of-safety multiple calculation and trading at trigger points for the timing of trades. The recommended number of companies that astute speculators should trade in at any one time is three, each representing 25 percent of total risk capital. This leaves 25 percent of total risk capital as a cash reserve.

15 Targeted Trades Per Year

Approximately 15 targeted trades are required to earn the astute speculative goal of +33 percent per year. This is calculated by first looking at Table 4 – 1: Reward-To-Risk Expected Payoff where ten trades are expected to earn +30 percent less commissions, consequently, the average earned on each trade is three percent. Eleven trades earn +33 percent but typically only 75 percent of the total risk capital is used for trading, resulting in a total of 11 trades divided by 0.75 equaling approximately 15 targeted trades required per year.

V. Stay With The Winners

Purchase corporate leaders in high ranking industries during a long-term stock market advance. The second or third-tier stock laggards in weak industries during a long-term downward trending market are the deadbeat companies that should be sold short. Never fight the line of least resistance in the stock market, instead, trade along with the long-term market trends and intermediate-term industry trends.

Enter long stock positions or short stock positions close to turning points. Let profits run as long as the stock continues to act properly. Remain with positions that confirm the initial plan, maintain an iron nerve and remain courageous.

Do not settle for being an unintentional investor. Stay away from listless stock drifters. Select stock that are active and moving, i.e., market leaders that have the highest probability for rapid advancement when buying and market losers that have the highest probability for rapid decline when short the stock, at the correct time.

Let Profits Run: Whether Long Or Short

Letting profits run is not the same thing as a "buy and hold" strategy. Asset-allocation investing is not the goal when speculating. Let the stock price run in the speculator's favor, either long or short, as long as possible while setting progressive stop-loss orders. The realization that an active winning stock will not lose money allows speculators to sit quietly while patiently waiting for their stock position to earn even more money.

While trading methodologies are vastly important, money management risk-reduction strategies are crucial. Money management is concerned with the speculative risk of the trade based upon trade size in relation to the total risk capital, drawdown, reward-to-risk ratio calculations, setting stop-loss order price points and the individual speculator's emotional trading zone. The five money management rules, if staunchly followed, ensure that astute speculators stay out of serious financial trouble and have money remaining when their stock trading days are behind them.

Program Trading

Program trading is best described as an arbitrage strategy where the purchase of equities on one market for instantaneous resale on another market captures profits from any inter-market price variations. Program trading is the concurrent trading of a basket of equities on different exchanges rather than focusing on just one stock on one exchange.

According to the program trading website www.programtrading.com, the NYSE specifies a program trade as: 1) a basket of S&P 500 Index common stock numbering fifteen or more; or 2) a basket of S&P 500 Index common stock with a total value of $1,000,000 dollars or more.

Program Trading Development

Program trading begins in the 1970's when basket stock orders are hand carried around to NYSE specialists on the floor. The use of computer assisted program trading has since made this manual process very efficient. Computer program trading has increased significantly since the early 1980's and dominates Wall Street trading today.

The investing public normally uses mutual funds when investing rather than purchasing stock directly through a broker. Mutual fund institutions rely on program trading to purchase or sell baskets of common stock as efficiently and effectively as possible.

Program trading developed as the result of the following four stock market conditions: 1) computer technologies drastically reduced trading costs; 2) trading a basket of common stock, e.g., the S&P 500 Index, reduces or eliminates the unsystematic risk associated with an individual stock; 3) institutions now dominate trading on the stock, futures and options exchanges; and 4) institutions expect to make short-term transactions at optimal price points.

Many institutional buy-side traders rely 100 percent on computer programs to make the decision on what to purchase and when. Portfolio managers at mutual fund companies are turning more and more toward computer generated models when buying and selling stock for their portfolios. Program trading computer technology allows brokerage company customers to make the trades themselves, thus saving on stock commissions.

Program Trading: 59 Percent Of All Trades

Because program trading accounts for a large percentage of the total trades being made each day on the major stock exchanges, it is important to understand how program trading operates. The total number of program trading shares purchased or sold are summed together to determine total program trading volume. The program trading volume is then divided by the total number of shares traded on the exchange to calculate the program trading percentage.

As of March, 2006, the New York Stock Exchange (NYSE) reports on their website www.nyse.com that program trading accounts for 58.6 percent of all trades made on the NYSE. This is up from 57.1 percent for program trading for all of 2005. Almost 59 percent of the trading on the NYSE is performed by a computer, similar program trading activity is expected on the National Association of Securities Dealers Automated Quotation (NASDAQ) and American Stock Exchange (AMEX) exchanges.

Computerized Program Trading Links Markets

The exchanges where program trading takes place typically trade the underlying stock on the NYSE, NASDAQ and AMEX exchanges, and derivatives consisting of stock options contracts traded on the Chicago Board Options Exchange (CBOE) or AMEX, and Standard & Poor's (S&P) 500 Index futures contracts traded on the Chicago Mercantile Exchange (CME). Program trades are required by the Securities and Exchange Commission (SEC) to be specifically identified as such when sent by computer to each exchange.

Computerized program trading is performed by large institutional financial firms who make high volume buy and sell transactions using a direct link between their computer system and the different exchange computers where the orders are executed. By this method the underlying stock exchange cash markets and derivative futures and options markets are coupled together so that market prices on different exchanges do not significantly deviate from another (futures and options are fully discussed in chapter 10).

Two Major Categories

Program trading falls into two major categories. The first higher percentage of total activity is by NYSE member firms who perform most of their program trading for their customers and merely act as customer agents. The second lower percentage of total activity is by NYSE member firms who participate in program trading for their own accounts, called proprietary trading.

Program Trading Algorithms

Program trading relies on computers to run algorithms, designed by quantitative specialists, to make quick decisions in order to take advantage of the fast changing stock and derivative markets. An algorithm solves optimally a mathematical model representing a large trading problem by using a goal seeking objective function utilizing a progressive or iterative problem-solving solution methodology. Computers make the buy and sell actions go very quickly but are under the ultimate control of human beings who do the actual model development and computer programming.

Program trading algorithms typically use short-term predictive methodologies to establish expected optimal predictive solutions for order timing, order size and on which exchanges transactions are to be preformed, all while decreasing the disruption on share prices. The algorithmic based computer system responds in real time to market price fluctuations.

The goal is to balance not having other traders recognize what purpose the algorithmic orders are serving as well as not significantly moving the share price with large buy or sell orders. Typically, computer transactions based on algorithms break up the order into very small blocks of perhaps 500 shares each and only intermittently send these orders out to the different exchanges.

Prices Divergences, Not Fundamentals

The computer is not programmed for and does no fundamental analysis of whether a company is overvalued or undervalued to support the computer's action. No political-economic conditions are analyzed to determine how to best proceed with the program trade. It is assumed that all the fundamental analysis is performed by investors and speculators, either in the cash markets or in the futures and options derivative markets. Computer program trading merely acts as a balancing scale among the separate cash and derivative marketplaces.

Computer programming orders are generated based solely upon price divergences, the reasons are immaterial and the fundamentals are unknown. By using computer technology, monitoring prices on both the futures & options markets and on the cash markets are performed continuously.

Interest rates and dividend rates are also tracked. Risk-free profits from the original spread between the futures contract and the underlying stock are captured during the unwinding at futures expiration when the initial spread rate dominates the interest rate on Treasury bills.

The efficient linking of the all markets via computer, including the cash or spot and derivative futures & options markets, lowers cost and increases trading liquidity. If prices deviate materially in the cash markets or derivative futures & options markets, based on mathematical algorithms, computers buy or sell to rebalance prices.

Program Trading Strategies

Program trading utilizes computer algorithms to implement the following four strategies: 1) a specific portfolio investment objective; 2) duration averaging; 3) portfolio insurance; and most importantly 4) index arbitrage which is a price divergent equalizer between the cash or spot equities markets and the futures and options derivative markets. Each of these strategies are described next.

1) Specific Portfolio Investment Objective

One way to understand specific portfolio investment objective is to assume that many individual investors decide to invest with a particular mutual fund. The mutual fund portfolio manager receives the investor's money and decides to purchase more shares of stock currently in the mutual fund's portfolio.

If this basket of common stock were automatically purchased using computer program trading, this is defined as a program trade satisfying this mutual fund portfolio manager's investment objective.

2) Duration Averaging

Duration averaging attempts to perform the "buy low, sell high" function via computer and works well enough when stock prices stay within a trading range, but misses out when stock prices break below price support or surge above price resistance levels.

The use of institutional computer generated scale-in and scale-out orders tend to reduce volatility and the movement of prices in either direction, therefore, stock prices typically stay within a trading range.

3) Portfolio Insurance

The goal of portfolio insurance is to lock in a set value of a portfolio's worth during a declining stock market, at the same time allowing for appreciation during an up trending market. A portfolio insurance strategy is to purchase a "put option" on a basket of common stock or the S&P 500 Index. The "put option" gives the holder the right but not the obligation to sell the stock basket or stock index at a striking price.

During a downward trending market, the "put option" is exercised at a higher price than the current market price, thus, saving money during the market's decline. If the stock basket or stock index increases in price, the "put option" is not exercised and all that is lost is the purchase price of the "put option."

4) Index Arbitrage

Index arbitrage is the most widely used strategy of program trading, being the equalizer between different cash and derivative markets, which involves identifying price inconsistencies among stock baskets, indexes and futures & options contracts. Advanced computer algorithms are used to hedge equity positions.

When traders in the futures or options markets cause prices to deviate from the underlying stock prices on the stock exchanges, the less expensive stock or derivative is purchased simultaneously with selling the more expensive stock or derivative, thus, locking in the arbitrage price differential for the computer program trader.

As an example, S&P 500 Index futures and the underlying common stock in the S&P 500 Index are at the same fair value, then, new information is foreseen which moves both markets upward. The futures market normally reacts faster than the prices for the underlying common stock, consequently, the need for index arbitrage to bring both stock and derivative prices back in line at fair value. The expensive futures are sold coincidently with purchasing a basket of the S&P 500 Index common stock.

A fully hedged position can be created by selling futures and buying the underlying common stock. Futures normally sell at a premium to the underlying stock because interest rates are typically higher than the dividend rate paid on the underlying stock.

Financial Futures & Options Expiration Dates

Financial futures normally expire quarterly on the third Friday in March, June, September and December. Options expire monthly, on Saturday following the last trading day which also occurs on the third Friday of the month (futures and options are fully discussed in chapter 10).

Upon futures expiration, the spread shrinks to zero because the value of the ending futures contract is required to equal the value of the underlying stock. This is called the "unwinding" of the hedged positions, i.e., selling the underlying stock while the futures expire.

Fair Value

Fair value is an important concept when performing index arbitrage because it ties the current value to the futures contract price. Fair value is the price which a stock, option, or futures contract should be purchased or sold. Fair value may be found for common stock by calculating its intrinsic value. Futures fair value, options fair value and options on futures fair value are specified using mathematical valuation models that are discussed in chapter 10.

The fair value for the S&P 500 Index, currently reported by CNBC on television, as this is written, is the link between the S&P 500 Index futures contract and the cash value of the S&P 500 Index. When actual futures prices are higher than fair value, traders believe S&P 500 Index will trade up in price and likewise, traders believe the S&P 500 Index will move lower when futures prices are below fair value.

Premium

The absolute price difference, whether positive or negative, between the S&P 500 Index futures contract price and the spot or cash price of the underlying stock in the S&P 500 Index is described as "the premium."

By knowing "the premium," the market momentum, either up-or-down, is determined. A market described as "holding a positive premium" means that for the majority of the time the premium is higher than fair value and the futures are expected to move higher.

The premium may not be high enough to trigger a buy computer program but the premium staying positive intraday, over the short-term, is an indication that a strong market is expected. Since futures are expected to lead the underlying cash markets, it is projected that the actual S&P 500 Index will also move higher.

Premium below fair value occurs in markets that are described as weak and "not able to hold premium." A market that has a consistently weak premium intraday is a market that is probably heading lower.

Importance Of Knowing Premium

It is important to know the premium because a feel for the market is developed. If the premium is currently 2.1 and it is known that a computer trading buy program will begin at 3.0 and the sell program at 1.0, the premium is watched and if it stays strong this bodes well for an increase in the futures contract price and eventually for the underlying S&P 500 Index price.

By knowing the premium, the timing of program trading may be identified. If the premium hits 3.0, the presence of buy programs are expected. If relative movement in the futures index and cash index results in program trading, it is preferable to have the premium remain above the buy point of 3.0 for more than a few seconds. Experienced program traders will not trade when premiums only momentarily touch trigger points because liquidity may not be sufficient in either the cash or futures market to justify a program trade.

To get an accurate S&P 500 Index premium calculation, all of the companies in the S&P 500 Index have to be open for trading, especially the largest companies, because the S&P 500 Index is value weighted. Very large companies in the S&P 500 Index such as General Electric, Microsoft, or Exxon Mobil not being open for trading would skew the premium number and make it unreliable.

Identifying When Program Trading Is Ongoing

It may be important to identify when program trading is ongoing. A program trading program may be in effect if the S&P 500 Index cash price begins moving up in leaps, with each leap slightly larger than the last. For example, the actual S&P 500 Index might leap up in increasingly larger increments in price: e.g., 1265.09, 1265.29, 1265.70 and 1266.30.

Program trades are normally transacted when S&P 500 Index prices reach certain threshold levels and not before. Consequently, program trading tends to generate volatile price changes. Because of this, restrictions on the timing of program trading are enforced.

Program Trading Curbs

Computer program trading is singled out as a reason why share prices experience high volatility. Computer trading is generally thought to have exacerbated the scary -22.6 percent, 508 point drop in the Dow Jones Industrial Average (DJIA) to 1,738 on October 19, 1987. Due to the magnitude of the computer generated buy and sell orders, the SEC decided that markets should be protected under certain conditions. As a result of this 1987 experience, the NYSE instituted the following program trading curbs or collars.

Program Trading Collars

Program trading curbs or collars are subject to Rule 80A on the NYSE and restrict but do not completely stop program trading. If the NYSE Composite Index (NYA) either increases or decreases 150 points or more in a day, program trading curbs are instituted. This is reported by the media as trading "curbs in" place. The trading curbs remain in effect throughout the entire trading day as long as the NYA remains 70 points away from the prior day's NYA closing price.

Once computer program trading curbs or collars are in effect on the NYSE, program selling can only occur on an uptick and program buying can only occur on a downtick. Rule 80A tries to direct derivative-related computer program trading to be performed only as a steadying influence, once trading collars are instituted.

In conclusion, program trading begins only when the premium is large enough for program traders to make money on the trade. The result of program trading is to force the premium back toward fair value.

Program trading is approximately 59 percent of total NYSE, NASDAQ and AMEX trading and typically occurs daily. Astute traders are aware of computer program trading activity to better understand short-term market volatility and use premium information to recognize strong or weak markets.

Summary

Money management focuses upon position size, or how many stock shares should be acquired in relation to the total amount of risk capital available to the speculator, and upon the downside risk of stock trading where speculators plan for the possibility of trading losses by using risk-reduction strategies. The three goals of money management are: 1) never put one's way of life at risk; 2) only risk as much money on one trade that will keep the mind clear; and 3) be able to keep the money once earned.

Money management rules are emphasized because it is not how much money speculators earn that is most important, instead, it is how much traders do not lose that determines speculative success. Five speculative money management rules keep trading risk exposure to an acceptable level and are presented with the highest priority rule listed first:

I. *Save Half The Profits*: Making money in the stock market is relatively easy, it is the end game of keeping the money earned that is difficult.

II. *Learn To "Say No" And Keep A Cash Reserve:* An astute speculator has neither the product or industry knowledge of the company trader or the low transaction costs nor the transaction speed of the floor trader, but has one overwhelming advantage—he or she does not have to speculate unless all the probabilities are in his or her favor—the power to "say no" is an invaluable asset. Speculators keep a cash reserve in order to take advantage of extraordinary market conditions when they occur.

III. *Protect Capital*: Do not focus on just making money, instead, speculators should focus on not losing their risk capital. Success in the stock market is dependent upon not losing a great deal rather than on winning a great deal, i.e., defense not offence is central. Speculators should protect their risk capital, make reward-to-risk ratio calculations that are at least four-to-one and always use stop-loss orders.

IV. *Focus Speculating:* Not every trade makes money. Drawdown is the term used to describe the probable amount of money lost as a percentage of the total risk capital used during trading in order to achieve the expected returns. The recommended number of companies that astute speculators should trade in at any one time is three, each representing 25 percent of total risk capital. This leaves 25 percent of total risk capital as a cash reserve. Approximately 15 targeted trades are required to earn the astute speculative goal of +33 percent per year.

V. *Stay With The Winners:* Speculate only in the high ranking industry leader on the way up. The second or third-tier industry laggards on the way up should be the leaders on the way down and sold short. Let both long and short position winners run for large gains.

Money management is concerned with the speculative risk of the trade based upon trade size in relation to the total risk capital, drawdown, reward-to-risk ratio calculations, setting stop-loss order price points and the individual speculator's emotional trading zone.

Program trading is an arbitrage strategy where the purchase of equities on one market for instantaneous resale on another market captures profits from any inter-market price variations. Institutions rely on program trading to purchase or sell baskets of common stock as efficiently and effectively as possible.

Approximately 59 percent of the trading on the NYSE, NASDAQ and AMEX is program trading performed by a computer based solely upon relative prices from one exchange market to another. The computer programming orders are generated on price divergences only, the reasons are immaterial and the fundamentals of whether the stock is undervalued or overvalued are unknown.

Program trading utilizes computer algorithms to implement the following four strategies: 1) a specific portfolio investment objective; 2) duration averaging; 3) portfolio insurance; and most importantly 4) index arbitrage which is an equalizer between the cash or spot equities markets and the futures & options derivative markets.

The NYSE has trading curbs or collars on computer program trading. If the NYSE Composite Index (NYA) either increases or decreases 150 points or more in a day, program trading collars are instituted which restrict but do not completely stop program trading.

8

Speculative Bylaws

Introduction

SPECULATORS NEED STOCK MARKET foresight in order to succeed. The most formidable competitor that a speculator has is himself or herself, consequently, knowing the best strategy that matches one's character, personality and lifestyle, not always expecting to win and being able to admit a mistake are all crucial for speculative success.

The ten character traits of the best stock market speculators are presented. Traders should ensure the ten speculative bylaws are followed by signing a contract with themselves. Astute speculators plan and schedule all their actions but also understand the importance of comparing their plan to what is actually occurring in the stock market.

Speculators should first rehearse by using simulator or paper trading to test their practical knowledge. Once simulator trading proves successful, speculating with limited funds using very small odd-lot trades is then recommended. Graduate to full-fledged round-lot stock trading only after odd-lot trading is profitable and the speculator is in full command of his or her nerves when trading.

Use A Robust Methodology

Speculators strive to foresee the stock market's future which makes speculating powerful, fascinating and even seem somewhat mysterious to outsiders. Think about what should take place in the stock market over the next three-to-six months. What are the consequences if the reverse should happen? What circumstances are in place if the market just bides its time? Speculators should contemplate all the possibilities, predict, foresee and plan based on all the probable developments so that they are ready to act according to the right circumstances.

Astute speculators are open to learning because almost everything that happens in the world has an impact on the stock market. The unforeseen is looked for and even expected in the stock market. While a market extreme may seem very unlikely, it can and will happen. Consequently, speculators should not limit their vision with artificial blinders and conventional restrictions.

Perfection or trying to find the optimal stock market solution methodology is counterproductive. Riches and perfection do not go hand-in-hand in the stock market, because, performing flawlessness in the stock market is an impossibility. Instead, look for the most robust methodology and stock market models that have proven profitable in the past, as discussed next.

Speculation Cannot Be Optimized

Significant financial or company facts known only to the trader do not ensure prosperity when speculating. Just as important for success is understanding and subjectively judging what import these facts will have on the stock market.

Success while speculating requires correct information, study, foresight and good judgment which is more than just pure facts being plugged into a mathematical formula that mechanically supplies answers. Methodology and calculations help, but no mechanical system can substitute for sound judgment which speculators can only acquire with in-depth study and practical stock market experience.

Looking for a foolproof mathematical system that ensures trading success is futile, because, a computer program can never replace a speculator's good judgment or experience in a fast changing social institution like the stock market. Speculators are required to think for themselves to deduce how the market will react to internal company and overall political-economic conditions, so they are situated properly as the price move occurs.

Successful speculation requires first knowing what other speculators are thinking and then making the trade before they act. It should be self-evident that trying to condense to mathematical certainty the thoughts in each and every speculator's mind, at any point in time, is pretentious and ultimately preposterous. For that reason, speculating in the stock market is not as straightforward as developing a mathematical algorithm. Consequently, each speculator is required to judge for themselves and trust in their own premises and robust methodologies to be successful when speculating.

Study Data, Not Opinions

Astute speculators consider objective truths, facts and data from reliable official sources the only information worth analyzing. Tips or subjective opinions, all by themselves, from any outside source whatsoever should be shunned as probable worthless propaganda.

The speculator must make proper calculations and use their own judgment when deciding on and taking correct action. Information is Wall Street's most precious product, consequently, good information is never just given away with no ulterior motive in mind. News in the media becomes public knowledge and does so for a reason which is probably not the easily understood surface reason believed by the investing public or by amateur speculators.

Look at the facts and data in corporate annual reports, from the stock market and from the U.S. government concerning fiscal and monetary policy. Make the appropriate methodology and model calculations to form an opinion based on these objective truths and facts. Speculative subjective judgments should be based upon making calculations using factual data and analyzing the results, not simply by believing someone else's opinions.

The most excellent safeguard against stock market loss is to sharpen one's judgment so that it comes within reach of complete correctness when making the buy or sell decision. The speculator must feel certain that they are correct and then take the appropriate action. The secret to hitting it big on Wall Street is to be correct at precisely the right time and then acting accordingly.

Speculative Priorities And Techniques

The correct speculative mindset is to first wait patiently for the appropriate stock market signals, have confidence in their validity, and then feel good about taking timely action regardless of the trade's eventual outcome. For example, if a stock or the stock market is at a historic high price this is a major occurrence. Regardless of what others say about why the price level should not be at this level and how nothing has changed to justify the new high price; believe it, the fact that prices are at a new all-time high should convince speculators that these high prices are warranted.

Decisions and actions in the stock market should be based, as much as possible, on information and reliable facts. Because the speculative game is so intellectual, quiet and privacy help speculators to properly weigh all the facts and develop the best plan. As new information becomes available, it is best not to be distracted in a noisy brokerage office or by a financial TV program when making crucial decisions. Keeping the mind clear without distractions from outside sources is a decided advantage for almost all traders.

Market Hysteria

When there is investing public hysteria and stock market news is placed on the front page of leading daily newspapers, this is normally a good indication that speculators should now be prepared to become contrarian. Always remain skeptical of conventional wisdom, especially when broadcast on the nightly business news or written about in the leading financial newspapers. Also, any unsolicited financial notices received in the mail, by fax, or over the Internet should be treated as possible propaganda.

At long-term boom bubble market tops and panic selling market bottoms, the investing public is often trading in a fit of emotional frenzy. One way to know when the correct time to oppose public frenetic trading is to wait patiently in anticipation of market prices continuing to gap-up toward a market top or to gap-down toward a market bottom. Patience is required because the market always seems to go higher at a market top and lower at a market bottom than the investing public or amateur speculators anticipate.

Averaging Down

It is not a good idea to naively average down in order to lower the average price of the stock being held, i.e., continuing to add to a losing stock position by buying more stock as the stock declines in price. The misinformed idea being that once the stock price returns to its prior level the speculator can get out of their position even. Unfortunately, the price of the stock can and often will go much lower before it ever comes back up in price.

Innocently averaging down is a suicidal strategy practiced only by speculative amateurs. It is much better to lose a little money by using a stop-loss order than to be stuck with a stock market laggard which may never return to its original price.

Interest Rates And Negative Divergence

Long-term and short-term interest rates should move in tandem and when they do not this is a negative divergence that needs to correct itself prior to the market being right for trading. Three-month Treasury bill (T-bill) and thirty-year Treasury bond (T-bond) daily closing interest rates are entered into a spread sheet program. For Treasury interest rates go to the U.S. Department Of The Treasury website at: http://www.ustreas.gov/offices/domestic-finance/debt-management/interest-rate/.

Both short and long-term Treasury interest rates should move in the same direction to confirm one another and indicate the market is right for speculation. Compare the daily three-month T-bill and thirty-year T-bond interest rates with their respective thirty-day moving averages (MA). If there is a divergence, e.g., the daily three-month T-bill rate is above its thirty-day MA and the daily thirty-year T-bond rate is below its thirty-day MA then no speculative trading position should be begun until these two interest rates begin to move together on the same side of their respective moving averages.

Charts Or Graphs And Positive Divergence

Always check the weekly price charts/graphs and trading volume bar charts/graphs, and check the 26 week moving average (MA) trend line before acquiring a position in a high probability stock. Enter a buy position on an undervalued stock only when the 26 week MA trend line is trending upward.

If the intermediate-term trend in the market is down, hits a turning point and then rebounds on the next leg upward, check the price action of the stock of interest. If the stock's price remains above its latest low point while the S&P 500 Index falls below its latest low price, the stock has more relative price strength than the overall market. This is an example of a positive divergence for the stock, mark it as a possible candidate for purchase.

Character And Personality Traits

A speculator's character and personality determine, as much as correct calculations and sound judgment, success or failure in the stock market. Possessing the will power to act on what the speculator knows, rather than just following the crowd, is important. Having initiative, integrity, an even temperament, thinking everything through to a reasoned conclusion, having a cool judicial mind and the courage to act properly serves the astute speculator well.

Speculators who are fearful, greedy, egotistical, easily led by crowds, nervous, trade impulsively and with haste are least likely to be successful traders. Also, whether the speculator possesses the iron nerve or stomach to overcome the travails and stress of speculation is unknowable until trading with money is actually attempted. Every trader has to address his or her unique human vulnerabilities within themselves that jeopardize their own speculative success.

The science of speculation can be taught but the art of speculation can only be improved upon through practice. Successful speculation is dependent upon finding a speculative strategy that works for each speculator which best matches their character, personality and lifestyle. The first step in finding a speculative strategy that works for the speculator is to know thyself, as explained next in the third art of speculation.

Third Art Of Speculation

The third art of speculation relies on first knowing yourself. Each speculator has to find a unique speculative trading approach that works for their own character, personality and lifestyle, additionally, they have to determine this for themselves. Knowing yourself allows speculators to develop a strategic plan with the highest probability for their own speculative success. Three different strategic approaches are presented in chapter 9 that speculators may use exactly or modify to suit themselves.

Selecting the best strategic approach to stock market speculation should be matched with personal temperament, predispositions, motivations and ambitions. Because the most formidable competitor that a speculator has is himself or herself, knowing who we are and what is the best personal approach for each of us is the third crucial speculative art, after correct timing and knowing how to sell.

One-Valued Orientations In Life Should Be Discarded

American society has a one-valued orientation toward life, i.e., always wanting to win, being perfect, or finding an optimal solution. The push for perfection in life is self defeating because it is impossible to always win, to always be the best, to always be courteous, or even to always be truthful and never tell any harmless white lies—even during the holidays.

Most people lose much more often than win and as a consequence feel more comfortable losing. Losers makeup excuses for losing rather than learning how to win. The soul resonates and attracts its biggest craving, in this case the consolation of losing. This is a dangerous mindset for speculators to have. Since people do not know how to deal with winning, they subconsciously avoid it and secretly crave the reassuring well-known position of failure.

Speculators, win or lose, get what they want out of the stock market. If speculators, deep down, cannot handle winning, they will always be losers. Or said another way, people feel comfortable when losing because it has happened so much in their lives and, therefore, secretly dread winning.

The best way to get out of this dilemma is to shed the one-valued orientation towards life. Since it is impossible to be perfect and to always win in the stock market, speculators should prepare themselves mentally

219

for that eventuality by rejecting one-valued orientations. Speculators may need to delve into their subconscious mind to make this needed change.

Subconscious Mind

The maxim should be, "don't be a loser." Secretly or subconsciously needing failure, because it is a known comfortable position, is self-defeating for speculators. A good way to bring the subconscious mind in line with the conscious mind is by using positive goal setting, e.g., visualize yourself with huge trading profits and think how you would react to possible criticisms from those who are now envious. Convince yourself that it is now acceptable and desirable to be successful and leave the comfortable and all too familiar loser position behind.

While stock market speculation is intellectual and both an art and a science, some good thinking does take place in the subconscious mind, i.e., that portion of the mind residing beneath conscious perception can be most elucidating. For example, if speculators think deeply concerning a current stock market position, so much so that they dream about it, the dream's meaning should be listen to and acted upon.

Trying to be perfect, either consciously or subconsciously, should now be rejected by astute speculators. Instead, feel good about being close enough—as explained next.

Be Close Enough

Maintain a positive frame of mind and a "close enough" stock market spirit when speculating. Will yourself to be close enough to shed the loser mantle. Feel that being close enough is the goal in your soul and be a success as a result.

Look for the middle two thirds of the trend's move and do not criticize yourself for not getting out at the exact top or back in at the exact bottom price. Perfection, optimization and always needing to win should be replaced with feeling good about being close enough to be a success in the stock market.

Cut Losses Early And Let Winners Run

Human beings hate to lose more than they like to win, perhaps because they have had more experience with losing. Since fear and the pain of a loss persists long after the pleasure of the win is forgotten, speculators do just the opposite of what should be done in the stock market. Incorrectly, amateur speculators hold their stock losers for a large loss and sell their stock winners for a small gain.

Amateur speculators plan how not to lose rather than how to win which is a losing strategy, instead, plan to win by being close enough. Being stubborn in the stock market is a major mistake, ultimately the most difficult competition to master is yourself. Instead, astute speculators learn how to "cut their losses early for a small loss and let their winners run long for a large gain."

Speculators typically have a more difficult time staying with a winning position that shows larger and larger daily profits then remaining with a continually losing position that he or she hopes may eventually turn around so that they can get out even. The wrong speculative tendency is to under stay a winning position and over stay a losing position.

Be Able To Take Small Losses Early

Not being able to take a small loss because the speculator always wants to win precludes traders from being a stock market success. Innumerable small stock losses must be endured in order to test theories and speculative judgment. The way to limit losses to inconsequential amounts is by using the stop-loss order, as discussed in chapters 4 and 7.

James R. Keene—called totally fearless when trading but in no way irresponsible—said that winning in a common stock position six times out of ten is sufficient to guarantee a fortune in the stock market. In the field of stock market speculation, where proper judgment and timely action guarantee wealth, it should never be thought of nor will it ever be an exact science. Too many issues, known and unknown, determine a speculative outcome. Consequently, speculative mistakes and omissions are always part of assessing the disposition of the stock market and ensures some stock losses.

The saying on Wall Street is true, "the first small loss is the best loss." Do not hold on to a small loss position as it grows into a catastrophic loss.

Do not be nonchalant about losses, actual money is being lost. The courage to act properly is required to take a small loss by design but is the wisest course to take when wrong, as explained next.

Courage To Act Properly

Talking knowledgably, convincingly and even brilliantly about what should be done with a stock and then remaining powerless to act is futile. Proper action is the goal of knowledge, consequently, make sure the action happens. The courage to act properly when you know you should act is never a forgone conclusion. Many traders can "talk-the-talk," but few can also "walk-the-walk."

Speculators require the courage to act properly when making speculative attempts, the courage to both win and fail, and perhaps most importantly, the courage to trade again after a stock market losing streak. Remember that constant losing begets more losing which begins to change one's trading psychology. To break this resulting pessimistic attitude, stop trading for a few weeks to review how you trade best and what you might improve upon.

One way that people cope with stress, who are overly nervous, is to freeze on the trigger and not be able to decide or to take appropriate action. This is the fight-or-flight dilemma. Also, the anxiety of doubt causes weak-willed speculators to focus on their worry and not on the important facts and correct judgment. To bolster courage, astute speculators should learn as much as possible about the stock market in order to know what not to fear.

Obsessing about failure or running scared clouds the mind, limits the opportunities and creates internal conflict. Mental and emotional energy are wasted upon nonproductive issues that adversely affect trading performance. Astute speculators, instead, resolve to develop an iron nerve and to be completely devoid of all nerves when trading.

Trading Psychology

Greed prevents speculators from turning paper profits into cash. Greedy speculators always think they deserve more. As the stock price makes a tremendous advance, their voracity, covetousness and selfishness instills a belief in them that they have the ability to quadruple the stock price again;

222

overlooking the fact that political-economic conditions, industry and company specific factors piled up the huge paper profits and not their own particular market prowess. Greediness is a sign that the speculator covets too much, thus, fostering a will to reach beyond their possible accomplishments.

Fear, greed, hope, worry, irrational emotions and speculative perceptions move stock prices for awhile, but the stock market is never mistaken for long and in due course responds to truth, reason and logic. Fundamental factors are consonant with long-term trends and speculator perceptions are often in agreement with intermediate and short-term price movements.

Prices in the intermediate or short term may move counter to fundamental facts due to emotional or inexperienced stock market participants. Traders are frequently wrong, the stock market is bigger than any one speculator and ultimately goes were it wants to go.

Non-rational emotions of fear or greed and the irrational emotions of the need for recognition and to save face, the need for perfection and stock trading addiction all may control a speculator's perceptions and actions in the stock market. Perhaps of the three irrational emotions, an oversized ego or the need for recognition and to save face so as not to look ridiculous is the most difficult irrational emotion to overcome, as explained next.

Need For Recognition And To Save Face

Be able to separate your ego or the need for recognition and to save face from making money in the stock market. If the speculator's ego is so important that not being able to admit a mistake takes precedent over making money, then speculators will lose money to save their own face.

Once speculators recognize that many trading winners will eventually be theirs, it becomes easier to accept small mistakes. Use stop-loss orders that limit the amount of money being lost on a losing trade. Be anxious to get out of small losing trades so that you can get into the next huge winning stock position. The watchword is, "I made a small mistake, so what, I want to get on with making money."

The most formidable competitor that a speculator has is himself or herself, consequently, not always expecting to win and being able to admit a mistake are crucial for speculative success. Getting control of one's emotions goes a long way toward speculative success, as discussed next.

Self-Control

Self-control is necessary to resist fear, greed, the need to save face and to ignore the opinions of others. Some speculators can accomplish this sometimes, others most of the time, but no one can do it all the time, consequently, frequent breaks are required to remain mentally focused and to stay emotionally fresh.

Acting cocky, especially to others, after a profitable trade is concluded should be scrupulously avoided. Act the same and keep silent counsel regardless of the outcome of the trade, good or bad.

Interestingly, a certain class of speculators like to boast about stock losses. These traders regard the stock market as a large casino betting game and proclaim to one and all, "Wow what a profit I had, but the stock went against me for an unexpected reason. Being a good sport, I will try again because I can take it." Being a good loser and bragging to others about stock market losses should be conscientiously rejected through the use of self-control.

Speculation can be addictive and is called "the white collar gambling disease." The money is secondary, what is wanted is the rush of the action and the excitement of the trade. The speculator is hooked after a hugely profitable trade and does not and cannot leave the game because he or she starts wastefully spending all their winnings. The fun now comes from risking more and more money until the amount of money risked is more capital than can be afforded to lose, ultimately resulting in the catastrophe of bankruptcy. If self-control does not work with the white collar gambling disease, professional help should be sought.

Poor Mental State

A poor mental state concerning the stock market works against speculators. If speculators get impatient with a stock or the stock market and do not allow time for key elements to align properly, this is a problem. Speculators cannot push, hurry along, or tempt the stock market.

If speculators get angry at the stock market and begin to take things personally, this is a irrational. Remember that the market neither knows who you are or cares anything about you, the markets are completely impersonal.

If speculators are unduly afraid of the stock market, especially at the wrong time, this is a problem. Speculators will never feel completely safe when trading, in fact, the most anxiety producing of the final good alternatives remaining, prior to making a purchase or short sale, is often the best choice. Risk can be managed using the reward-to-risk ratio, stop-loss order, focus speculating and money management rules. Also, if speculators are too optimistic, they should learn to reduce their optimism by 50 percent until projections are closer to the outcomes experienced.

How To Change A Poor Mental State

The way to change a poor mental state is to perform the following exercise. Speculators should rise from their chair and walk out of the room for a short period of time. When returning to your desk, do not sit down but visualize yourself in the chair working. Envision objectively your bearing, what you are wearing, how you are moving, your scent, the noises you hear and the taste in your mouth.

Imagine how all these personal attributes would change if you now had the correct mental state of mind. Then make it happen, e.g., change your clothes, comb your hair, take a shower, brush your teeth, call a friend, repeat a mantra, sing a song, or read a poem. Now sit in the chair again with your new persona which possesses an improved mental state of mind.

Traders should be objective, should not be stubborn or too rigid in their opinions and be flexible in their thinking. Resolve to be open and to see everything without prejudice. Repeated failure is having beliefs that do not change, i.e., the trader is in an intellectual rut. Instead, learn to break this destructive cycle by changing your thinking and beliefs, as explained next.

Changing Thinking And Beliefs For Success

Traders' thinking, beliefs and values get played out in the stock market and help determine their trading results. Values are subjective priorities that rank concepts as well as objective truths. In this way all objective truths become subjective truths to the individual trader (please see chapter 12 in *The Astute Investor* for more on this topic). If traders look deeply enough into their trading style they are getting what they want to out of the stock market, be it either profit or loss.

Even though the speculator may not recognize it, what it, or agree with it, their trading operations will match their subjective values and priorities. If trading results are poor, review the reasoning producing defective decision making and poor judgments. Concentrate on your subjective values, concepts and the prioritizing of objective truths. To achieve success, thinking and beliefs leading to poor results have to be changed, i.e., the best speculators do not stay in an intellectual rut.

Handling Losing Streaks

Trying to trade through a losing streak is emotionally draining and should be avoided. A losing steak is best handled by planning a full retreat to get out of all stock positions. A losing streak speculator should take a break from the stock market to clear their mind and to see the market from a different perspective.

Never try to play "catch up" when trading resumes. Trying to regain all one's losses at one time will almost certainly result in complete failure. Start with amounts of money that are a quarter of normal trading with the idea that winning trades and black ink will give you confidence and get your stock market trading rhythm back—only then return to normal trading patterns.

Even after winning over a period of time, it is always best to take some time off. It is difficult to carry on trading at a high level for more than a few months. Instead, take some time off and only return by speculating with smaller amounts of money.

Regrettably, the biggest losses seem to come after the biggest gains. Believe that the complete test of a profitable sale includes how the money is subsequently used. Patience should be emphasized to be a successful trader, as explained next.

Patience

The stock market is always there, beckoning speculators to take positions in order to make money. The number of prospects for gainful exchange seem limitless. It is impossible to take advantage of all these opportunities, or even a small percentage of those offered every day in the stock market.

Patience is required to wait for just the right time to act when the preponderance of the indicators are in the speculator's favor. Use patience to engage in only those stock positions that are most likely to be profitable.

Speculators should reward their patience with a small treat—e.g., seeing a movie, eating ice cream, listening to music, or taking time off—while waiting for all of the key prerequisites to line up properly prior to making a trade. The treat is money or time well spent because the waiting for just the right moment significantly improves the probability of a profitable trade.

The same basic speculative principles and methods apply for a long-term move as well as an intermediate-term move. Those making money speculating in the stock market have the patience to delay taking action until an outstanding opportunity for profit presents itself. The discipline to stay to plan is required for patient speculators, as discussed next.

Discipline

Discipline is required for successful speculators. Have the discipline to consistently follow the speculative plan, schedule and bylaws (discussed later in this chapter) regardless of the eventual trading outcome. Maintain the discipline not to trade impulsively or to get emotional, but to remain focused by staying faithful to your plan and schedule.

Have the discipline to stay with winning positions. A misleading saying on Wall Street is; "No one ever goes bankrupt by taking a profit." This saying is further reinforced because traders love to take profits. The saying sounds good but it is poor policy which leads to chronic trading and cutting winners off before they have a chance to make a considerable amount of money, instead, remain disciplined to stay with winners.

Play A Lone Hand

It is best to play a lone hand when speculating in the stock market. Do not listen to rumors, opinions or tips from market pundits. Make up your own mind and then keep your failures and triumphs to yourself. Maintain silence concerning your speculative affairs. Hard work and study, patience, poise and silence are virtues requiring encouragement that need to be part of a speculator's character.

Astute speculators should be able to size up a situation on their own and determine the action that different persons will take, i.e., how the investing public, amateur and professional speculators will manage their money prior to them actually doing it.

A lone hand necessitates having silent discussions with yourself. Examine the conclusion arrived at and whether it would be more prudent to take another course of action or do nothing at all. Pride of opinion leads to losses for speculators, instead, practice humility, as explained next.

Practice Humility

Humility is forced upon speculators the minute they believe that they are the market leaders, normally, the slighted stock market turns and takes a big bite out of their bankroll. Have a high regard for the stock market, let it confirm its trend of least resistance. Keep your journal current, recapitulate what happened during the day and write down what went right or wrong and why.

The reality of speculating in the stock market is that speculators are wrong a considerable number of times. Whether right or wrong, study and be accepting of the lessons learned. Experience, after acquiring the correct knowledge, is required and is the best practical teacher.

Remain humble while either winning or losing. Always have a high regard for the person on the other side of the trade. Stock speculation has many well-informed participants who compete against you for profits and will often succeed.

Typically, there is a dupe on one side of a stock trade or the other; when a speculator does not know which side that is—they are the dupe. When more knowledgeable traders are on the opposite side of a sock transaction, they are going to win.

A good strategy to guard against being an easy target is to analyze the other side of the trade from your own. Ask yourself when buying, "Why have others decided to sell and what do they realize that I may have overlooked?" Truthfulness with yourself is imperative here, subdue your pride of opinion and look for only the reality of the situation.

Planning and Scheduling Are Important

Planning and scheduling require developing your own ideas and having the discipline to consistently act upon them; but, at the same time if the action on the tape says that you have made an error you have to be willing to change quickly and go the other way. Proper trading balances confidence with flexibility.

Develop a plan and schedule and see if the stock market agrees. Comparable conditions in the market repeat themselves in similar chart patterns. The investing public and speculators often cause the same price patterns, learn to spot this familiar patterns best seen on graphs or charts and trade along with them. Speculators should formulate a subjective opinion after doing their own analysis, make a plan and schedule and then let the market tell them if they are correct.

Implementing the plan and schedule one minute and discarding it the next, whatsoever the rationale, is just plain poor practice and should be avoided. Impulsiveness is one common speculative pitfall, bad judgment and poor timing are two more. Observe and observe again, stay flexible and try never to oppose the market.

Speculative Bylaws

Dickson G. Watts, reportedly, is the first to publish speculative laws and rules when speculating in the market. He was the president of the New York Cotton Exchange and a successful speculator during the late nineteenth century. Some fifty years later, Jesse Livermore publishes his book listing rules on how to trade in the stock market. Both sets of laws and rules are combined and form the basis for the speculative bylaws presented here.

Proper speculation requires intellectual exertion and planning to reduce risk as much as possible, unlike gambling, e.g., betting on American roulette, which relies entirely on blind luck. Good fortune in business or in stock market speculation is welcome, but chance should not be thought of as a significant part of the problem if speculation is to be performed properly. Only allow for a margin of error in your speculative strategy to accommodate likely occurrences. To be most successful, carry out speculation in accordance with the following ten speculative bylaws.

Ten Speculative Bylaws

Speculative bylaws are necessary because speculation looks relatively easy to the uninitiated who incorrectly think of speculation as simply gambling in a large casino called the stock market. Instead, proper knowledge and following tested bylaws are key to reducing risk and achieving market success.

Trading bylaws encompass successful speculative conditions that have served stock traders well in the past and are expected to continue to serve them well in the future. The following ten bylaws govern how speculators should behave when trading in the stock market and should be treated as commandments.

The best strategy to making money is to simply follow the ten bylaws for speculative success. Disregard any of these bylaws at your own peril, especially when first starting out as a speculative novice. After many years of trading experience, when speculators know they are experts, the bylaws may be bent—but never broken. The bylaws are listed beginning with the most important first:

1. *Keep the mind clear.* Keep stress at bay, think for yourself, never take tips. Make sound, trustworthy subjective judgments using significant objective truths and facts based upon correct premises and proper calculations.

2. *Have a plan and schedule, do the analysis, do not trade impulsively.* Trading is a science as well as an art. Always make the required calculations based on pertinent data, check the charts and evaluate all of the applicable risks prior to arriving at a judgment. Know the political-economic conditions, interest rate spreads and yield curves, long and intermediate-term trends, the strongest and weakest industries and the company's margin-of-safety multiple. Never go directly from a long position to a short position, always go to a neutral cash position first and take time to plan and schedule prior to making the next trade.

3. *Trade on trigger points.* Timing is the primary art of speculation or the "art of arts." Being too early can be as ruinous as being too late when trading. The question is always, "Do I really what to be in this position, yes or no?" The investing public and most speculators are optimists and trade on their perceptions which then become their reality. Learn to make the trade when reality overtakes perceptions and the expected reality becomes real. Reality eventually always wins in the stock market, so trade on it.

4. *Use reward-to-risk calculations, stop-loss orders and money management rules.* The second speculative art is learning how to sell or cover positions properly. Use reward-to-risk calculations, stop-loss orders and drawdown to plan potential stock gains. A strategy of risk-aversion in

the area of losses and risk-seeking in the area of profits is necessary. Astute speculators always protect their money using money management rules so that they have risk capital available to trade with and have money remaining when their trading career ends.

5. *Know yourself, select an approach to trading that fits your character, personality and lifestyle.* The third speculative art is realizing that in the stock market you are competing against yourself and you are your own toughest competitor. Since there is an infinite capacity to sabotage your own trading, select the speculative strategy that works best for you and have the discipline to stay with this strategy.

6. *Let trading volume, turning points and market conditions confirm your plan and schedule.* Learn how to read the tape in relation to trading volume and turning points. You cannot know more than the composite mind that is reported on the tape. Do not fight the tape by using pride of opinion to try to prove that you are right and the tape is wrong, instead, practice humility. Discipline your ego by being willing to admit mistakes freely.

7. *Judge the news based on your assessment of what the average speculator will think about the average speculator's appraisal of market or stock expectations.* A stock or the stock market, based on perceptions, can remain undervalued or overvalued for an extensive period of time. Learn that the news is judged based on how speculators react to the news and not on the news itself.

8. *Do not trade on margin.* Do not borrow money to trade in the stock market. On the buy-side, use a 100 percent cash account and on the short-sale side, only trade up to 100 percent of the funds available in your account. To be under the influence and control of creditors is expensive and clouds the mind and corrupts judgment. Having a clear mind and good judgment in the stock market are the most important requirements, not how much money you expect to earn on a single trade.

9. *Do not be a chronic trader.* The stock market cannot be beaten if you are a chronic trader and are always in the market. When in doubt, pause, or reduce the amount of the stock position. Have patience to wait for the appropriate time to act and then have the courage to actually make the proper trade. Always keep a ready reserve of cash for the outstanding opportunity that the stock market intermittently presents to all speculators.

10. *Do not obsess about making money in the stock market.* A good way to keep the mind clear is not to fixate on money, instead, concentrate

on the proper trading methodology. It is a paradox in the stock market that the less concerned traders are about money, the better they will do and the more money they will ultimately make. Trade correctly and profits will subsequently follow.

The ten speculative bylaws should be copied and attached to your computer screen or another prominent location so that they are always available to remind you of the proper approach to stock market trading. How to ensure the ten speculative bylaws are scrupulously followed and enforced is presented next.

Sign A Contract With Yourself

A good way to reinforce the discipline required to consistently follow the ten speculative bylaws is to sign a contract with yourself. In the contract you pledge to follow the speculative bylaws, regardless of the trading results. If the outcome of the trade is poor, you are not to blame—the bylaws are held responsible. This is a good way to save face with yourself. If the bylaws are broken, for any reason, a constructive penalty specified in the contract must be paid to yourself, upon your honor.

Speculative Bylaw Conclusions

The motivation that draws most speculators into the stock market is to become wealthy, unfortunately, this also becomes a reason for their downfall. Speculators become so obsessed about money that they cut their profits short and let their losses run. This is just the opposite of the strategy required to be a successful speculator, resulting in pain, suffering and possible bankruptcy.

Do not quickly read and then forget the bylaws. In stock speculation only a small fraction of those who try, succeed. The ten speculative bylaws give astute speculators an advantage over the uninformed; however, as Rene Descartes (1596-1650) instructs, it is the application of the bylaws that is most crucial. Only skilled speculators will take the bylaws to heart and implement them correctly—to only the truly talented will these bylaws become truly advantageous.

The Best Speculators

The best stock market speculators think: 1) money is only a means to keep score; 2) losing periodically in the stock market is going to happen regardless of how smart I am; 3) stock trading is best treated as a fun but serious game; and 4) planning, scheduling and hard work are required to succeed.

The best traders all share similar character and personality traits. Successful traders closely observe the markets for comparable conditions that have taken place in the past and build models based on their findings. They test their robust models, and projected outcomes are compared to actual outcomes. Any methodology or model mistakes are then quickly corrected.

Winning speculators understand their aim is both outsized gains and survival when trading. There is no "they" who are out to get them, consequently, successful speculators take responsibility for their actions. Speculators should understand the markets are bigger than anyone and will eventually go where they want to go. Winning traders believe they are just along for the ride, but are ever vigilant regarding intermediate and long-term turning points.

Controlling Stress

The intellectual side of trading requires learning and following all the speculative bylaws. However, there is a portion of successful trading that relies on iron nerve. If traders get upset stomachs as a result of stock trading, so that they cannot take the stress and strain of trading, they may not have nerve enough to be a speculator. To acquire the nerve to be a speculator, for stressed-out traders, try being a semi-investor first.

There is a difference between trying to avoid large losses using stop-loss orders and being scared to take losses. If speculators are frightened to lose they will never be able to play the stock market game properly, or said another way, "Scared money does not make money." Losses in the stock market are a fact of life, deal with it. If traders cannot accept some small speculative losses while trading, do not speculate but rather be a semi-investor or an investor.

Astute speculators do not see common stock or the stock market, but focus instead on reward-to-risk calculations, setting stop-loss order price points and following money management rules. The trader should never fall in love with the stock, remember, common stock are made to be sold.

A character trait found in the foremost speculators, including Jesse Livermore, is the facility to realize when they are completely right, to feel this with certainty and then to load up on the winning position. The courage and iron nerve necessary to pile on a position at the right time divides the merely proficient speculators from the truly extraordinary and is why cash is kept in reserve. A summarized list of the ten desired character and personality traits of the best stock market traders is presented next.

List Of Ten Desired Character And Personality Traits

Ten character and personality traits of the best stock market speculators are summarized as follows:

1) The best speculators have discipline, know the speculative bylaws and have the self-assurance to remain obedient to these bylaws.

2) Success in the stock market is not an option, it is the only legitimate goal, speculators require a passion to succeed.

3) Self-control is used to ensure that in the stock market, money takes precedence over the need for recognition and to save face, consequently, mistakes are freely admitted.

4) One-valued orientations that always require winning, perfection or optimization are rejected and being close enough by attaining the more secure middle two thirds in any market move is embraced.

5) Patience is rehearsed and practiced because the stock market cannot be beaten with chronic trading.

6) Once the risks are known and analyzed, winning traders have the utmost confidence in their judgment and have the courage to act properly—regardless of the trade's eventual outcome.

7) Traders always keep a journal, analyze all their trades and determine in writing what worked or did not work and why.

8) The best speculators never take tips and prefer playing a lone hand by planning and scheduling their stock market operations in order not to trade impulsively.

9) The best speculators practice humility and reject pride of opinion, i.e., the tape confirms what should be done in the market. To achieve success, thinking and beliefs leading to poor results have to be changed, i.e., the best speculators do not stay in an intellectual rut.

10) The best speculators are always reading, always learning and trying to improve their robust methodology and plans and schedules through observation and testing.

Astute speculators resolve to develop the above ten character traits, be completely devoid of all nerves and acquire the iron nerve necessary to be an excellent trader. Mental preparation requires practice runs through all of the potential risks prior to taking a stock position. The best novice traders what to feel they have won the speculative game prior to beginning, consequently, they use simulator trading to practice—as explained next.

Simulator Or Paper Trading

The adage on Wall Street and in most endeavors is, "begin in haste and repent at leisure." To trade successfully requires specialized knowledge and extensive experience. Speculators can learn about stock market trading by just beginning which is common but very expensive and not recommended. The preferred method is to gain practical experience first through simulator or paper trading.

Simulator or paper trading should be a required activity for all novice speculators. Trying to learn a complicated profession like stock market speculation only from books is unrealistic. Intellectually, novice speculators all feel that they are much farther along in understanding how to speculate in the stock market by reading books than is actually proven once they begin to trade with money. Simply knowing how to speculate does not make anyone an expert, for that, practical experience is required. And the best way to build up practical experience is to perform fictional trades with real data but not with real money.

No Capital Required

Simulator trading, paper trading, or virtual trading is a simulated process where speculators rehearse trading and gain practical real world experience without risking their money. Simulator or paper trading allows budding speculators to test the ten speculative bylaws, money management rules, use different trading methodologies, test their judgment, discipline, conviction and produce a simulated trading record that may be analyzed.

Simulator or paper trading requires no capital because imaginary money is used to simulate the trade. Practice trades are a learning device that require speculators in training to make timely decisions, just like in a real brokerage account. Rather than just reading about speculation, traders can practice and make decisions about promising stock trades and then see the consequences of their actions based on real life market situations.

Simulator trading is considered a final examination before going out into the unforgiving capitalistic world to risk one's own funds. Speculative application during simulation is the real world activity that brings all the knowledge together to help form the complete speculator. Any deficiencies are now quickly uncovered and a remedial course in this deficient area may be administered. A feel for the markets is developed using a dry-run exercise where all the decisions and actions are the same but where there are no financial consequences.

Simulator Trading Accounts

Some online Internet stock brokerage firms and other organizations allow speculators to open free or low cost "simulator trading accounts." All trades use imaginary simulator money but the computer does the resulting entry and exit price calculations and informs the account holder of all simulated profits and losses, just like in an actual brokerage account. The orders are entered and the simulated trades are a result of realistic broker instructions, including the designation of the specific company, share quantity and all buy, sell and limit order instructions.

The best thing about this is the accuracy that the simulator account affords, i.e., the computer is completely accurate and market data cannot be fabricated or the results modified by conveniently forgetting a trade, therefore, gaming the results is not possible.

A positive aspect of the simulator account is that how to use buy-market orders, short-sale market orders, buy and sell limit orders, stop-loss orders, progressive stop-loss orders, reward-to-risk calculations and money management rules may be freely practiced without financial consequences. Where to get this simulator trading experience without risking hard earned money is discussed next.

Simulator Stock Trading Websites

As this is written, Charles Schwab brokerage has a free StreetSmart.com trading simulator on there website. Go to: http://www.schwabat.com/ to bring up the sign-in page screen. A demo of Schwab's StreetSmart.com trading platform is available by clicking on <u>Interactive Demo</u> located on the right-hand side in the green box on the sigh-in page. Click the "I agree" radio button at the bottom of the sign-in page to launch Schwab's simulator program.

Investopedia, as this is written, has a nominal charge of $5 dollars per person for a six month membership to open a simulated trading account on their website at: <u>http://simulator.investopedia.com</u>. Investopedia reports that their stock market simulator has been in operation since 2003 and has helped over 250,000 users learn about and practice simulator stock trading.

Simulator Trading Steps

Attempt the difficult speculative enterprise only after practicing first. Only after a long rehearsal, including the analysis of why trades either worked or went wrong, should money be used when trading in the stock market.

Market professionals advocate learning about and practicing speculation for two or three years prior to beginning in earnest. Study the overall market, industries, individual stock, make the calculations and read the price graphs and volume bar charts. Novice speculators should gain experience using simulator trading by following these six steps:

1) First become an learned investor by reading *The Astute Investor* and know the macro issues that determine the long-term trends in the stock market.

2) Study the micro issues of speculation and know the intermediate-term industry trends by reading *The Astute Speculator*.

3) Develop a trading methodology that fits your character, personality and lifestyle.

4) Open an Internet simulator trading account.

5) Keep a journal of why the trade is made and the simulated result of the trade. Record the daily open, high, low and closing prices along with daily trading volume figures for each stock followed. In the journal record all profits, losses and assumed commission costs along with the explanations of why success was achieved or errors were made. It is important to take everything into account while simulator trading that you would while performing actual trading.

6) Astute speculators (AS) should continue simulator trading until they can consistently perform three times more profitably than the S&P 500

Index over the same time period, e.g., S&P 500 Index result: +5%, AS result: +15%; S&P 500 Index result: -5%, AS result: +10%.

Simulator trading using a website based trading system, while not perfect, does significantly boost the prospects that speculators will become successful traders. Unfortunately, simulator trading success by itself is no guarantee when trading with real money. Keeping the mind clear is easy when simulator trading because the stress of using money is not present, i.e., fear is not an issue, greed is not present and patience is endless. How to make simulator trading more lifelike is discussed next.

How To Make Simulator Trading More Lifelike

Because there is no risk of loss involved, simulator stock trading can be an empty exercise if not conducted properly. To simulate having the iron nerve necessary to risk your own money, make a substitution for money. Commit to performing a disagreeable but beneficial task if the trade should lose simulated money, e.g., 30 stomach crunches (a type of sit-up), cleaning the car, or walking briskly around the block. The consequence should not be too ornery, but still be significant enough so that you think about your trying task prior to putting on the trade. To make this work, put these commitments in the signed contract with yourself and always honor them.

Simulator trading, while good training, is not the real thing and should only be thought of as minor league play. Simulator trading in relation to the real thing means little when judging success. To gain actual real world experience requires trading real money, because, it is impossible to tell how collected speculators' nerves will be until money is at risk. Start out slowly with small odd-lot trades when actual money is involved, as explained next.

Trading With Money

Making pretend profits on simulated trades is risk free and should not be trusted. The emotional attachment associated with putting hard earned cash at risk clouds the mind and makes judgment and timely action difficult. Risking actual money in the stock market tests the speculator's nerves and stomach. Having the iron nerve required for trading is the final test for a speculator.

Odd-Lot Trading

Once simulator stock trading is consistently three times more profitable than the returns from the S&P 500 Index during the same time period, speculators graduate to real trading using real money. Open an Internet trading account at one of the online discount brokers (e.g., TD Ameritrade at www.tdameritrade.com, Scottrade at www.scottrade.com, or Charles Schwab at www.schwab.com) and start trading in odd lots of less than 100 shares for each trade. The total cash risked during trading should be small, approximately $800 dollars.

The $800 dollar limit allows trading approximately 20 shares of an average price per share stock on the NYSE of $37.55 and a $25 dollar trade execution cost (20 shares x $37.55 + $25 = $776.00). Trading twenty shares in one stock is acceptable because speculators are trying to learn to control their nerves while trading for real using their hard earned money.

Money Makes Trading More Difficult

Speculators are often astonished that money makes stock trading so much more emotional and, consequently, prior simulator trading results now look unrealistic. Trading $800 dollars or less is a good first step because it diminishes the effect that trading with money has on the speculator's psyche and trading acumen.

A trader only gains the required confidence he or she needs after earning money trading in the stock market using their own unique strategy matched to their specific character, personality and lifestyle. The added dimension of money severely effects judgment, being able to maintain a clear mind, arriving at good decisions and taking timely action.

Full-Fledged Speculation

Once small odd-lot trades are consistently three times more profitable than the returns from the S&P 500 Index during the same time period, with trading being made with conviction and traders in full command of his or her emotions, only then should traders consider themselves a full-fledged speculator and move up to trading round lots. This may take anywhere from three months to three years, or never, depending on the speculator's nerves when trading.

The patience to go from: 1) gaining the required investment and speculative knowledge; 2) to successful simulator stock trading account practice; 3) to successful small odd-lot trading with limited funds; and 4) to full-fledged speculator is well worth the time and effort. Be honest with yourself concerning the appropriate graduation times from each step along the way. As a consequence of using these four speculative steps responsibly, extraordinary stock market success is now a good possibility for the novice speculator.

Summary

Speculators strive to foresee the future which makes speculating powerful, fascinating and even somewhat mysterious to industry outsiders. Riches and perfection do not go together in the stock market because performing flawlessness in the stock market is an impossibility, consequently, use a robust methodology rather than an optimization approach.

The best mindset when speculating is to first wait patiently for the appropriate stock market signals, have confidence in the signals' validity and then feel good about taking timely action regardless of the eventual outcome of the trade. Planning requires developing ideas and having the discipline to consistently act upon them. Have a plan and schedule but learn to react to what the market is saying through tape reading.

Each speculator has to find a unique speculative trading approach that works for their own character, personality and lifestyle, additionally, they have to determine this for themselves. Selecting the strategic approach to speculating should be matched with personal predispositions, motivations, temperament, disposition and ambitions.

A speculator's character and personality determine, as much as correct calculations and sound judgment, success or failure in the stock market. The most formidable competitor that a speculator has is himself or herself, consequently, knowing the best strategy that matches one's character, personality and lifestyle, not always expecting to win and being able to admit a mistake are all crucial for speculative success.

The ten desired character traits of the best speculators are: 1) discipline; 2) need to be successful; 3) self control; 4) being close enough is embraced; 5) patience; 6) confidence; 7) keeping a journal; 8) playing a lone hand and never taking tips; 9) practicing humility and rejecting pride of opinion;

240

and 10) always learning and improving. Astute speculators resolve to develop an iron nerve and be completely devoid of all nerves when trading.

Traders' beliefs and values get played out in the stock market and help determine trading results. Even though the speculator may not recognize it, what it, or agree with it, their trading operations will match their subjective values and priorities. A good way to bring the subconscious in line with the conscious mind is by using positive goal setting, e.g., visualize winning.

Bylaws are necessary and encompass speculative traditions and regulations that have served stock traders well in the past and are expected to serve them well in the future. A summary of the ten speculative bylaws are:

1) Keep the mind clear.
2) Have a plan and schedule, do the analysis, do not trade impulsively.
3) Trade at trigger points.
4) Use reward-to risk calculations, stop-loss orders and money management rules. Cut losses quickly and learn to let profits run.
5) Know yourself, select an approach to trading that matches your character, personality and lifestyle.
6) Let trading volume, turning points and market conditions confirm your plan and schedule through tape reading. Discipline your ego by being willing to admit mistakes freely.
7) Judge the news based on your assessment of what the average speculator will think about the average speculator's appraisal of market or stock expectations.
8) Do not trade on margin.
9) Do not be a chronic trader.
10) Do not obsess about making money in the stock market.

The preferred method to gain speculative practical experience is first through simulator or paper trading. Successful simulator stock trading is considered a final examination before going out into the unforgiving capitalistic world to risk your own hard earned money in the stock market. Only after a long rehearsal, including the analysis of why trades either worked or went wrong, should money be used trading small odd-lots in the stock market.

Once small odd-lot trades are consistently three times more profitable than the returns for the S&P 500 Index over the same time period, with trading being made with conviction and no longer jangling the nerves or upsetting the stomach, only then should traders consider themselves a full-fledged speculator and move up to trading round lots.

9

Speculative Strategies

Introduction

SPECULATORS RESPOND DIFFERENTLY to the stress of stock trading, consequently, each trader has to select a speculative strategy that matches their own character, personality and lifestyle. The following three successful strategies are presented as possible models.

Persons using the panic or contrarian specialist strategy are semi-investors making a transition from investing to speculating and purchase leading, high-quality companies with stellar track records at long-term market bottoms. The box theory strategy is for speculators who find stock trading nerve wracking and want to reduce unwanted market news to zero. Speculators using the tandem trading strategy are iron nerved, good at identifying pivot or turning points and believe that "timing is everything."

No one can tell a stock trader precisely what their best speculative strategy is, instead, each trader has to determine this for themselves. Select one of the strategies presented or combine different attributes from the three strategies discussed to develop your own personalized approach to trading in the stock market.

Select An Appropriate Strategy

Speculators are their own most challenging competition. Every speculator's character and personality traits are different, as discussed in chapter 8. How each person responds to the pressures of trading in a volatile stock market is unique, therefore, traders have to judge their own speculative capabilities.

Each speculator's emotional control necessary for successful speculation requires diverse approaches to the same problem. Speculators who know themselves find it easier to develop their own speculative strategy because no one else can tell traders exactly what strategy will work best for them.

Three different strategies for trading are presented here with the intent that astute speculators may not what to follow any one approach exactly, but may be eclectic and pick and choose which parts are appropriate that match their character, personality and lifestyle.

Strategy A: Panic Or Contrarian Specialist

The first strategy is a transition from investing to speculating where traders are termed semi-investors. Buying stock initially occurs at a long-term stock market bottom. The semi-investor approach is often termed trading for the "long pull."

Daily, semi-investors ask themselves this question, "Is there a panic in the stock market today?" If the answer is "no," non-action is required. If the answer is "yes," the long anticipated semi-investor's plan is simply implemented with no further thought required.

The semi-investor feels comfortable with the panic or contrarian specialist strategy because timing is not as crucial and the stress when trading is radically reduced to perhaps only a few times a year, consequently, the semi-investor's trading nerves are only minimally affected.

Semi-Investor

The semi-investor's approach is to "buy low, sell high" by patiently waiting for specific long-term opportunities to arrive and then seizing control using the appropriate action at the correct time.

The semi-investor feels more comfortable waiting patiently in cash for possibly 1-3 years until the market hits a long-term bottom and prefers putting his or her money in leading, high-quality companies with stellar track records. Normally, the position is acquired over many weeks on a scale-in basis using buy-limit orders and the trigger is a panic low selling climax point in the overall market.

It is assumed here that the semi-investor is an accomplished astute investor and knows when the stock market is in a long-term bottoming stage 2. For those who want to review how to use the S&P 500 Index Nine Month Moving Average Trend Line and confirming indicators, yield curves and fiscal and monetary policy to determine the stock market's stage— please see chapters 4 and 7 in *The Astute Investor*.

Four Accounts

The semi-investor divides his or her capital into four different accounts: 1) living expenses; 2) an emergency fund consisting of two months pay; 3) total risk capital held in a money market account to put into the stock market at the appropriate time during a market panic; and 4) a save half the profits fund at a bank to set aside stock trading profits which should never be touched accept to purchase a bond annuity to live on later in life (please see Chapter 11: At Retirement in *The Astute Investor* for more on bond annuities).

The semi-investor buys active stock and likes to reduce risk to a minimum by purchasing three leading, high-quality companies with stellar track records. At the beginning of stage 3, when the market begins its long-term uptrend, allocate equal amounts of the total risk capital (i.e., 33 percent for each stock) when purchasing three leading, high-quality active stock companies.

Scale-in orders are typically used for buying because the semi-investor may not feel confident in determining the exact low price of each stock. The methodology presented next may be replicated to select the three leading, high-quality companies for long-pull trading. The following example using Intel Corporation explains the semi-investor's approach.

Panic Or Contrarian Specialist Example: Intel Corp.

This particular semi-investor understands science and technology and feels very comfortable speculating in high-tech companies. It is expected that the computer industry will be at the forefront of the information, telecommunication and Internet revolutions that are ongoing worldwide, and semiconductors are the foundation of the computer industry.

Intel Corporation (NASDAQ: INTC) is the leading semiconductor company and a leading, high-quality blue-chip member of the Dow Jones Industrial Average (DJIA). Consequently, the semi-investor selects Intel for analysis using the annual reports available from Intel on their website at www.intel.com for the years 1998 through 2002.

Market Low Panic Point

The S&P 500 Index experienced a head and shoulders bottom reversal pattern by reaching an intraday price low of 776 on July 24, 2002 (left shoulder), 769 on October 10, 2002 (head) and 789 on March 12, 2003 (right shoulder).

Following the Nine Month Moving Average (MA) Trend Line for the S&P 500 Index, the overall market indicated its long-term decline in November of 2000. Our semi-investor had over two years to prepare for the eventual purchase of Intel's stock at a panic low that occurred during March of 2003.

Intrinsic, True, Or Fair Value Calculation

Prior to purchasing stock, the semi-investor calculates the company's intrinsic, true, or fair value and margin-of-safety multiple to determine if the company is undervalued. Begin by looking at sales revenue, net income and diluted earnings per share growth.

From 1992 to 2002, sales revenue for Intel increased by approximately +15 percent per year, net income by almost +15 percent per year and diluted earnings per share by approximately +20 percent per year. Net income dropped off during the recession year of 2001 but remained positive. See

Table 9 – 1: Intel Corp. - Sales Revenues & Net Income (in billions of dollars) below for 1998 – 2002.

Table 9 - 1: Intel Corp - Sales Revenue & Net Income
(in billions of dollars)

Year	1998	1999	2000	2001	2002
Sales Revenue	25.1	29.4	33.7	26.5	26.8
Net Income	**6.1**	**7.3**	**10.5**	**1.3**	**3.1**

The semi-investor looks for a leading, high-quality company that is undervalued with a margin-of-safety multiple close to or over two. Start by calculating Intel's free cash flow (FCF).

Free cash flow (FCF) is calculated from the cash flow statement and is defined as cash from operating activities (COA) minus total capital expenditures. Traders who are looking for a step-by-step refresher on the intrinsic, true, or fair value calculation procedure, please see chapter 6 in *The Astute Investor*. The data for Intel are shown in Table 9 – 2: Intel Corp. – Cash Flow Statement (billions of dollars).

Summing the total capital expenditures and subtracting from the cash from operating activities indicate positive FCF from 1998 to 2002 as shown in Table 9 – 3: Intel Corp. – Free Cash Flow (billions of dollars).

Table 9 - 2: Intel Corp. - Cash Flow Statement (billions of dollars)

Year	1998	1999	2000	2001	2002
Cash From Operating Activities	**9.19**	**12.13**	**12.83**	**8.79**	**9.13**
Purchase of Property and Equipment	(3.56)	(3.40)	(6.67)	(7.31)	(4.70)
Purchase of Investments*					
Maturities and Sale of Investments*					
Proceeds from Sale of Assets		(0.80)	(0.98)	(0.26)	(0.33)
Acquisitions, net of cash acquired	(0.91)	(2.98)	(2.32)	(0.88)	(0.06)
Cash from Investing Activities*					

*Investment accounts not pertinent for the calculation of Total Capital Expenditures and Free Cash Flow (FCF).

Table 9 - 3: Intel Corp. - Free Cash Flow (billions of dollars)

Year	1998	1999	2000	2001	2002
Cash from Operating Activities	**9.19**	**12.13**	**12.83**	**8.79**	**9.13**
Total Capital Expenditures	(4.47)	(7.18)	(9.97)	(8.45)	(5.09)
Free Cash Flow (FCF)	**4.72**	**4.95**	**2.86**	**0.34**	**4.04**

By averaging the FCF results for 1998 to 2001 and using $3.2 billion dollars as a base, a growth rate for FCF is estimated at a positive six percent per year. Because Intel's FCF has the lowest growth rate when compared to either sales revenue or net income growth, a six percent growth in Intel's FCF is a conservative assumption over the next ten years.

Row four in Table 9 – 4: Intel – Stage 1: Expected Discounted FCF to Today's Prices (in billions of dollars), presented on the next page, shows Intel's growth of FCF over the next ten years from $4.28 billion dollars to $7.23 billion dollars. Present worth factors assume a long-term interest rate of five percent which is used to discount future year FCF calculations.

Table 9 - 4: Intel - Stage 1: Expected Discounted FCF to Today's Prices (in billions of dollars)

Future Yr	1	2	3	4	5	6	7	8	9	10
Prior Yr's FCF	4.04*	4.28	4.54	4.81	5.10	5.41	5.73	6.07	6.43	6.82
Growth Rate/Year	6%	6%	6%	6%	6%	6%	6%	6%	6%	6%
Free Cash Flow	4.28=	4.54	4.81	5.10	5.41	5.73	6.07	6.43	6.82	7.23
Present Worth Factors	0.95	0.91	0.86	0.82	0.78	0.75	0.71	0.68	0.64	0.61
Present Worth of FCF	**4.07#**	**4.13**	**4.14**	**4.18**	**4.22**	**4.30**	**4.31**	**4.38**	**4.36**	**4.41**

* Actual Free Cash Flow (FCF) of Intel in Year 2002

= Multiply $4.04 billion dollars x 1.06 = $4.28 (rounded off) billions dollars

Multiply $4.28 billion dollars x 0.95 = $4.07 billion dollars

First & Second Stage Intrinsic Values

The first stage intrinsic value is the sum of all of the present worth FCF's in the last row of Table 9 – 4 which equals $42.5 billion dollars. The FCF in year eleven is assumed to increase by five percent over year ten, or 1.05 x $7.23 = $7.5915 billion dollars. To calculate the present worth from year eleven for a uniform series of all future FCF values, divide the $7.5915 billion dollars by the capitalization rate of three percent which equals $253.05 billion dollars.

Bring the $253.05 billion dollars to 2002 prices by multiplying by the present worth factor of 0.58, which equals $146.769 billion dollars and is Intel's second stage intrinsic value. Intel's intrinsic, true, or fair value in 2002 dollars is the sum of stage 1 and 2 which equals $42.5 + $146.769 = $189.269 billion dollars.

Market Value Capitalization

The market value capitalization is performed as of December 31, 2002 to determine how speculators are valuing Intel in the stock market. Intel's market value capitalization is the number of diluted shares outstanding, 6.759 billion shares, times the stock price on 12/31/02 of approximately $15.50 per share, equaling $104.764 billion dollars.

Bargain Value Calculation

The intrinsic, true, or fair value for Intel is compared to its market value capitalization. Intel's intrinsic value is higher than its stock market valuation, $189.269 - $104.764 = $84.505 billion dollars, therefore, Intel is undervalued with a positive $84.505 billion dollar bargain value.

Because this is a semi-investor strategy, the margin-of-safety for a leading, high-quality company with a stellar track record should be close to or over two for Intel to be considered a good candidate to invest 33 percent of total risk capital at an expected long-term market bottom.

Margin-of-Safety Multiple

The margin-of-safety multiple is calculated by dividing Intel's intrinsic value of $189.269 billion dollars by its market value capitalization of $104.764 billion dollars, equaling 1.81.

Because the margin-of-safety multiple is almost two this is considered appropriate for a long-term semi-investor position in a leading, high-quality blue-chip corporation that is included in the Dow Jones Industrial Average (DJIA). Ten additional crucial factors necessary for study are presented next.

Ten Additional Crucial Factors

Ten additional crucial factors for Intel are checked next: (from the December 31, 2002 financial statement).

1) *Current Ratio: 2.87* – The current ratio is a test for short-term solvency, creditors would like a safety cushion value of 2.00, this measure for Intel is excellent.

2) *Debt-to-Equity Ratio: 0.25* – Intel is using $0.25 dollars of liabilities for every $1.00 dollar of shareholder equity which makes Intel a conservatively leveraged company. An effective limit for manufacturing companies is often set at a one-to-one debt to equity ratio.

3) *Return-on-Equity: +8.8%* - Intel had net income of approximately $3.117 billion dollars on sales of $35.468 billion dollars in 2002. Astute speculators prefer to have ROE over 15 percent for a manufacturing company.

4) *Operating Profit Margin: +16.4%* - Intel had a positive $4.382 billion dollar operating profit on sales of $35.468 billion dollars in 2002. Astute speculators prefer the operating profit margin in the 15-to-25 percent range, Intel's number is acceptable at the low end of this range.

5) *Diluted Net Earnings Per Share: +$0.46* – Over the past five years, diluted EPS have averaged $1.20. Diluted EPS have remained positive and are reported as +$0.19 in the recession year of 2001.

6) *Continued good service is apparent.* Intel is a leader in semiconductor manufacturing and is expected to remain so.

7) *Intel's management* is doing a good job translating top line sales growth (+15% per year) into bottom-line net income growth (+20%) over the past ten years.

8) *Intel's marketing/sales/distribution* organization is judged to be good, with sales growing by approximately 15 percent per year over the past ten years.

9) *Intel* is a leader in the semiconductor manufacturing category, however, the U.S. semiconductor industry is highly competitive.

10) Any interviews with customers, vendors, employees, etc. are reported positive.

Intel is an appropriate candidate for the semi-investor at the long-term market low. Intel may be purchased on a market order or a scale-in buy-limit order during a stage 2 market panic. Once Intel's stock price begins to climb, a progressive stop-loss order should be pushed upward as the price advances. Intel may also be analyzed as a contrarian investment, as presented next.

Six-Step Contrarian Analysis: Intel Corp.

Being contrarian is simple in theory but challenging and disconcerting to implement in practice. Opposing the market has many pitfalls and should only be undertaken with the proper methodology. Please see chapter 9 in *The Astute Investor* for a complete review of how to implement a contrarian strategy. The following are the required six steps to identify a contrarian stock and is applied to Intel as of December 31, 2002.

Step 1: Within a depressed industry, find a well managed stock with good prospects that has fallen at least fifty percent in price. The semiconductor industry is depressed during the general market downturn from 2000 to 2003. Intel peaked at approximately $75.00 per share in 2000 and is priced at approximately $15.50 on 12/31/02 which is an 80 percent reduction in price.

Step 2: The stock price should be depressed but the earnings should be less so, resulting in a low but respectable price-to-earnings (P/E) ratio. Intel's diluted P/E ratio for 12/31/02 is $15.50 divided by earnings of $0.46 per share equaling a very respectable 33.7 for a high tech, blue-chip DJIA growth company.

Step 3: A price-to-sales (P/S) ratio less than one qualifies the stock as a contrarian buy. The (S) is calculated by dividing the annual sales by the total number of diluted shares outstanding, $26.8 billion dollars divided by 6.759 billion diluted shares equals $3.97 sales/share. The 12/31/02 share price is $15.50, divided by $3.97 equals 3.9 which is higher than stipulated but still respectable for a blue-chip company that is part of the DJIA.

Step 4: A price to free cash flow (P/FCF) less than ten is considered a strong contrarian candidate. Positive FCF companies can continue paying dividends, repurchase stock if share prices drop too far, or self-invest in their own company to take advantage industry conditions. FCF for 2002 is $4.04 billion dollars, when divided by 6.759 billion diluted shares equals $0.60 per share. The 12/31/02 share price is $15.50, divided by $0.60 equals approximately 26 which is higher than stipulated but still respectable for a blue-chip DJIA company.

Step 5: The price-to-book value (P/B) less than one is a strong contrarian stock candidate for purchase. The book value is calculated from the left side of the balance sheet which is the property, plant and equipment net of accumulated depreciation which is then divided by the total number of diluted shares outstanding, i.e., $17.847 divided by 6.759 billion diluted shares equals $2.64. The share price of $15.50 is divided by book value of $2.64 equaling almost six which is higher than stipulated but still respectable for a blue-chip DJIA company.

Step 6: Looking for a high dividend yielding common stock is another important factor. Intel is paying $0.08 per share with a dividend yield of 0.5 percent. The dividend yield is low but respectable for a high tech growth company. The dividend payout has increased each year over the past ten years and Intel's management is directing that dividend increases should continue, at perhaps an increased rate.

Intel: Four Additional Contrarian Factors

Four additional contrarian factors help determine if Intel is a good semi-investor stock for purchase.

Factor 1: GARP stands for "growth at a reasonable price" which is a comparison of Intel's growth rate to its P/E ratio. Sales revenue over the past ten years has been growing by almost 15 percent and net income by 20 percent. Intel's P/E ratio calculated earlier is 33. Contrarians prefer companies growing faster than their P/E ratio. Intel's P/E ratio is higher than stipulated but still respectable for a blue-chip company that is part of the DJIA.

Factor 2: The debt-to-equity ratio should be low and preferably with no debt on the books. As calculated earlier, Intel's debt-to-equity ratio is 0.25 which is low and considered very good.

Factor 3: Insider purchases should be investigated. Insiders purchasing a significant number of shares is considered a positive indicator. It is determined that company directors and top management have been purchasing stock at this time, making Intel a strong contrarian candidate.

Factor 4: Technical common stock, in general, are avoided by contrarians due to their high multiples. While Intel is a high-tech company with a high P/E multiple relative to its growth rate, it is a very safe blue-chip DJIA stock and may be considered a good speculative trade for a semi-investor.

The panic or contrarian specialist combines the margin-of-safety multiple, ten additional crucial factors, the six-step contrarian analysis and the four additional contrarian factors to conclude that Intel is a leading, high-quality, blue-chip DJIA stock with a stellar track record that should be purchased for the long pull at a long-term stock market bottom. How Intel's purchase worked out in practice is presented next.

How The Semi-Investor Performed In Intel

During the March, 2003 panic low, Intel's price hovers around $15.50 and our semi-investor purchases half of his or her position at the market and scales-in the remaining purchases using two buy-limit orders. Soon, Intel's stock price begins going up on increasing volume. The progressive stop-loss order is put on when the stock is 10 percent above where the stock was purchased. The progressive stop-loss order is raised but trails Intel's stock price increases, by setting it 10 percent behind Intel's current price level.

By the end of 2003, Intel tops out at approximately $34.50 per share and our semi-investor is stopped out at the progressive stop-loss order price of $31.05 during a reaction in Intel's stock price. Assuming the average price of Intel's stock to our semi-investor is $15.50, the speculative investment yields a plus +100 percent return in roughly nine months. In keeping with the number one money management rule, half of the Intel profits are placed in the bank separate from the semi-investor's risk capital.

The semi-investor should identify three leading, high-quality companies to purchase, each representing 33 percent of total risk capital, when the long-term stock market bottom entry point is indicated. The recommended three semi-investor stock positions offers the safety of spreading the risk rather than putting all one's money into any one stock.

Strategy B: Box Theory

Nicolas Darvas (d. 1977) develops a successful method for stock market speculation. Darvas is a renowned ballroom dancer who travels the world performing at major venues. He finds stock market speculation fascinating and works part time at his lucrative stock picking avocation. Beginning with just $25,000, Darvas earns $2.25 million dollars in just 18 months by speculating in the stock market (www.nicolasdarvas.org).

Darvas finds that he is very impulsive and susceptible to rumors when speculating. Upon visiting and trying to trade stock at a stock broker's office, after becoming somewhat successful on his own, he loses -$100,000 dollars in just a few weeks.

Darvas goes from winning in the stock market to losing and he makes changes after analyzing his trading results. Rereading his journal of trades at this time he is stuck with the lunacy of his actions, they follow his unreasoning instincts and out of control emotions. Darvas exclaims, "My ears are my enemy!" Hearing rumors, getting tips and fighting the imaginary trading ghosts all make Darvas trade impulsively with disastrous results.

Darvas realizes that he attempts to read into things too much and second guesses himself with disastrous consequences. Darvas is a nervous trader who has to shield himself from market news, as discussed next.

Darvas's Zero News Approach

Darvas adopts a style of trading that reduces the unwanted news of the stock market to zero. He requests that his broker cable him at whatever hotel he is staying at on his dance tour with the open, high, low and closing prices for the five to eight common stock that he follows at any one time. On no account should his broker try to contact him in any other way than by telegram and only with the stock price information as instructed.

Darvas believes that trading by telegram versus calling a broker on the phone has the following advantages: no confusion, no tips, no rumors and no broker suggestions allow Darvas to remain emotionally disconnected from the stock market, as a result, this permits him to make winning trading decisions on his own.

Darvas trains himself to identify, looking only at financial stock tables, the early stage upward trend in stock prices so that he can share in the price rise without ever knowing or caring why it is happening. He concentrates on stock price information, which becomes like an x-ray for Darvas, to the exclusion of all news, tips, or market rumors.

Prices are compared for the five to eight companies under review and to the action of the overall market as represented by the Dow Jones Industrial Average (DJIA). Darvas reviews the DJIA to get an indication of whether the overall market is either strong or weak, because, the overall market has a major influence on all stock prices. Unexpected violent moves in a particular stock's price Darvas attributes to the action in the overall market. Darvas also closely follows the stock's trading volume, as described next.

Good Steady Volume

A stock's trading volume determines its active nature. It is only active stock issues that interest Darvas because they are the ones where excessive speculative profits can be realized.

Darvas gets his stock trading volume information by subscribing to *Barron's* weekly newspaper, it is forwarded to him as he travels while giving dance performances. The advent of the Internet now makes this unnecessary as volume information is readily available on websites such as http:// bigcharts.marketwatch.com/. However, the astute speculator is still looking for active stock movement indicated by using trading volume.

The question is, "How active does a stock have to be to get attention?" The answer, the stock should display "good steady volume." However, the definition of good steady volume is contingent upon the volume history of the stock in question.

If a stock's trading volume averages 5 million shares per week and then suddenly jumps to 20 million shares per week for approximately four weeks, this represents a 400 percent increase in weekly volume and an example of "good steady volume" which is excellent evidence of changed circumstances for this now active stock.

Wall Street Works While Darvas Sleeps

Darvas gives dance performances at night and sleeps during the day. He leaves word at the hotel switchboard to have no calls passed through to his room. With Darvas's approach the daily action in the stock market occurs while he is in bed, permitting Wall Street to work while he sleeps. Since Wall Street cannot contact him, Wall Street never makes him anxious, nervous, nor causes him to act impulsively.

While Darvas sleeps, the stock market is in session but it in no way concerns him. Darvas delegates the stop-loss order as his surrogate protector that safeguards his money if something unexpected occurs in the market. If a change in position is warranted, Darvas sends a telegram to his broker explaining the required action.

Darvas's Trading Day

Upon arising at 6:00 p.m. and just before going to dinner at 7:00 p.m., Darvas requests his broker's telegram at the hotel's front desk and buys a newspaper with closing stock market prices. Darvas immediately throws away the newspaper's market news as being only rumors, opinions, or stock market tips. Reading the articles and commentaries by Wall Street pundits might lead Darvas to make a mistake, consequently, he keeps and studies over dinner only the daily newspaper's financial stock tables, the weekly trading volume data found in *Barron's* and his broker's telegrams.

Darvas's approach could be used by persons who work during the day and have time after dinner to review the price and volume action on selected common stock. Rather than getting cables on stock from a broker, the price and volume data should be reviewed for analysis on a technical analysis website such as http://bigcharts.marketwatch.com/. Then use a discount broker with all buy and sell orders carried out over the Internet. Darvas uses the following money management rules to help protect his risk capital.

Darvas's Money Management Rules

Darvas uses a money management rule that restricts his stock market total risk capital to only as much as he can afford to lose without changing his lifestyle. Also, once the initial capital from dancing is accumulated for stock market trading, no additional funds are ever added to his total risk capital from his full-time employment. In this way he keeps his mind clear to make difficult decisions during stressful trading situations.

Darvas assumes he will be wrong half the time and consequently his pride of opinion has to be mollified to accept this fact. The necessary strategy to be successful when winning half the time is to have large profits and small losses. Therefore, Darvas takes an unemotional diagnostician's approach to speculation that does not rely on chance but endeavors to reduce risk as much as possible prior to making the stock trade.

Quick-Loss Weapon

Darvas decides his objectives should be to purchase active stock with good steady volume at the correct time and hold for a large gain; but, if things go wrong, to exit with a small loss.

Darvas institutes the "quick-loss weapon." Stock purchases are made close to breakthrough resistance levels by using buy-limit orders and as soon as the trade is finalized an automatic stop-loss order is in place a fraction below the purchase price to limit losses. Using this approach, Darvas assumes he will never lose sleep over a losing stock position.

Never Sell A Winning Stock Without Reason

Discipline not to sell a rising stock had to be gained because Darvas considers himself a financial coward who feels compelled to sell a stock just as it becomes profitable. He declares instead to never sell a winning stock if it has not done anything wrong and without a very good reason, e.g., the fact that it is at a high price is not an acceptable reason.

The progressive stop-loss order is raised in parallel with the stock's price increase. The progressive stop-loss order increase is only moved close enough to the current price so that inconsequential downward movements in the stock's price does not trigger it and force him out of the position.

Keep A Journal

A journal is kept with the reason for purchasing the stock entered. When the stock is sold, another short journal entry explains why it is thought either a gain was made or a loss sustained. The goal is to learn from and not to repeat any of Darvas's prior trading mistakes.

The tools that Darvas uses include analyzing both a stock's price and volume data, using the buy-limit order to get good fill prices, using the stop-loss order on all positions set a fraction below the purchase price to limit losses and using the box theory—as explained next.

Box Theory: Staircase Method

Darvas prefers to speculate in common stock he understands and observes that individual companies have personalities that if learned are easy to predict. He likes common stock that behave consistently and logically, typical of the qualities he looks for in his friends. Some stock prices act so bizarrely that they are impossible to predict, so, Darvas shuns these particular stock issues. Also, any stock that causes Darvas to experience two losses is blackballed forever.

The appropriate pattern looked for in a stock begins first with greatly increased trading volume. If an inactive stock suddenly becomes active with "good steady volume" and the price trend is clearly upward, the trend is likely to continue in that direction.

It is observed that intraday stock prices of active stock issues tend to move within a series of boxes that stack next to one another like an up staircase. Graph 9 – 1: Boxes In An Up Staircase shows how the boxes look during an uptrend.

Graph 9 – 1: Boxes In An Up Staircase

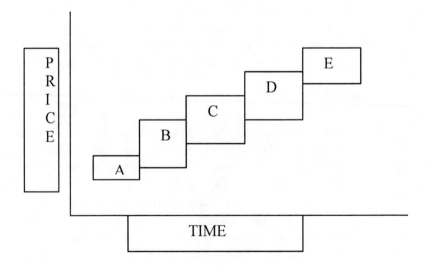

The trading range and box formations are evaluated to determine whether stock should be bought, sold, or held. The upward staircase pattern in Graph 9 – 1 demonstrates the required box pattern necessary to indicate whether an active stock is performing correctly for purchase. Within box A, the stock's price oscillates between $18 dollars and $20 dollars based upon intraday price fluctuations, i.e., highs and lows for the day and not based on opening and closing prices for the day. The area enclosed by the daily intraday price swings for the stock defines the box.

If the stock's intraday price does not bounce up and down within a box, it is discarded as inappropriate because it is not acting according to the box theory. No lively price action within a box indicates a stock that is a listless drifter and therefore a stock that will not perform as required. The box theory requires stock prices that experience bold quick advances which excludes 90 percent of all stock issues.

After a period of time, a stock acting correctly will break through the top price of box A at $20 dollars and start bouncing within the intraday high and low prices of box B at $19 to $23 dollars. This process continues until the boxes A, B, C, D and E stack up like a staircase. The correct method for deciding on the dimensions of each box is presented next.

Dimensions Of Each Box

Determining the dimensions of each box is crucial to the box theory. When a stock breaks out from a preceding box to the upside, the new intraday price point reached and not equaled or exceeded for three consecutive trading days defines the new box high price point.

Darvas explains his procedure when common stock is traded in fractions based on 1/8 of a point. Now that trading takes place in decimals of 1/100 of a point, the methodology here is modified slightly. Accordingly, stock prices at or within $0.12 of one another are considered to be identical. The following example in Table 9 – 5: Box Dimension Example is instructive:

The example common stock's intraday price hits $35.12 on March 22 and two days later reaches $35.00 on March 24. Because both prices are at or within $0.12 of one another over three consecutive trading days they are considered equal and a new box high price has yet to be determined.

The lower limit of the breakout box is only set once the upper limit is determined using the three consecutive day rule. Setting the lower limit is the reverse of how the upper limit is established, i.e., the new intraday low price should not be equaled, at or within $0.12 of one another, or broken through for three consecutive trading days.

Table 9 - 5: Box Dimension Example

Date	Intraday Low	Intraday High
March 20	$30.33	$32.45
March 21	33.48	34.16
March 22	34.37	35.12*
March 23	34.06	34.97
March 24	34.18	35.00*
March 27	34.25	34.67
March 28	34.35	36.02
March 29	36.00	38.19**

* Prices within $0.12 of one another and considered the same.
** Box high price point still not set.

If the stock has intraday highs over three consecutive trading days of $38, $37, $36, the stock has a new high price limit of $38; and now if intraday lows of $34, $35, $35 occur over the next three consecutive trading days, the stock has new low limit of $34. This means the stock is in the new $34/$38 box. The stock may stay within this box for a few weeks.

From here the continued advance might be consecutive intraday highs of $43, $44, $43, $42, therefore, the stock has a new high limit of $44; and now consecutive intraday lows of $39, $38, $39, $40, the stock has new low limit of $38. This means the stock is in the new $38/$44 box. Intraday prices fluctuate but all inside this new box. Also, it is apparent that the stock's price continues to trend higher into higher priced boxes which is the correct action under the box theory.

Box Theory: Implementation

As the boxes stack up one on top of the other like a staircase, the stock is now a candidate for purchase. If the stock price bounces between the upper and lower price limits of the new box, everything is as it should be and the speculator feels confident concerning the stock's behavior. Once the dimensions of the box are determined, the stock's price can act anyway it wants within the confines of its particular box. A stock not lively and bouncing, however, is worrisome and should be rejected as a possible purchase candidate.

When a stock is within the new higher $38/$44 box, everything is fine and the stock is a good candidate for purchase. But, if the stock now drops to $37.95 this stock is quickly removed as a possible purchase contender because it is acting improperly. The once advancing stock is dropping back in price to a lower box which invalidates the box theory. Stock is only wanted for purchase when moving into higher boxes, never lower boxes.

If a stock attains its historical all-time high price and is acting properly within the box theory, it may be purchased. The all-time high price breakthrough is the buy point, never the 52 week or even the five year high point in price. This reduces the overhang in stock supply since speculators are not waiting to unload their stock to get out even. This stock is now in "strong hands." Buying at the all-time high may be best accomplished using an automatic buy-limit order placed $0.15 above the all-time high price.

Different stock issues have different price movement personalities. Some stock moves over a small range of price swings of perhaps five percent while other stock have wide-swings of perhaps ten percent. While the ranges differ, the box theory implementation does not. Once the box lower and upper limits are determined and set, no stock can break below the lower limit and still remain a purchase candidate. A stock breaking below the lower limit of the box should be sold immediately, using a previously set stop-loss order as explained next.

Stop-Loss Orders

Stop-loss order price points should never be placed within the price limits of a box. The question for astute speculators is how far below the box breakout point should the stop-loss order price point be placed. With the box theory and purchasing active stock only as it breaks through to an all-time high price, the stop-loss order price point should be placed $0.15 below the upper limit of the box that the stock has just broken through. The stop-loss order should be placed right away following the stock's purchase.

The appropriate handling of raising progressive stop-loss order price points is to wait until the stock establishes its new upper and lower price limits before raising the progressive stop-loss order price point. Once the new higher box range is established, the progressive stop-loss price point should be moved up to $0.15 below the new lower limit price of the new box. In this way the stock is immediately sold if it does something it should not do, i.e., moves down in price to a lower priced box.

Techno-Fundamentalist Theory

So far, the technical side of the box theory explains price and trading volume action for the active stock under study. Another important aspect of the box theory is based upon the fundamental assessment of the company's prospects.

During a long-term stock market downtrend, Darvas watches companies that give ground grudgingly. He examines the earnings of these companies and finds that most are improving their earnings or the expectations of future earnings. This is where he combines his technical approach with the fundamentals of increasing earnings, called the "Techno-Fundamentalist Theory," as a reason for purchasing an active common stock.

Darvas likes growth stock companies because they tend to be active issues. He also likes companies with increased earning power as a result of innovative new products that are likely to significantly change the cost structure or product demand in their industry.

Improving earnings forecast over the next 20 years is considered a good fundamental reason to purchase a stock. If an active stock company belongs to a vibrant new growth industry where its earnings could easily double or quadruple in two years, this is a strong recommendation to purchase the stock.

Box Theory Conclusions

Darvas's decisions in the stock market may turn out to be right or wrong but no longer have an emotional pull on him. If correct, terrific, if wrong— a stop-loss sale is made which occurs automatically and consequently does not hurt his ego. Pride of opinion no longer matters because Darvas no longer feels self-satisfied if his stock pick goes up in price nor depressed if it should decline in price.

Darvas does not attempt to identify the long-term turning points in the overall stock market. However unwittingly, Darvas's box theory allows him to exit the market toward a long-term market top because stop-loss orders take him out of positions as the downward staircase of prices commence which precludes him from purchasing additional common stock. Google Inc. is presented next as an example when using Darvas's box theory.

Box Theory Example: Google Inc.

The following are recommended steps to identify what stock to purchase using the box theory. Additional astute speculator steps are added to explain how the box theory fits within the astute speculator methodology.

This example uses data based upon purchasing Google Incorporated (NASDAQ: GOOG) stock shortly after the company went public with its IPO during August, 2004. The steps proceed from the macro issues concerning the long-term trend in the stock market, to the industry ranking, to the analyzing Google's margin-of-safety multiple for purchase.

Long-Term Trend Favorable

Darvas uses the poorly diversified DJIA as a simple means of determining what the overall market is doing, however, he should not mind if we use the following scientific approach to answering this same question.

Step A. Make sure the long-term trend is favorable. Astute speculators realize that approximately 50 percent of a stock's price is determined by the overall political-economic conditions that affect all common stock issues alike. Astute speculators will only purchase a stock if the market is in Stage 2: Accumulation - Bottoming or Stage 3: Mark-Up – Uptrend.

Use only the well diversified S&P 500 Index and the proper perspective of monthly data to see that the long-term trend in the stock market is upward during August, 2004. The S&P 500 Index Nine Month Moving Average (MA) Trend Line trends upward at this time and signals that the stock market is in Stage 3: Mark-Up – Uptrend.

Confirming indicators on the S&P 500 Index monthly chart such as: 1) monthly data higher-highs and higher-lows; 2) two month moving average trend line being above the nine month moving average trend line; and 3) the Moving Average Convergence Divergence (MACD) blue line (12,26) being above the red line EMA (9) all confirm the stock market is in Stage 3: Mark-Up – Uptrend. August, 2004 is the correct time to purchase common stock in leading companies.

Industry Position Favorable

Step B. Make sure the industry ranking is favorable. The Internet industry ranking, available on websites mentioned in chapter 6, is in the top 25 percent of all industries during August, 2004, making the leading company in this new vibrant industry favorable for speculation.

Google is an Internet search engine corporate leader which is free to grow at a phenomenal rate. Google's earnings are growing by approximately 100 percent per year which means earnings could quadruple in two years. Google is developing innovative products that should have a major impact on the world economy for many decades to come. This satisfies Darvas's fundamental requirement for innovative new products in a new fast growing industry for the company under consideration.

High Margin-of-Safety Multiple

Step C. Make sure the company's stock has a high margin-of-safety multiple. Approximately 40 percent of the stock price is directly determined based upon internal company specific factors called unsystematic risk.

While Darvas did not calculate intrinsic, true or fair value and margin-of-safety multiple, a review of earnings for Google is mandatory and located in the prospectus issued at the time of the IPO in August, 2004. Astute speculators make the intrinsic, true or fair value and margin-of-safety multiple calculations which determine that Google is undervalued with a margin-of-safety multiple over three.

Actual Price And Volume Action

Google, Inc., founded by Larry Page and Sergey Brin, is the leading Internet search engine company that offers advertising services and approximately, as this is written, 8 billion searchable Web pages for its users. Google, Inc. began trading as an initial public offering (IPO) during August, 2004 at approximately $96 per share.

Google initially sold off into September, 2004, but weekly volume went from approximately 10 million shares traded per week during September, 2004 to over 40 million shares per week every week during October, 2004, a 400 percent increase, while the stock continued to reach new all-time highs of $125 per share. Google fits Darvas's definition of an active "good steady volume" stock in a fundamentally strong market and vibrant new industry with bright prospects for new products as well as being a very profitable company with excellent earnings potential.

Google's Results

Google is purchased at $125 with the boxes piling up in an up staircase as the stock advances in price. Progressive stop-loss orders are raised until the stock breaks through the lower limit of the top stair step box at approximately $400 per share. This is a plus +320 percent return over 15 months using the box theory.

Box Theory: Short Selling

Darvas did not have the expertise nor feel psychologically suited to sell stock short, but there is no reason why the box theory methodology explained here cannot be turned upside-down to identify margin-of-safety overvalued stock candidates when the long-term trend in the stock market is downward and the selected laggard stock is in the bottom 25 percent of industry rankings. The company's shares would experience "good steady volume" while stock prices would break through the lower boundary of boxes and move lower like a down staircase.

Strategy C: Tandem Trading

Jesse Livermore is a stock market legend who develops the top-down tandem trading strategy. Livermore has an iron nerve and believes that in the stock market, "timing is everything." The question is never "if" a stock will move but "when" it will move, either up, down, or in a sideways trading range.

Livermore believes that every aware speculator receives the same basic information, therefore, winning and losing in the stock market is dependent upon correct comprehension and interpretation of the facts presented.

Livermore's Trading Day

Livermore quietly reads his newspapers early in the morning and uses two hours prior to the market's opening to plan his day. He looks for facts and new information on which to base his trading, never relying on headlines or anyone else's opinions.

Livermore watches the market and trades in approximately three companies at a time. He waits patiently until the proof of the correctness of a trade is confirmed and everything looks to be in his favor.

Tandem traders should at all times go along with the line of least resistance in the market, i.e., "the price trend is your friend." Because industry analysis is so important when tandem trading, the following discussion presents the salient points.

Industries

Search out leading industries for potential stock market candidates. Keep records on the industry of interest. Enter industries with purchases that demonstrate potential leadership and reject lagging industries, except when short selling.

Shun weak companies in weak industries, except when short selling, and choose instead the leading stock in the strongest industry when taking a long position.

Tandem Trading: Two Leading Companies

Leading companies within the same high ranking industry tend to move in concert, never in a divergent way. The importance in tandem trading of always monitoring the two stock leaders in an industry gives a feeling of confidence in the speculator's ability to correctly interpret what is occurring and how best to take advantage of a company's price and volume patterns.

Visualizing the two leading companies tracking together gives confidence to the speculator and contributes to making a sound judgment. When the leader and sister stock actually move together in tandem, it is twice as difficult to ignore and gives a verification of the proper pattern signals.

Learn what the prominent stock issues are and follow them closely. The current leaders represent the active issues and are where the speculator's attention should be focused. This also keeps the number of stock issues that need to be monitored small and manageable.

Favored Industry Movement At Market Tops

How favored industry groups perform at a long-term stock market top is informative. Favored industries during stage 3 in a long-term stock market uptrend will often breakdown prior to the overall market peak. This is how Livermore predicts the stock market panics of 1907 when he makes $3 million dollars and the stock market crash of 1929 when he makes $100 million dollars.

Leading industries normally change from one major long-term cycle to the next, as explained in chapter 6. Be on the lookout for the next leading industry during the upcoming long-term cycle in the stock market.

Five Tandem Trading Steps

The following five tandem-trading steps taken by Livermore prior to making any purchase or short sale are incorporated into the astute speculator methodology.

Step 1: Make certain the market is right. Speculators should check the line of least resistance to make sure they are trading along with the long-term trend of the market. Astute speculators check the S&P 500 Index Nine Month MA Trend Line and all confirming indicators to determine the stock market's stage.

Step 2: Make certain the specific industry group is right. Look at the line of least resistance for the industry under study and go with the trend. The industry group should be in the top 25 percent of all industry groups when purchasing common stock, in the bottom 25 percent when selling stock short.

Step 3: Tandem trading requires comparing both the leading company in the high ranked industry and the second leader sister stock in the same industry. The first and second industry stock leaders are checked side-by-side and should be trending upward together. Look for the stock price chart patterns of both industry leaders to track one another almost exactly. Any graphical deviations or serious fundamental financial differences precludes making the purchase.

When selling short, compare both the leading company in the low ranked industry and the second leader sister stock in the same industry. The industry leader and the second leader sister stock should be tracking downward together almost exactly. Select the second or third-tier laggard common stock in this low ranked industry to sell short.

Step 4: When buying common stock, only purchase active high-ranking industry stock leaders with margin-of-safety multiples over two. When short selling common stock, short only the active low-ranking industry stock laggards with margin-of-safety multiples preferably at zero.

Step 5: Look at all the information presented in the prior four steps simultaneously to get an overall picture of whether the trade should be made. Ask yourself, "Is this the best trade at this time?" Be circumspect and patient, wait for just the right time and then act accordingly.

Patience

Over a speculator's career, having the correct knowledge is the number one asset but close behind in importance is the need to cultivate patience when trading. Livermore makes it a point to emphasize the importance of patience and waiting for the stock market to position itself properly for the next big advance or decline.

Prior to purchasing a stock, the most difficult aspect of trading is sitting and waiting patiently for the market to open itself up to the most auspicious time to make a purchase or a short sale. Chronic trading speculators lay the groundwork with their inevitable speculative mistakes. Recognize the speculative mistakes made by others and use them to make money. Or as poker players say, "Play your opponents, not the cards." The speculator's job is to take advantage of these speculative mistakes at just the right time by having cash available.

Keep A Journal

A journal is kept where daily open, high, low and closing prices along with total trading volume figures are recorded for each stock under study. Recording price and volume figures gives speculators a clear picture and a feel for probable stock market events. Records help formulate plans to predict coming stock market movements. At least once a year, all trades should be reviewed in the speculator's journal to understand why each trade either worked or failed.

Plan, anticipate and predict what the market or a stock should do but learn to react and take action based on what the market indicates by its price and volume behavior. Knowing the right stock market patterns is an important means of gaining stock market insight, as presented next.

Chart Patterns

Stock traders' human nature does not materially change through time. Speculation on Wall Street remains the same because all past mistakes are continually repeated by new traders who are ruled by their emotions which continually trumps their reason. So while the traders themselves do change, how traders act and react as a consequence of worry, hope, greed, fear and ignorance remains constant. This common reaction to trader's emotions produces recurring shapes or price patterns that constantly repeat when viewed on charts or graphs.

Tandem trading speculators have enough experience to look at their journal price and volume entries to see recognizable patterns emerge. Today, with the effortlessness of drawing stock graphs on the Internet, these graph patterns are that much easier to visualize.

The investing public or amateur speculators never want to sell stock below its peak price, nor do they ever want to sell a stock showing them a loss. Consequently, the investing public sits tight holding stock as it drops in price until a hoped for rally will return it to their purchase price and they can get out even. This is the reason that a double top reversal pattern constantly recurs on different stock market charts where the stock price pauses and then declines just short of the prior price high point.

Familiar stock price and volume patterns for active common stock trigger the following speculative actions:

1) The chart pattern is conveying a certain state of affairs that may be coming to fruition.

2) The chart pattern looks familiar and prompts the speculator to examine his or her notes to review the last significant price advancement in comparable circumstances.

3) The chart pattern indicates that with prudent investigation and expert judgment a profitable decision should be reached.

That stock patterns on charts repeat through time is irrefutable. Astute speculators should familiarize themselves with actions of the past because it enhances the ability to respond correctly to similar patterns in the future. Correctly observing past chart patterns allows the speculator to foresee expected future price movements and to profitably position his or her trade to take advantage of the anticipated development.

Stock patterns are never perfect but do serve to put the probabilities in the speculator's favor. Keeping a journal of stock prices and trading volume of interest helps speculators develop a feel for the stock's price action and traders should profit by using this recording method.

Trading Volume Changes

Trading volume changes are the heralds of new things to come. Changing stock volume proclaims a new condition or that an abnormality is about to occur in the stock market.

Increased volume is almost always either accumulation or distribution, it is the speculator's job to determine which. As the stock's price either advances or declines on increased volume, accumulation or distribution is easy to judge; however, if a stock moves sideways on increased volume, accumulation or distribution is more difficult to determine.

Is heightened volume action pointing toward a market's boom-bubble top with a subsequent decline to follow, or does the increased volume portend overwhelming speculative interest in a stock that will force the stock price higher in coming months.

The investing public, to their peril, incorrectly views heavy volume at a boom-bubble market top as the sign of a lively vigorous market. At the conclusion of a long-term stock market decline, when the market is in stage 2, heavy volume signifies accumulation as common stock are transferred from "weak hands" to "strong hands."

Common stock is never distributed on the way up during Stage 3: Mark-Up – Uptrend but only during Stage 4: Distribution - Topping or Rounding Over and on the way down during Stage 1: Mark-Down – Downtrend. The reason for this strategy by stock market professionals is that they know the psychology of the investing public of looking to purchase stock at seemingly bargain prices. Consequently, trading volume is heavy during Stage 1: Mark-Down – Downtrend because the investing public continues to buy what they think are price bargains and speculative professionals want to sell their overvalued declining stock.

Trading Volume Changes And The Reasons Why

Livermore cares nothing about why a stock becomes active, only that it is active or it is not active. The reasons why trading volume becomes heavy in an active stock may not become public until long after the stock's move and long after the opportunity to make money in the stock has passed.

Time is wasted searching for the reasons why something is happening to a stock's price while it is happening. Hold fundamentally sound stock positions but recognize that the timing of stock moves is an art, speculators should let the stock's price and trading volume supply them with the proper timing clues.

Heavy trading volume is the empirical evidence that something new is afoot. Determine later exactly why heavy volume occurs when it does. Increased volume with no advance in the stock's price is a warning that the issue will stall out at its top price, i.e., stock is being distributed from professional speculators to the investing public.

A significant difference between amateur and professional speculators is how they view trading volume. Amateurs either overlook volume entirely or read its consequences incorrectly. The astute speculator's motto is, "Be ever alert to trading volume changes and know what they mean."

Tandem Trading Pivot Points

Pivot points or turning points are price support and resistance levels. Pivot points and active markets go hand in hand and should be understood as one confirming the other. The radical difference of opinion between buyers and sellers at pivot points results in trend changes at these price level points.

Increased trading volume for a particular stock at a pivot point should be 150-to-500 percent of normal average volume. Livermore describes two different types of pivot points.

Reversal Pivot Points

Reversal pivot points mark the end of a long-term trend for a stock or the stock market, either upward or downward. The reversal pivot point is the ideal psychological time to begin the "long-pull" trade to take advantage of the new major long-term trend in the market.

Reversal pivots points, typically, are linked with a noticeable swelling in the volume of shares traded. The increased trading volume coincides with a phalanx of selling met with a blitz of buying.

Continuation Pivot Points

Continuation pivot points are intermediate-term trend reversal points which signifies that a counter trend is ending and the intermediate-term trend will now track along with the long-term trend in the market.

A continuation pivot point is evidence that an intermediate-term trend is reversing course and corroborates the move in the long-term direction.

Passing Through Pivot Points

Monitor the follow-through as the stock's price passes through a pivot point. If a purchased stock becomes listless and begins to drift after passing a resistance pivot point, there are many times when Livermore would decide the stock is not acting properly and would switch to the short side of the market.

When predicting stock market movements using pivot points, if a stock's price acts erratically after passing through a pivot point, this is a red flag indicating peril, consequently, always use a stop-loss order to guard against this eventuality. Go long or short close to the pivot point, however, if the risk becomes too much, let the stop-loss order take you out of the position at a small loss.

A speculator is required to have a plan and schedule in mind as to how they will act if something is triggered in the stock market, however, take no action nor make any commitments until the market confirms the plan by its action. Livermore is an inveterate tape reader and likes to analyze stock price movements based upon pivot points. The following support, resistance and trading range examples explain Livermore's tape reading methodology.

Support Example

If stock XYZ is in a downward trend and bounces off support at $50 dollars per share and then rallies to $55 dollars, $50 dollars might be a pivot point. Assume the stock now meanders for awhile by backing and filling and then shoots upward to $59 dollars. The stock to date has yet to tell us anything about confirming the $50 dollar pivot point. Assume further the market overall becomes dull and listless for a few days with low volume but then picks up and the XYZ stock becomes active and quickly drops four points and continues downward until it approaches the possible pivot point price level of $50 dollars.

Here is where the price action on XYZ should be closely monitored. If the XYZ stock is going to continue its downward trend it should sell down 3 points below the possible pivot point of $50 dollars to $47, prior to having another rally of significance. If so, the stock may be shorted at $47 for a continuation of the downward trend. If, however, XYZ does not reach the possible pivot point low of $50 dollars and rallies to $53 dollars, XYZ should be purchased as soon as it reaches $53 dollars per share.

Resistance Example

Once a stock hits a new high price, say $35 per share, and then sells off for a few years and then something positive happens for the company that causes its stock to break through resistance at $35 dollars on heavy volume—it is time to buy just above the pivot point of $35 with a stop-loss placed just below this $35 dollar resistance level.

Trading Range Example

An IPO may be brought out at $45 dollars per share and immediately sell off. Over two or three years the stock's price may bounce between $25 and $45 dollars. The pivot point on the downside is $25 dollars per share and if it once sells below the $25 dollar pivot point, the stock may be shorted because it is very likely that it is due for a terrific drop in price. Why? Because even though the speculator may not be aware of it or the information is not made public, the company is probably experiencing increased internal problems.

Pivot Point Patience

Whenever Jesse Livermore waits patiently in cash for the stock price to arrive at almost the exact pivot point before starting to trade, Livermore always makes money. He believes that acting close to the pivot point is beginning trading at the right time and because the position is accumulated at the correct time, he never has to sit with a loss.

The pivot point acts as a personal guide telling speculators the appropriate move to make and when. Now the only problem is to hold on and watch the market develop, knowing in advance that the market's action indicates when to get out with profits intact.

Additional Factors

Livermore's experience when trading convinces him that the largest stock price moves occur during the last two weeks of a stock's major advance and the last 48 hours is often the most explosive. Price spikes often occur during the last 48 hours on heavy volume of at least 150 percent of normal trading volume. Price spikes are an aberration and a glaring danger signal that says, "exit this active stock position." Consequently, it is very important to patiently wait for these moves to develop and then to set a very tight progressive stop-loss order price point to capture outsized gains.

Trading in the stock market is fundamentally different than all other professions and should be treated as such. Livermore believes that management insiders are too close to their own companies and are poor judges of their stock's worth, such as the Enron bankruptcy example presented in chapter 1. Business executives know about their products, companies, industries, vendors and customers but know almost nothing about the stock market and fool themselves that they know more than they do.

Once the plan and schedule are in place and the market signal is given, Livermore directs the speculator to have the discipline to follow the plan. Be committed to the trade and only let market action determine the results. Tandem trading professionals should be winning 60 percent of the time on their stock positions, with small losses when losing and with large gains when winning.

Summary

Each speculator's nerves have to be taken into account when trading common stock. Because we are our own biggest competitor, knowing who we are and what is the best personal approach when speculating is a crucial factor for our success. The following three successful strategies are presented as possible models:

Strategy A: Panic Or Contrarian Specialist—A transition from investing to speculating. The long-pull semi-investor feels more comfortable waiting until the market hits a long-term bottom and prefers putting his or her risk capital in leading, high-quality companies with stellar track records.

The semi-investor divides his or her capital into four different accounts: 1) living expenses; 2) an emergency fund consisting of two months pay; 3) risk capital held in a money market account to put into the stock market at the appropriate time during a market panic; and 4) a save half the profits fund.

The panic or contrarian specialist combines the margin-of-safety multiple, ten additional crucial factors, the six-step contrarian analysis and the four additional contrarian factors when evaluating leading companies. At the beginning of stage 3, when the market begins its long-term uptrend, allocate equal amounts of the total risk capital (i.e., 33 percent for each stock) when purchasing three leading, high-quality companies with stellar track records.

Strategy B: Box Theory—For the emotional speculator who wants to reduce the unwanted and upsetting news of the stock market to zero. Open, high, low and closing prices for each stock tracked are entered in a journal and studied. A "good steady volume" increase of 400 percent for approximately four weeks over normal average weekly volume is excellent evidence of changed circumstances for a stock.

Box theory money management rules are strictly enforced and the "quick-loss weapon" stop-loss order ensures that speculators never lose sleep over a losing stock position. A techno-fundamentalist theory is used which relies on identifying a new vibrant industry and a fundamental assessment of the leading company's earnings growth rate in that industry. Stock market speculation using the box theory may be conducted part-time as a secondary occupation.

Stock prices of active issues tend to move within a series of boxes that stack next to one another like an up staircase in an up-trending stock market.

Once the dimensions of the box are determined, the stock's price can act anyway it wants within the confines of its box and is considered normal.

Strategy C: Tandem Trading—For the iron nerved speculator who waits patiently until the proof of the correctness of a trade is confirmed and believes that "timing is everything." Tandem speculators have enough experience to look at their journal price and volume entries to see recognizable chart patterns emerge. Changing volume proclaims a new condition or an abnormality is about to occur in the stock market.

Tandem trading requires comparing both the leading company and the second leader sister stock in the same industry. Pivot points or turning points are price support and resistance levels. Reversal pivot points mark the end of a long-term trend. Continuation pivot points are intermediate-term trend reversal points which indicate that a counter trend is ending and the intermediate-term trend will now track along with the long-term trend in the market.

All the tandem trading fundamental and timing conditions have to be in the speculator's favor, including:
1) The market's long-term trend.
2) A high or low industry ranking.
3) Matching the leader and sister stock chart patterns.
4) Purchase the high ranking industry leader or short the low ranking industry laggard company.
5) The prior steps all must support one another.
6) Use reversal and continuation pivot points for clues on timing.
7) Set appropriate stop-loss order price points.

Each speculator may select one of the three successful strategies above to implement, or mix and match different aspects of the three to find a strategy that works best for their own character, personality and lifestyle.

10

Futures And Options

Introduction

THE FUTURES MARKET serves hedgers and speculators with standardized commodity and financial futures contracts. Futures hedging strategies aim to earn above market returns and/or to reduce risk while price spread strategies are based on commodity seasonality. The four main duties of a futures exchange are: 1) price settlement; 2) contract standardization; 3) buying and selling liquidity; and 4) the transfer of risk.

Options exchanges are listed, and call and put options are described. How the options price is determined, based upon the underlying stock's price and other factors, is presented. Good options strategies are explained and recommended for use that have the possibility for unlimited gain and limited loss.

Options on futures are derivatives on derivatives that are twice removed from the underlying cash or spot market. Learn the decision choices available to buyers of options on futures. The pitfalls with futures and options contracts are explained, i.e., high cost, long learning curve and fixed expiration dates. How to best use futures, options and options on futures is discussed.

Futures Market

Hedgers are producers or end users of a commodity. Hedgers and speculators all play a role in the futures market. The futures exchange function is to bring buyers and sellers together using futures contracts—whether they are producers, end users, or speculators.

Hedgers and speculators in the futures market attempt to forecast, for successive months over the next twelve months for most futures contracts, the price of soft commodities (agricultural and food), physical commodities (energy and metals) and financial futures (equity, foreign currency, and interest rate indexes).

Standardized futures for seasonal agricultural commodities such as wheat, corn or barley allow the inherent riskiness of a perishable commodity to be transferred from the producer to the speculator, from the end user to the speculator, from the producer to the end user, from the end user to the producer and from speculator to speculator. Speculative trading in the futures market requires specialized knowledge of that commodity or financial index for the futures speculator to be consistently successful.

Futures Contract

Futures contracts are standardized for soft and physical commodities with regard to quantity, quality, destination and expiration date. The four main attributes of the futures exchange are: 1) price settlement; 2) contract standardization; 3) buying and selling liquidity; and 4) the transfer of risk. Standardization encourages futures trading and, therefore, market liquidity. Both the buyer and seller are committed and obligated to satisfy the terms of the futures contract on its expiration date.

The commodity or financial index underlying the futures contract is termed the "spot" and trades in the spot or cash market at the "spot price." Commodity futures contracts have set expiration dates, called the final settlement or delivery date, but many other terms of the contract vary which makes each commodity contract unique unto itself. Financial futures such as equity, foreign currency, and interest rate indexes normally expire quarterly on the third Friday in March, June, September and December.

The futures price is the preset price of the futures contract while the price of the underlying asset in the cash market is termed the settlement price. Typically, the settlement price moves toward the futures price on the contract's final settlement date.

As Jake Bernstein explains, a futures contract is a legal commitment between a buyer and a seller covering a specific commodity or financial index on a particular exchange, such as the Chicago Mercantile Exchange (CME) or the New York Board of Trade (NYBOT). Commodity futures require the seller to deliver a particular commodity of a specific grade and quantity to a certain destination on a fixed delivery date, or its cash equivalent.

A commodity is not automatically delivered to the futures contract buyer on the contract's final settlement date. Futures contracts covering a commodity are assigned for delivery over four to six weeks during a "notice period." When delivery does take place, the buyer simply receives a warehouse receipt and gets billed for insurance, transportation and storage costs. It is reported that only five percent of futures commodity contracts actually get assigned and result in the delivery of the actual commodity.

Initial And Maintenance Margin

The futures market relies on initial margin where perhaps five-to-fifteen percent of the contract's value is committed up front to control the entire value of the futures position. Initial margin requirements are lower for hedgers who have title to the underlying commodity or for speculators who have counterbalancing futures positions. Since the futures contract requires the actual transaction to take place at a later date, no money, other than margin, changes hands until the futures contract comes due on its final settlement date.

Both the buyer and the seller put up the initial margin for the contract on the exchange where the trade takes place which guarantees the contract to the satisfaction of both the buyer and seller. The initial margin from the buyer and seller purchases nothing, but is deposited with the exchange broker and acts like earnest money for the transaction. The initial margin is held by the broker on account over the life of the futures contract.

During the interim leading up to the delivery date of a futures contract, market conditions may vary significantly. Each exchange where a futures trade takes place guarantees all contract payments, consequently, when market conditions change materially the exchange may require additional money be added to the initial margin account—called maintenance margin—to protect the exchange's position. A listing of the major futures exchanges is presented next.

Major Futures Exchanges

A short description of the seven major futures exchanges and a listing of the futures contracts and options on commodity and financial futures contracts that each exchange offers, follows:

Chicago Mercantile Exchange (CME) www.cme.com, founded in 1898, trades both futures and options on futures. Food such as dairy products and meat, and agricultural commodities such as wheat, oats, barley and rice are traded on the futures market. Financial futures for the S&P 500 Index which is very important to program traders as presented in chapter 7, S&P 400 Index, NASDAQ 100 Index and Russell 2000 Index are traded on the CME. Financial future indexes for U.S. Treasury bills, notes and bonds' interest rates and foreign currencies are also traded on the CME.

New York Mercantile Exchange (NYMEX) www.nymex.com includes the New York Commodities Exchange (COMEX). The NYMEX focuses on physical commodity futures for energy products such as oil, gasoline, natural gas, coal and electricity, as well as the following metals: gold, silver, platinum and copper.

New York Board of Trade (NYBOT) www.nybot.com trades futures and options on futures in internationally traded agricultural commodities including: cocoa, coffee, cotton, sugar and frozen concentrated orange juice—as well as foreign currency index futures.

Mid-America Commodity Exchange (MACE) www.midam.com, founded in 1868, trades futures contracts in agricultural products such as soybeans and food such as pigs, as well as precious metals and limited financial futures.

Minneapolis Grain Exchange (MGEX) www.mgex.com, founded in 1881, trades futures and options on futures in agricultural products such as wheat, corn and soybeans.

Kansas City Board of Trade (KCBT) www.kcbt.com, founded in 1856, trades futures and options on agricultural futures in wheat and financial futures in the Value Line Index.

Philadelphia Board of Trade (PBOT) www.phlx.com is the futures exchange subsidiary of the Philadelphia Stock Exchange (PHLX), specializing in market data products.

The mechanics of the futures trade for each exchange listed above is handled by clearinghouse corporations which are described next.

Futures Clearinghouse Corporations

Typically, each of the futures exchanges establish their own clearinghouse corporation. To be a member of an exchange clearinghouse, firms typically have to be members of that specific exchange. Each clearinghouse corporation assists in the trade execution by conveying money, handing commodity deliveries and certifying the completion of all contracts.

Each clearinghouse corporation assumes the responsibility for all trades made on their exchange. Buyers and sellers agree on price and futures contract terms but after the transaction is made for future delivery, the clearinghouse corporation alone assures that the trade is satisfactorily finalized—not the buyer or the seller of the futures contact.

The futures clearinghouse corporation is the exchange's hub in collecting and paying out funds to member firms as transactions are made and futures contracts become due. If a member firm's client or the member firm itself does not make good on the futures contract when due, the clearinghouse corporation steps in and guarantees the maturing contract using the combined capital of all the member firms of the specific exchange.

Futures Trading Mechanics

Brokers on a futures exchange understand the regulations of a futures trade but typically are not trained in, nor do they normally offer, futures trading advice. Futures security analysts are usually in charge of giving advice on futures contracts.

Commissions are set on all futures contracts and priced based upon a "round turn" contract once concluded. Commissions are not collected by the broker until the futures contract comes due and is closed out on its expiration date.

Market orders are usually filled in a few minutes after reaching the exchange trading floor. If a futures market is very volatile, it may be declared a "fast market." In a "fast market" floor traders are not obligated to fill orders within a set time frame and may wait for better order fill prices.

Futures traders should be guarded about placing market orders in a "fast market" as they can be very costly to fill at good prices. Price setting orders such as buy or sell stop-limit orders are best to use to assure good fill prices in a "fast market," but the downside is that they may not be filled or executed at all.

A market if touched (MIT) order specifies a set purchase price only if the current price drops to the lower set price. The fill or kill (FOK) order directs the pit broker, a.k.a the floor broker on the futures exchange, to attempt to fill the order three times at a specified price, after that the order is killed or cancelled if not successful.

Contingency orders, a.k.a. if-then orders, allow a futures speculator to initially put in multiple orders that are dependent upon one another and if one order is completed then the other orders are automatically cancelled. For example, on a long position, when a contingency stop-loss order at a lower price and a sell-limit order at a higher price on the same futures position is in place—the execution of one of these orders automatically cancels the execution of the other order.

Contingency orders ensure that the same futures contract is not sold twice at two different prices in a very volatile market. One cancels the other (OCO) contingency orders are specified to accomplish this and set up beforehand with the brokerage company.

Futures Fair Value Calculation

Futures fair value is a speculative assumption based upon a calculation that includes the current spot or cash price times the cost of interest paid on the futures contract until expiration less dividends paid by the companies in the stock basket. Corporate dividends are subtracted because the futures contract pays no dividends associated with the underlying stock in the basket.

The theoretical and actual futures prices experience short-term variations due to supply and demand factors, however, theoretical and actual price divergence gets resolved through trading by arbitragers.

Futures Strategies

Futures strategies attempt to be on the correct side of either rising or falling prices where speculators can either go long, go short, or use price spread strategies to take advantage of divergent price movements on different futures contracts.

Futures hedging strategies aim to earn above market returns and/or to reduce risk while price spread strategies are based on commodity seasonality. Hedge funds use hedging strategies, as explained next.

Hedge Funds

Hedge funds are open-end investment companies sold to large institutions and high net-worth individuals. Hedge funds are speculative enterprises whose objective is to earn above market returns and/or to reduce risk.

A hedge fund may invest in common stock, bonds, commodities, equity indexes, interest rate indexes, foreign currency indexes, or in foreign stock markets. Typically the hedge fund manager is permitted to borrow money, buy long or sell short and use futures, options and options on futures. Hedge funds account for approximately 30-to-50 percent of all trading on major stock, futures and options exchanges.

Hedge funds may use purchase-long and sell-short strategies, concurrently. Within a specific industry, strong company stock are purchased while at the same time the weak company stock in the same industry are sold short.

Hedge funds are not regulated by the Securities and Exchange Commission (SEC), consequently, disclosure of information to their customers is voluntary. Hedge fund managers are typically paid 20-to-30 percent of the fund's profits and an annual fee of two percent of the assets under management. Hedge funds may use any of the following speculative hedging practices.

Hedging Strategies

Hedging is a common strategy practiced by hedgers, i.e., both producers and end users of a commodity as well as speculators. Producers and end users reduce their risk by hedging their position in both the futures market and the spot or cash market.

Hedging is practiced by an end user who expects to purchase a required commodity for their production process at a future date. Protection from a possible commodity price increase is planned for because the company has signed a fixed-price contract for the future delivery of their end product.

The position in the futures market is normally opposite to the position in the spot or cash market, consequently, the commodity price is determined in advance prior to its actual use, perhaps three months in the future. Price risk is transferred from an individual or company setting up the hedge to the speculator taking the other side of the futures trade.

Since the end user's company does not have the commodity on hand to fill the signed contract order, the company is said to be "short" the commodity. The end user now takes a "long" position in the futures market to lock in the price for the commodity's delivery at a future date for use in their production process.

If actual prices do increase for the required commodity, the company loses money in the cash market but makes it up with a gain in the futures market and their position is hedged.

A price decline in the cash or spot market reduces the value of commodities actually held, however, a hedged position in the futures market allows the producer or end user to recoup these losses.

The profit on the futures position offsets the losses in the commodity being held in storage. Likewise, a rise in the commodity's price increases the value on the held commodity and reduces the value of the hedged futures position to allow the businessperson to come out essentially even.

Basis

"Basis" describes the relative difference between the movement of spot prices and futures prices over the term of the contract. A perfect hedge has a constant basis. Cash prices and futures prices should normally track as one. While this is what should happen in theory, it does not always work out that way in practice. The following factors change the basis resulting in a difference between cash and futures prices:

1) The commodity is limited to one specific grade in a futures contract but the cash or spot market typically has multiple grades, consequently, the grade of the commodity required by the end user may change relative to the price of the commodity specified in the futures contract.

2) Futures contracts are reflective of national conditions while the producer or end user may have to purchase commodities in a regional market which may experience a price differential.

3) The farther in time the futures contract price is from the cash price, the less they track together.

4) The quality and quantity of the commodity specified in the futures contract may not exactly match the needs of the end user for their production process.

Hedging protects on the downside but also restricts profits if prices should go in the producer's favor over the duration of the futures contract. Thus, asymmetrical movement of the cash and futures markets can cause problems. Futures price spreads based on seasonality, along with basis, also complicate hedging in the futures market, as described next.

Price Spread Strategies

At certain times of the year, based on seasonality, futures price spreads on different futures contract expiration dates of an identical or similar commodity fluctuate. Prices may not change in an identical fashion on different futures exchanges, therefore, price spread strategies may be used profitably.

Fluctuating futures price spreads for a commodity presents an opportunity to make money using a spread strategy which requires buying one futures contract while selling another futures contract.

Premium

Normally acting futures markets have prices in the spot month, i.e., the month closest to the expiration date, very near to the cash price for the identical commodity. Typically, each futures contract at later and later expiration dates have higher commodity prices, called a premium, due to inventory carrying costs such as storage fees, insurance and interest charges.

Price Inversion

A non-typical futures market has futures price inversion, i.e., prices for later future contract months are successively lower, not higher. Price inversion results from high demand for the commodity in the cash or spot market which drives the commodity price materially higher thus inducing those holding the actual commodity to sell in the spot market.

This commodity shortage is called a "short squeeze" because spot prices increase due to a normal market shortage or due to individuals trying to corner the market by driving up prices artificially. In any case, the short squeeze requires those short the commodity to purchase to cover their position.

The speculator must know the conditions that cause one futures contract to change will also cause another contract to change in like fashion. What is looked for is a relative change in the futures contracts moving in the same direction. Fluctuating price spreads may be guarded against using the following strategies.

Intra-Commodity Spread

The first futures price spread strategy is called an "intra-commodity spread," in which a position is taken for a commodity in each contract month where the price premium is higher than the inventory carrying cost. Thus, the July contract may be purchased and the September contract for the same commodity may be sold short.

As the premiums on the futures contracts narrow and prices come back in line, the trader gains due to a positive change in the difference between futures contracts for July and September expiration dates. The real price of the commodity is not an issue, only the relative price changes of the premiums are critical.

Inter-Commodity Spread

The second spread strategy, called "inter-commodity spread," requires buying one commodity and selling a similar but different commodity. It is projected that prices for the two comparable commodities will track one another, but the premiums are expected to change at a different rate. For example, if sugar rises too high in price, a corn syrup substitute may be used for sweetening purposes.

Typically, either the short or the long position makes money. What is expected is that one of the positions makes more money than the other loses. In-depth knowledge of how the two similar commodity markets interconnect is required to make the inter-commodity spread strategy successful for the futures trader.

Straddles

Price spread strategies are also called straddles which is more descriptive of what is actually taking place. The speculator is straddling the market like a politician straddling an issue, seemingly supporting both sides of the issue at the same time. The left leg is on one side of the issue while the right leg is on the other side.

An expression heard in commodity trading is called "lifting a leg." This means that one leg of the spread is removed, either the short or the long position, thus allowing the other to continue. Also, rather than entering both sides of the spread at the same time, the speculator may "leg into" a position. "Legging in" or "legging out" of spread positions normally happens when traders carry a net losing position and wish to avoid additional losses.

Price spread trading strategies have low profit potential, but a strong benefit of trading commodity spreads or straddles is that they are reliable with respect to seasonality. In addition, spreads offer good timing indicators especially as a confirming factor in supporting the validity of market trends. Price spread behavior gives market professionals a heads up of what is likely to occur in a particular commodity or index.

Fundamental Analysis For Agricultural Commodities

For agricultural commodities, the U.S. Department of Agriculture (USDA) publishes crop reports which estimate yield quantities that are helpful in understanding supply factors and doing analysis. Private corporations also do agricultural research.

The amount and type of fundamental data needed for analysis to be a success when trading a particular agricultural commodity can be overwhelming, including knowing: 1) the long-term weather forecast; 2) the agricultural commodity's current and future supply and demand; 3) the state of the U.S. and world economy; 4) suitability of using alternative agricultural commodities; 5) storage capacity; and 6) interest rates for calculating carrying costs.

Even professionals and economists specializing in a particular agricultural commodity have a difficult time understanding the interactions of all the important factors previously listed.

Commodity Specialization

Due to the scope and breath of the knowledge required to intelligently trade commodities, such as agricultural, food, energy, or metals, it is a lifetime occupation for futures speculators who typically specialize in one commodity. Producers and end users of the commodity have an advantage since they are in the industry and have expert knowledge concerning either the supply or demand side of the futures contract when setting prices.

Unless the speculator is willing to spend their entire professional career understanding and trading futures in a specific commodity, trading commodity futures contacts without professional help from a commodities expert is not recommended for astute speculators.

Options Market

A holder of a stock option has the right but not the obligation to either purchase or sell a stock at a predetermined price over a specified time period. A call option allows the holder to buy the underlying stock at a specific price, called the striking price, and the put option allows the holder to sell the underlying stock at the striking price. Both call and put options on stock may be traded at any time up until the options expiration date.

As Lawrence G. McMillan explains, options may either be sold, called writing the option, or purchased, called being the holder of the option. Speculators expect an upward price movement in the underlying stock when purchasing or holding a call option and a downward price movement when purchasing or holding a put option. Speculators expect a upward price movement in the underlying stock when writing a put option and a downward price movement when writing a call option.

Listed Options

Listed options are traded on options exchanges and require the following five pieces of information to describe the option, e.g., "2 INTC Sept 20 call." This is a call option for Intel Corporation for two options contacts each representing 100 shares of the underlying stock or 200 shares total, at a striking price of $20 dollars per share, due to expire on Saturday following the last trading day which occurs on the third Friday in September.

All Intel options which expire at different expiration dates are of one class. A series represents a portion of a class of options that expire at the same time and at the same striking price. Listed options expire on Saturday following the third Friday for successive months throughout the year.

Cash-based options, as opposed to commodity based futures options, have no material commodities as a basis for the options contract. Cash-based options are normally associated with the stock market and if exercised only cash, not stock, is required on the expiration date.

When exercised, the cash-based option holder receives cash based on the difference between the stock's closing price and the options striking price. For example, "INTC Sept 20 call" options, if the underlying price for Intel's stock is at $24 dollars per share, the exercised option would pay: 100 shares x ($24 - $20) = $400 dollars, less any commissions.

Note: When a number before the stock's symbol is absent, the number of options contracts is one—representing 100 shares of the underlying stock.

American & European Options

There are two ways to exercise listed options depending on the type of option traded. The American option may be exercised throughout the contract's scheduled duration while the European option is only allowed to be exercised on its expiration day.

All stock options use the American exercise feature. Institutions use stock index futures to hedge their portfolios and want protection throughout the scheduled duration of the option on financial futures, consequently, the S&P 500 Index and other financial index options on futures use the European exercise feature when options on futures are used (discussed later in this chapter).

The five major options exchanges are listed next where common stock options and equity, industry, foreign currency and interest rate index options are traded.

Major Options Exchanges

Chicago Board Options Exchange (CBOE) www.cboe.com, founded in 1973, lists and trades options for many common stock companies that trade on the NYSE, NASDAQ and AMEX stock exchanges. In addition, stock indexes and exchange traded funds (ETF) and futures contracts are traded on the CBOE.

American Stock Exchange (AMEX) www.amex.com is often thought of as a stock exchange but has moved aggressively into trading listed options on domestic common stock, foreign common stock using American Depository Receipts (ADR), i.e., a negotiable certificate drawn on a U.S. bank representing a foreign corporation that may be traded on a U.S. exchange in U.S. dollars, industry indexes, international stock indexes, exchange traded funds (ETF) and HOLDRS, i.e., common stock or ADR's grouped in a particular industry.

The AMEX trades LEAPS (Long-term Equity Anticipation Securities) that are both put and call options which expire anywhere from more than 9 to 24 months in the future. In addition, FLEX options are offered which permit common stock and financial index options customization based upon such factors as exercise price and expiration date.

International Securities Exchange (ISE) www.iseoptions.com lists and trades options on stock and financial index options. The ISE is a fully electronic U.S. options exchange using a screen-based trading system. International Securities Exchange (NYSE: ISE) is a corporation and came public with its IPO during March of 2005.

Pacific Exchange (PCX) www.pacificex.com trades approximately 1,700 stock options, financial index options and is a totally electronic exchange with an agreement with Archipelago which provides the trading platform for the Archipelago Exchange (ArcaEx) which in turn has ties to ArcaEx of the NYSE Group.

Philadelphia Stock Exchange (PHLX) www.phlx.com, founded in 1790, trades stock options and 19 industry index options including the Semiconductor Index (SOX), the Bank Index (BKX), the Oil Service Index (OSX) and the Gold/Silver Index (XAU) as well as standardized and customized currency options on the Euro Dollar, Australian Dollar, British Pound, Canadian Dollar, Japanese Yen and the Swiss Franc.

Options Clearinghouse Corporation

Options Clearing Corporation (OCC) www.optionsclearing.com is the clearinghouse corporation for the AMEX, CBOE, ISE, PCX and PHLX as well as being owned by these exchange members. The OCC clears transactions for listed stock options and options on equity, foreign currency and interest rate indexes.

The relationship between the underlying stock's price and the option price on the equity is determined by how much the options premium surpasses its intrinsic value. How to calculate the time value premium for a call option is presented next.

Call Time Value Premium Calculation

The initial option premium paid by the buyer of the option to the writer is set initially at purchase. For a "INTC Sept 20 call" example, Intel's options contract premium is $3 when Intel is trading at $18 and the striking price is $20 dollars per share. Please see Table 10 -1: Intel Corp. – Call Time Value Premium Changes, shown on the next page.

Assuming that Intel is trading initially out-of-the-money at $18 dollars per share, the call time value premium (TVP) = call option premium – intrinsic value, or $3 = $3 – $0.

A call with a underlying stock price above the striking price is termed "in-the-money." For the "INTC Sept 20 call" example, if Intel is trading at $22 dollars on the NASDAQ, the intrinsic value of the option is calculated: intrinsic value = stock price - striking price or $2 = $22 - $20, as shown in Table 10-1.

The call TVP calculation when Intel reaches $22 dollars per share is: call TVP = call option premium – intrinsic value: $3 = $5 – $2. Another way of calculating the call TVP = call option premium + striking price – stock price or $3 = $5 + $20 – $22, resulting in the same $3 answer.

Table 10 – 1: Intel Corp – Call Time Value Premium Changes

Intel Stock Price	INTC Sept 20 Call Price	Intrinsic Value	Time Value Premium
12	½	0	½
14	1	0	1
16	2	0	2
18	3	0	3
# 20	4	0	4
22	5	2	3
24	6	4	2
26	7	6	1
28	8½	8	½
30	9½	10	* -½

Time Value Premium is at its highest at parity.
* Calls, deeply in the money, often change hands at a discount relative to intrinsic value. Those who purchase calls typically want to pay a less expensive premium with the expectation of higher percentage returns in a stock that is yet to make an upward price run rather than putting money in a stock that has already significantly increased in value.

The time value premium is normally at its highest price when the underlying stock price and the striking price are equal, making the intrinsic value equal to zero. In our example in Table 10-1, Intel's stock is trading at $20 dollars per share. This is important because the time value premium drops off in price on either side of its highest price at Intel's $20 dollar price parity.

The call option price premium changes from $0.50 to $9.50 dollars as Intel's underlying stock price changes from $12 to $30 dollars, as shown in Table 10-1. When a call is out-of-the-money, the call time value premium equals the option premium. The equation is: call time value premium = call option premium – intrinsic value. The intrinsic value is equal to the stock price less the striking price. When a call option is out-of-the-money, the intrinsic value is equal to zero.

Options Price Determination

Determining the options price is a combination of factors associated with the underlying stock as well as how the option itself is structured. The following four major and two minor factors, in order of importance, go into the pricing of an option:

Major Factors

1) The underlying stock's price is the most important factor in relation to the options striking price, because, if the difference between the two prices is very large then all other factors pale by comparison. As the options contract approaches its expiration date, the relationship between the underlying stock price and the options striking price take on increased importance until the expiration day of the option where they are the only two factors that matter.

2) The different options striking prices are determined to appeal to both the options writer, for sufficient premiums charged, and the options holder for expected price movement. An active options market insures liquidity and is the second most important factor.

3) The length of time remaining until the options expiration date is the third most important factor. For a call option, the premium or cost of the option prior to the expiration date is the total of the intrinsic value and the time value premium.

Options are termed a wasting asset which means that the time value premium decays in value as the option approaches its expiration date. The rate of decay is in proportion to the square root of the time remaining. That means that the time value premium of an option with four weeks remaining decays at twice the rate of an option with eight weeks remaining.

Speculators assume that selling out-of-the-money options is a good way to collect the value of the time value premium as it wastes away toward an options expiration date. Unfortunately, this may be negated if the volatility of the underlying stock increases. This is a good example of how the interaction of factors complicates the making of money when trading options.

4) Premiums on put and call option contracts incorporate volatility in their prices, i.e., the more volatile the stock price, the higher the options price. That means that with all other factors being equal, a highly volatile

stock like Google Inc. commands a higher options price than a less volatile stock such as a sedate utility company's stock. This is expected since the buyers of Google options have a higher probability to make more money, therefore, writers demand and purchasers pay a higher premium. The underlying stock's volatility completes the four major factors that go into calculating the options price.

Historical & Implied Volatility

Options volatility is an central speculative concept. Historical volatility refers to changes in the underlying stock price in the past while implied volatility predicts the underlying stock price change over the future duration of the options contract.

Both historical and implied volatility get factored into the options price whose price range tends to increase as the contract approaches its expiration date. Unfortunately for the options trader, it has been shown that implied volatility relies on a trader's perception and is often a poor forecaster of the final volatility of the option.

Vega is the measure which explains how much an option price changes as a result of a one point change in the volatility of the underlying stock.

Minor Factors

1) The first minor factor is the risk free interest rate, as determined by the 3-month Treasury bill (T-bill). Financing to carry options is a factor in their pricing and should be taken into account.

2) Options do not pay dividends, even on an underlying stock that does. A stock with no dividend does not concern itself with this factor when calculating its options price. However, a stock paying a large dividend lowers the price of call options which is very important to the writer of calls. This point is covered more extensively later in this chapter.

Major And Minor Factor Interactions

The interplay of the four major and two minor factors above impacts actual options pricing, as one factor increases the options price the other factors may tend to reduce the options price. Figuring out this factor interplay is most challenging. Non-quantifiable issues also impact options pricing, as explained next.

Non-Quantifiable Issues For Options

The major and minor options factors mentioned above are only those which are quantifiable. Non-quantifiable issues also play a part when pricing options. For example, when speculators' sentiment is positive on the stock market, call premiums increase noticeably due to increased demand from buyers.

When the long-term trend in the market is downward and market sentiment is poor, call premiums tend to shrink due to increased supply and/or lower demand. Since speculative sentiment tends to be volatile, its influence on the options market is difficult to predict. A way to measure speculator sentiment is to calculate the put/call ratio, as presented next.

Sentiment Indicator: Put/Call Ratio

The put/call ratio (PCR) tracks speculator sentiment and is calculated by dividing the number of put options contracts traded per day by the number of call options contacts traded on the same day. The volume in puts divided by the volume in calls equals the PCR. A put/call ratio equal to one (PCR = 1) means that speculators are evenly divided between those who expect the stock's price to increase versus those who expect the price to decline.

The CBOE reports daily PCR's on their website at http:// www.cboe.com/data/PutCallRatio.aspx, scroll down the page and click on CBOE Total Exchange Volume and Put/Call Ratios. A PCR less than one means speculators are optimistic and expect stock prices to increase. Likewise, a PCR over one signifies pessimistic options traders who expect a price decline.

The PCR is a good contrarian sentiment indicator because the emotions of speculators tend to be revealed in this ratio. As speculators become overly pessimistic concerning market prospects, the number of put contacts purchased increases dramatically in anticipation of a further market decline. Using PCR data to construct a 10 week moving average gives an intermediate-term view to the PCR data.

Delta Or Hedge Ratio

The delta of the option, a.k.a. the hedge ratio, specifies how much call options will either increase or decrease in value when the underlying stock changes by one point in price. A delta of one stipulates that the underlying stock price is well above the options striking price while a delta of zero signifies a deeply out-of-the money call option.

A stock at its striking price normally has a delta of between 0.5 and 0.625 of a point. In general the strategy is—the shorter the time horizon of the option under consideration for purchase, the higher the delta value should be.

The "up delta" refers to how much the call option will increase when the underlying stock increases by one point. The "down delta" is how much the call option will decrease if the underlying stock goes down by one point. If the up delta is 0.625 while the down delta is 0.375 for stock options, this indicates a good purchase ratio.

Delta is important to the call option buyer because how much the option is expected to move with one point change in the underlying stock's price, either up or down, helps the speculator determine which stock option to purchase.

Delta And Equivalent Stock Position

Call or put option positions can be translated into the equivalent number of shares owned of the underlying common stock, either net-long or net-short. The equivalent stock position (ESP) equation is equal to the number of options contacts times delta times the number of shares per option.

For example, "10 INTC Sept 20 calls," ten Intel call option contracts are purchased and the delta is 0.55. The ESP is 10 contracts x 0.55 delta x 100 shares = 550 shares net long of Intel's stock. Owning ten call option contracts for Intel is the equivalent of owning or being long 550 shares of Intel. The put calculation is the same, but the resulting equivalency is a net short position.

Options Strategies

The following are available call and put option strategies that speculators should understand. Only good option strategies that are recommended for use should be implemented by astute speculators.

Call Buying

Speculators most frequently purchase calls or write covered calls, of the two, call buying is the much preferred strategy. The risks are limited when purchasing calls, because all that may be lost is the call premium and the commission charges, while the rewards are unlimited as the stock increases in price.

Successful call buying requires selecting, at the precise time, the stock that will increase significantly in price over the duration of the options contract. Leverage is the main selling point when purchasing call options. A sizable profit may be earned with little upfront money required when purchasing call options, unfortunately, the option can also expire worthless with the speculator's entire monetary position lost. Consequently, money management rules should be strictly followed when purchasing call options.

Call option buyers typically purchase options that are way out of the money because the premium is inexpensive. In-the-money call premiums are more expensive than out-of-the money calls on the same stock but may be the better choice. Having limited funds should not be a criterion when selecting the appropriate options contract.

Covered Call Writing

Covered call writing is the selling of call options while simultaneously owning the same number of shares of the underlying common stock. The covered call writer should believe that the stock is in an upward trend or at least neutral on the prospects for the stock's price.

Novices believe the risk of owning a stock is decreased when writing covered calls and may erroneously believe that covered call writing is a relativity safe enterprise. However, this is not the case since the downside risk of the stock plunging in price is still with the stock owner. The company can go bankrupt and all the covered call writer collects is the option premium while losing all the money in his or her long stock position.

The maximum profit potential from writing covered calls equals the striking price less the stock price plus the call premium. For the "INTC Sept 20 call" example, with the stock price at $18 dollars that would be $5 = $20 - $18 + $3. The downside break-even point equals the stock price less the call premium: $15 = $18 - $3.

Cover call writing has a limited upside gain potential since all that can be earned on one contract for the Intel example is $500 dollars ($5 x 100 shares), regardless of how high Intel's stock rises in price, however, the probability of this trade being in the writer's favor is predictably a high percentage.

Normally, speculators use a covered call writing strategy when looking to increase income on the stock owned. Unfortunately, the downside risk of bankruptcy for the company is unlimited and even though slight in probability this makes covered call writing a limited upside gain and unlimited downside risk strategy, consequently, astute speculators should avoid covered call writing. If what is wanted is short-term income, investing in 3-month T-bills is often the better strategy.

Uncovered Call Writing

Speculators selling call options without owning the underlying stock or any corresponding securities such as convertible bonds, convertible stock or other similar call options with different striking price terms are considered to be writing uncovered or naked calls.

The margin requirement on uncovered call writing varies between 10-to-20 percent of the common stock price plus premium, depending on whether the stock is trading above or below the striking price of the call option. Also, each brokerage firm may place additional requirements such as maintaining a minimum amount of money in the speculator's account and requiring the speculator to prove minimum option competence prior to permitting naked call writing.

Uncovered call writing should not be confused with short selling the underlying stock. When short selling, the downside risk is unlimited as with naked call writing but the upside profit possibility is substantial which is unlike uncovered call writing. However, because the naked call writer does not pay dividends on the underlying stock, there are some occasions when naked call writing out earns short selling of high dividend common stock.

Uncovered or naked call writing has only a limited profit possibility while at the same time offering the risk of unlimited loss, consequently, uncovered call writing is not recommended to be practiced by astute speculators.

Put Buying

The purchaser of a put option contract holds the right but not the obligation to sell the underlying common stock at the striking price at any time over the duration of the options contract. The availability of listed put options on options exchanges is narrower and of a more recent occurrence than listed call options, but all underlying stock with exchange listed put options also have corresponding listed call options. Listed puts and calls for a stock have the same expiration dates and striking prices.

Purchasing a put is the expectation of an underlying stock decline within the duration of the contract's expiration date. Five Intel put options, with the aforementioned expiration date and striking price, is written as: "5 INTC Sept 20 put."

An in-the-money put is when the underlying stock price is beneath the striking price and vice versa for the out-of-the-money put. The put time value premium (TVP) for in-the-money Intel put options equal the put option premium plus the stock price less the striking price. With Intel currently selling at $18 dollars per share and the put premium of $3 dollars, the put TVP = $3 + $18 - $20 = $1. The largest put TVP is when the underlying stock price and the striking price are equal.

It is interesting to note that call options normally sell for a higher premium than put options when the underlying stock and the striking price are identical. Also, in-the-money puts lose TVP more quickly than in-the-money calls.

Dividends, especially, increase put premiums. Because dividends are not paid on puts, high dividend paying common stock translates into higher prices for the puts but lower premiums for the calls.

Buying a put has a limited possibility of downside loss and a unlimited possibility for an upside gain which is desirable. Prior to purchase, put options should be analyzed and ranked based on delta or hedge ratio volatility. Consequently, a full-service brokerage firm is useful when purchasing puts.

Protected Short Sale

A protected short sale may be thought of as a synthetic put. The underlying stock is sold short while a call option contract in the same stock is purchased at the money. This acts like a put option and protects the speculator on the unlimited risk of a short sale. This strategy is particularly effective in markets where call options are plentiful and liquid while put options are either not available or too expensive.

Holding a call option on a stock that is held in a short position limits the risk which is calculated by adding the striking price of the call to the call price less the stock's price. For example from Table 10 - 1, "INTC Sept 20 call" price at the money is $4 dollars while the striking price and stock price are both $20 dollars. The total risk on the synthetic put position is 100 shares x $4 = $400 dollars.

If Intel's price goes to $12 dollars at expiration, the total profit on the position would be equal to the striking price of $20 dollars less the expiration price of $12 dollars less the cost of the call option of $4 dollars, or $20 - $12 - $4 x 100 shares = $400 dollars.

Reverse Hedge

The reverse hedge is also called a simulated straddle and involves purchasing twice the number of call option contracts than the number of shares held short on the same underlying stock. Profits come when the stock price either increases or decreases significantly enough during the duration of the call options.

A stock that is listlessly drifting is a poor reverse hedge candidate. The reverse hedge strategy is only used when underlying stock does not have listed put options on an exchange.

Straddle Buying

A stock with listed calls and puts may perform the same reverse hedge described above, called a straddle, by purchasing both puts and calls on an underlying stock with the identical striking price and expiration date. If in our example, Intel's price is at $20 dollars and the "INTC Sept 20 call" is priced at $4 dollars and the "INTC Sept 20 put" is priced at $3 dollars.

The straddle position cost for Intel is, $4 + $3 = $7 dollars, plus commissions. Profits are made if the price falls to $12 dollars, i.e., the profit on the position is the striking price less the price at expiration times 100 shares less the cost of the put and the call options: ($20 - $12) x 100 shares - $400 - $300 = $100 less commissions.

If Intel's price goes up to $30 dollars at expiration, the profit on the straddle position would be the expiration price less the striking price time 100 shares less the cost of the put and call options: ($30 - $20) x 100 shares - $400 - $300 = $300 dollars less commissions.

Both the reverse hedge and the straddle buying strategy example presented here have a built-in loss limit of $700 dollars plus commissions and an unlimited profit potential. The reverse hedge and straddle buying strategies should only be used for very volatile underlying stock.

Ratio Writing

Ratio writing requires combining two position classes. The first position is to own the underlying shares of the common stock. The second position is to write both covered and uncovered calls, normally for twice the number of long shares held. Half of the calls are written slightly lower than the current stock price and half of the calls are written slightly higher than the stock's current price. Typically, the speculator believes the outlook of the underlying stock is neutral and writes calls where the stock's current price is close to the striking price.

The maximum profit occurs if the stock expires exactly at the higher call option contract striking price and both call premiums are collected less commissions. However, this strategy has a limited premium reward and a large upside and downside risk and is not recommended for astute speculators. Ratio call spreads are similar to ratio writing and are described next.

Ratio Call Spreads

The ratio call spread is the purchase of call options close to but lower than then current underlying stock price while simultaneously selling call options at a slightly higher striking price than the current stock's price. Typically the ratio is, one call option contract is purchased for two call option contracts sold.

Ratio call spreads are a better strategy than ratio writing because the speculator is buying a significant amount of intrinsic value associated with purchasing the lower striking price call options while at the same time selling a substantial amount of the time value premium wasting assets in the call options being sold at the higher striking price.

The maximum profit occurs if the stock expires exactly at the striking price of the written call option contracts, resulting in the call premium being collected less commissions plus the difference in price of the purchased call's striking price and the stock's price at expiration date.

The downside price risk is limited, but unfortunately, the risk to the upside of a underlying stock price advance is unlimited. Consequently, with only limited profit possible and unlimited losses due to an upside price advance, astute speculators should shun ratio call spreads.

Call & Put Spread Strategies

Call spread strategies involve the simultaneous buying and selling of call options while put spread strategies involve the simultaneous buying and selling of put options. Both put and call spread strategies, described next, have different names depending on the terms of the options being either bought or sold.

1) *Vertical Spreads*: expiration dates are identical with different striking prices. A type of vertical spread that is very popular is called a "bull spread" which is used when the speculator believes the market is trending upward.

The bull spread involves purchasing a call at a striking price and selling a call at a striking price higher than the purchased call. A conservative bull spread has both the purchase call and the sale call in-the-money. The aggressive bull spread has the current stock price less than the higher striking price while a very aggressive bull spread has both calls out-of-the-money. Bull spreads are better than covered call writing because they have both limited upside gain and limited downside risk of loss.

2) *Horizontal Spreads*: also called a time spread, the striking prices are identical with different expiration dates. A "calendar spread" describes a type of horizontal spread that requires the sale of a call option at the same time purchasing a more distant call option all with the same striking price.

The calendar spread assumes a neutral market with the profit coming from the wasting away of the near-term options value at a faster rate than the far-term options value. Purchasing a calendar spread assumes that volatility in the markets remains quiescent. Increased volatility swells the striking price spreads which reduces the effectiveness of the calendar spread. Calendar spreads have both limited upside gain and limited downside risk of loss.

3) *Diagonal Spreads*: both the striking prices and the expiration dates are different. Typically the long position side of the spread should come due prior to the short position side of the spread. The analysis of diagonal spreads becomes very complicated very quickly and involves a combination of both the vertical and horizontal spreads discussed above.

Collar Strategy

Instituting a collar strategy is for speculators who have a profit in a underlying stock and begin to worry about the upside potential for the stock. An out-of-the-money call is written at the same time and out-of-the-money put is purchased. The speculator typically is able to accomplish this at no cost because the call premium received compensates for the put premium and commissions paid. The downside risk of loss is limited along with the upside gain when using collars.

LEAPS options contracts are often the best use of collars. The striking price of the calls over the underlying stock price in relation to the striking price of the puts can be relatively large, offering better upside gain possibility versus potential downside risk of loss.

Straddle Buying

Straddle buying is similar to using collars but here the speculative profit strategy uses call options contracts where traders lock in profits when anticipating additional upside market gains. In this case, a put is purchased to ensure profits at the same time allowing for more upside appreciation in the underlying stock.

Straddle buying limits the downside loss in an existing position showing a gain while at the same time allowing for possibility of more upside profits.

Options Strategy Review

The options strategies described in this chapter are separated into the following three categories termed poor, specialized and good options strategies.

A) *Poor options strategies* have the possibility for limited gain and for unlimited speculative loss and include: covered call writing, uncovered call writing, ratio writing and ratio call spreads. Astute speculators are recommended never to use these strategies.

B) *Specialized options strategies* have the possibility for limited gain and for limited loss and include: bull spreads, calendar spreads and collars. Astute speculators should use these strategies on a limited basis for a specific purpose only.

C) *Good options strategies* have the possibility for unlimited gain and for limited loss and include: call buying, put buying, protected short sale, reverse hedge and straddle buying. Astute speculators now have the possibility of making outsized gains with limited risk which is the purpose of speculation, therefore, these strategies are recommended for use.

Options On Futures

Options on futures contracts are derivatives on derivatives that are twice removed from the underlying spot or cash commodity and financial index markets. First is the cash or spot market, second is commodity or financial futures on the cash/spot market and third is the options on the futures on the cash/spot market.

Options on futures are treated just like stock options and give the buyer of an option the right but not the obligation to either buy or sell a futures contract at a set price, irrespective of the actual futures contract closing price on the final settlement date. As with common stock options, there are two types of options on futures: 1) put options; and 2) call options.

Put options give the holder or purchaser of the option the right but not the obligation to sell the underlying futures contract at a set striking price. The call option gives the holder or purchaser the right but not the obligation to buy the underlying futures contract at a set striking price. Striking prices are set by the exchange in standardize price increments. All options on futures have a set expiration date which is the last day the option can be exercised and is determined by the exchange.

Intrinsic Value

The underlying value of a futures contract is the intrinsic value of the futures option. For example, if an options trader purchases a put option on the CME with the right to sell in three months December wheat at a striking price of $4 dollars per bushel and one month later the price goes to $3.50 per bushel, the put option holder would sell the option at a profit and the original seller of the futures option now becomes long wheat at $4 dollars per bushel.

The intrinsic value in the above example is $0.50 profit times the standard contract quantity amount of 5,000 bushels, or $2,500 dollars per contract. At $3.50, a $4 put striking price is termed to be "in-the-money." If the price of wheat goes up to $4.50 per bushel, the intrinsic value of the futures put option contract is zero and is said to be "out-of-the-money."

In-and-out-of-the-money futures options are often incorrectly priced on the exchanges. The premiums for out-of-the-money futures put options are normally under priced while out-of-the-money futures call options are usually overpriced.

When Exercised

Most options on futures are traded prior to the expiration date. For example, the put option on futures buyer may sell the option showing a profit to another speculator who believes the underlying cash commodity price is going lower.

A trader will sometimes sell a futures option while at the same time hold the opposite position in a futures contract—this is termed "covered futures option writing." Who decides to exit a futures options contract and when is discussed next.

Exit Decisions Belong To The Buyer

The seller or writer of an option on a futures contract makes no decision about when to terminate the futures options contract once the transaction occurs, i.e., all further choices belong to the buyer who may elect one of three following alternatives:

1. The futures option buyer allows the option to expire worthless, this is a forgone conclusion if the futures option closes out-of-the-money.

2. The futures option may be offset by selling or writing an identical futures option at the same striking price. For example, if the purchaser bought a put, a call cannot be sold to offset the original put position, i.e., buying a put requires selling a put.

3. The futures option may be exercised. A futures option that is in-the-money and showing a profit should certainly be exercised for the buyer's advantage.

Options On Futures: Advantages & Disadvantages

Rather than trading futures, options on futures offer the speculator limited and quantifiable risk as well as offering speculators a means to hedge their futures positions.

The disadvantages of futures options trading is that making money is more difficult in futures options than in the underlying futures contracts. The reason for this is that cash prices have to move far enough to cover the premium charged on the futures option for the futures option to be in the money and to show the options futures trader a profit.

Commissions on options on futures tend to be high relative to other financial instruments. Futures option traders normally acquire long-term positions and since trading volume is low, commissions tend to be high. Therefore, prior to selecting an options on futures broker make sure to do some comparison shopping on brokerage fees.

Another downside to trading options on futures is that the entire position can be lost if the option closes out-of-the-money, this requires strict money management rules to protect risk capital when trading options on futures.

Purchasing Options On Futures

The futures options buyer has no margin cost but does have to pay the premium to buy the put or call option and eventually has to pay a commission to a broker. For the futures options buyer there is never a chance of a margin call from a broker which is a plus.

The futures options price is the sum total of what can be lost on the position. The good money management rules of never meeting a margin call and knowing the sum total of the money at risk are automatically enforced when purchasing options on futures.

The futures options purchaser may have lower odds of making money than the call writer but when they do make money they may make a considerable amount. For example, if a trader sells a call option on wheat futures for 15 cents, that is the writer's profit regardless how much wheat increases in price.

Writing Options On Futures

A Wall Street belief is that "eighty percent of all options on futures expire worthless." This statement may or may not be true, there is no research known by the author that explains whether the futures options purchasers receive their moneys worth for holding the option.

For example, if an option on a futures contract is purchased to hedge an existing futures position and it expires worthless, presumably, the futures option served its purpose of reducing risk over the option period and was valuable. Also, most options on futures buyers exit their positions when they have a profit prior to the expiration date. How many options on futures expire without fulfilling their planned purpose is impossible to know without individually interviewing futures options buyers.

Time Until Expiration

Time until expiration adds value to a futures option which then begins to waste away until it is zero at expiration. The option writer has a time value premium when the futures option is originally sold that begins to waste away as the option moves closer to its expiration date. The reason for this is that the further from the options expiration date the more likely that the cash price will move in the option purchaser's favor, therefore, increasing the futures options intrinsic value and profits for the option holder. An out-of-the-money option on a futures contract two moths from expiration is valued higher than the same option only two weeks from expiration.

The volatility of the underlying market adds value to a futures option contract. Added volatility increases the possibility of large price swings and consequently increases the premium that the purchaser is willing to pay for the put or call futures options contact. The higher premium offsets the higher risk that the writer accepts in a volatile market.

The futures option writer collects a premium which represents the entire profit on the trade. And while writing options on futures may seem less risky than purchasing the same options on futures, the upside rewards are limited.

Options On Futures Margin Requirements

The writer or seller of a futures option does have a margin requirement just as if he or she actually held the underlying futures contract. This is required because if the futures option holder exercises the option, the writer instantaneously holds a futures contract which more than likely shows a loss because the holder would not exercise the option except at a profit. Initial margin and additional maintenance margin, if the market goes against the futures options writer at any time, are demanded by the broker.

Waiting for futures options to expire is often a very emotional experience for the options writer. Writing options on futures may be a good way to make many small gains, however, the one big loss can wipe out all these gains. In conclusion, writing options on futures is generally more risky with less total reward than when purchasing options on futures.

Futures, Options And Options On Futures Problems

The problem with trading in the futures market for commodities is that it requires a long learning curve in order to be consistently successful. With the options market, the put and call premiums are expensive and the same protection is achieved in the stock market at no expense by using stop-loss orders.

Options on futures are derivatives on derivatives that combine the problems with both futures and options. Other factors restraining the use of the futures, options and options on futures contracts are explained next.

Fixed Expiration Dates

The derivative markets, i.e., futures, options and options on futures, whether buying or selling, have a fixed expiration date on all contracts, consequently, there is normally an equal probability for gain or loss at the contract's close which is a gambling situation. The first art of speculation, managing the "when" of trading, is severely limited with fixed expiration dates. Limiting risk as much as possible, the goal of astute speculation, is impossible to accomplish when gambling with fixed expiration dates.

Common stock ownership on the NYSE, NASDAQ, and AMEX stock exchanges have no fixed expiration dates which permits time to be the speculator's friend. Probabilities can be put in the speculator's favor by speculating in common stock rather than gambling with futures, options, or options on futures based on fixed expiration dates. Consequently, wanting to put the highest probabilities in the speculator's favor, speculating in common stock on the major stock exchanges is the favored strategy for astute speculators.

Leverage

Futures, options and options on futures allow the use of leverage which is believed to be a handicap to trading rather than an asset as generally thought. Leverage costs money, distracts the mind and a relatively small price move can wipe out a speculative position with the futures or options contract expiring worthless. Losing the entire stake for a speculator puts him or her out of business.

Wasting Asset

Purchased options or options on futures are a wasting asset of the time value premium. When purchasing a call option, unless the stock rises significantly and quickly, based on the time value premium, the profit is missed when the stock advances after the expiration date of the option. Time should be the speculator's friend, not their enemy as the call options time value premium wastes away.

Requires Specialized Training

The legendary stock trader James R. Keene felt it was impossible for him to win consistently enough to make money when speculating in commodities. Keene lost everything he owned in the Chicago grain futures market. Perhaps the most acclaimed stock speculator ever, Jesse Livermore, lost the bulk of his $3 million dollar fortune in bad cotton trades in the commodities market which eventually forced him into personal bankruptcy.

The commodity futures or options on futures market requires a long learning curve in order to be consistently successful. Unless the speculator is willing to concentrate their entire professional career understanding and trading futures or options on futures for a specific commodity, such as agricultural, food, energy, or metals, trading commodities without professional help from a commodities expert is not recommended for astute speculators.

Summary

The futures market serves hedgers (producers and end users) and speculators with standardized commodity and financial futures contracts. Hedgers and speculators in the futures market attempt to forecast, for successive months over the next twelve months for most futures contracts, the price of soft commodities (agricultural and food), physical commodities (energy and metals) and financial futures (equity, foreign currency, and interest rate indexes). Both the buyer and seller are committed and obligated to satisfy the terms of the futures contract on the final settlement date.

The futures exchanges bring buyers and sellers together—whether they are hedgers or speculators. The four main duties of a futures exchange are: 1) price settlement; 2) contract standardization; 3) buying and selling liquidity; and 4) the transfer of risk.

Commodity futures require the seller to deliver a particular commodity of a specific grade and quantity to a certain destination on a fixed delivery date, or its cash equivalent. The commodity underlying the futures contract is termed the "spot" and trades in the spot or cash market at the "spot price."

A hedge fund may invest in common stock, bonds, commodities, equity indexes, interest rate indexes, foreign currency indexes, or in foreign stock markets. Typically the hedge fund manager is permitted to borrow money, buy long or sell short and use futures, options and options on futures.

Hedging is practiced by producers, end users and speculators who attempt to increase profits and/or to reduce their risk by protecting their position in both the futures and the spot or cash market. Hedging only approximates conditions for a producer or end user and only protects against major risk factors in the market. Comprehensive coverage of all risk is not possible using hedging since the risk of commodity price fluctuation is merely exchanged for the smaller risk of a relative basis change between cash and futures prices.

Futures price spreads of the identical commodity between different futures contract expiration dates fluctuate based on seasonality. Prices may not change in an identical fashion on different futures exchanges, therefore, price spread strategies may be used profitably. Example futures price spread strategies include: intra-commodity spread, inter-commodity spread and straddles.

The options price, in order of importance, is based upon the underlying stock's price, the options striking price, the length of time remaining until the option reaches its expiration date, the underlying stock's volatility, the risk free interest rate and the cash dividend. The options strategies described in this chapter are separated into the following categories termed poor, specialized and good options strategies.

A) *Poor options strategies* have the possibility for limited gain and for unlimited speculative loss and include: covered call writing, uncovered call writing, ratio writing and ratio call spreads. Astute speculators are recommended never to use these strategies.

B) *Specialized options strategies* have the possibility for limited gain and for limited loss and include: bull spreads, calendar spreads and collars. Astute speculators should use these strategies on a limited basis for a specific purpose only.

C) *Good options strategies* have the possibility for unlimited gain and for limited loss and include: call buying, put buying, protected short sale, reverse hedge and straddle buying. Astute speculators now have the possibility of making outsized gains with limited risk which is the purpose of speculation, therefore, these strategies are recommended for use.

Options on futures are derivatives on derivatives and twice removed from the underlying spot or cash market. Options on futures give the buyer of an option the right but not the obligation to either buy or sell a futures contract at a set price, irrespective of the actual futures contract closing price.

There is a major difference between speculating in stock index futures or stock options and in common stock on the NYSE, NASDAQ, and AMEX stock exchanges. Common stock ownership on the stock exchanges have no fixed expiration dates as with financial futures and stock options which permits time to be the speculator's friend. Put and call stock option premiums are expensive and the same protection is achieved in the stock market at no cost by using stop-loss orders.

The commodity futures market requires a long learning curve in order to be consistently successful. Unless the speculator is willing to concentrate their entire professional career understanding and trading futures in a specific commodity, such as agricultural, food, energy, or metals, trading commodities without professional help from a commodities expert is not recommended for astute speculators.

Conclusion

Introduction

THE ART AND SCIENCE necessary to accomplish the twin goals of earning +33 percent per year by speculating in the stock market, in both good times and bad, and then retaining the profits which is the real end game, for a new life interest, leisure, or a comfortable retirement are presented. Eleven key scientific speculative factors and three speculative arts and the techniques necessary to master these arts are explained.

The best stock market speculators think: 1) money is only a means to keep score; 2) losing periodically in the stock market is going to happen regardless of how smart I am; 3) stock trading is best treated as a fun but serious game; and 4) planning, scheduling and hard work are required to succeed. Ten speculative bylaws are emphasized. Money management rules are presented because it is not how much money speculators win that is most important, instead, it is how much traders do not lose that determines speculative success.

Three strategies for trading stock over the intermediate term are presented: 1) panic or contrarian specialist; 2) box theory; and 3) tandem trading. Speculators cannot be told what his or her strategy should be, but are required to know themselves in order to arrive at a trading strategy that works best for their character, personality and lifestyle.

Learn about speculating in the stock market first, then practice using simulator trading, next implement odd-lot trading with limited funds and only then graduate to trading round lots. Eight astute speculator book firsts are listed.

Practical Benefits

Stock market speculation is an effort to reduce trading risk through knowledge and then balance being suitably venturesome without overreaching. *The Astute Speculator* gives speculators what they most need to know and where to find current data on the Internet to perform their model calculations, formalize their judgment and make their own stock trades.

A challenging but reasonable goal when speculating is to earn three times the average super-long-term S&P 500 Index return of approximately +11 percent per year, i.e., a speculative +33 percent per year. Try not to overreach, to expect to earn more than +33 percent per year, especially in the beginning of a speculative career, is unrealistic. Eleven key scientific speculative factors and three speculative arts and the techniques necessary to master these arts are presented. Once the money is earned, the second goal and real end game requires retaining the profits by using stop-loss orders and money management rules.

Robust speculative methodologies are explained. The crucial highlights of speculating, with examples, in ways that are practically useful to speculators over an intermediate-term planning horizon are presented. The practical benefits presented in *The Astute Speculator* rest on the theoretical foundations of the discounted news theory (DNT) and the discounted market hypothesis (DMH) presented in *The Astute Investor*, rather than the efficient market hypothesis (EMH) and the random walk theory of stock prices.

Speculative Arts And Scientific Factors

The underlying rule for success in the stock market is no different than in any other speculative commercial enterprise, i.e., "buy low, sell high." Common stock should be thought of as the speculator's merchandise, only purchase common stock with sound fundamentals that are going up in price and are expected to be sold at a profit.

Speculation, when performed properly, is not gambling like betting on American roulette. Speculation is a socially necessary profession. Production, distribution and exchange risks are already present in the economy, the only question for the businessperson is who shall assume these risks. Speculators bear risks that other persons wish to lay off. Both sides of a speculative exchange may profit over an extended time period.

Eleven Key Scientific Speculative Factors

Analysis for trading in the stock market requires the understanding of the following eleven key scientific speculative factors:

1) Knowing the difference between systematic risk versus unsystematic risk.

2) Knowing what stage the overall stock market is in and knowing the long-term stock market trend.

3) Determining whether the stock market is either undervalued or overvalued.

4) Yield curves, interest rate spreads and what affect they have on the stock market.

5) Knowing the political-economic conditions and how they affect the stock market.

6) Appreciation of human nature and trader psychology.

7) Understanding how the investing public responds to the news and the discounted news theory (DNT).

8) Knowing crowd psychology and when to be contrarian.

9) Intrinsic, true, or fair value and the margin-of-safety multiple calculations for common stock evaluation.

10) Understanding the discounted market hypothesis (DMH).

11) Identifying industry rankings and intermediate-term trends using turning points.

The scientific speculative factors are either presented in *The Astute Investor*, when following the practical ten-step method for investment success, and/or in this book. Prior to becoming an astute speculator, the eleven key scientific speculative factors must be completely understood because it is impossible to become an excellent speculator without first gaining this expertise. Only then should the following three speculative arts be attempted.

Three Speculative Arts

The following three speculative arts and the techniques necessary to master these arts are crucial to becoming a successful stock market speculator:
1) How to time stock buying or short selling over the intermediate-term using turning points and trigger points.
2) How to sell or cover a stock position by taking the emotion out when using stop-loss orders and money management rules.
3) Knowing yourself and what strategy will work best for you based on your character, personality and lifestyle.
A short review of each chapter's conclusions is presented next.

Speculative Conclusions

The motivation that draws most speculators into the stock market is to become wealthy, unfortunately, this also becomes the reason for their downfall. Speculators become so obsessed about money that they cut their profits short and let their losses run. This is just the opposite of the strategy required to be a successful speculator, resulting in pain, suffering and possible bankruptcy.

The best stock market speculators think: 1) money is only a means to keep score; 2) losing periodically in the stock market is going to happen regardless of how smart I am; 3) stock trading is best treated as a fun but serious game; and 4) planning, scheduling and hard work are required to succeed. Astute speculators should be as comfortable being short in the stock market, at the right time, as they are going long—a summary discussion follows.

Short Selling

"Sell high, buy low" describes the correct procedure when short selling. The same objective as long buyers follow, however, the actions are in reverse order. Short sellers constantly test the long stock positions and the direction of the market to find the truth of the market.

Short sellers are often vilified as being un-American but astute speculators believe that without short selling markets would be even more volatile then they are currently. Short selling deflates boom-bubble buying at market tops and buying to cover creates market liquidity at panic-selling market bottoms.

The investing public and most traders speculate only on the long side of the stock market. Astute speculators should feel comfortable selling stock short, as well. Because there are so few short sellers in the stock market at any one time, the only way for short sellers to win is to have the help of those in long positions who sell their stock.

Timing on Wall Street is the primary art or "art of arts." The major concern for speculators selling stock short is always "when," the "what" to sell short is always of secondary importance and the stock's price or "how much" is received for the shorted shares is only number three in significance. Many speculators have the story right but the timing wrong and, consequently, have lost all.

Timing is the chief failing for short-sale traders, to help, wait for a trigger point. A short-sale trigger point for a short-sale candidate is typically the fulfillment of what is expected. Speculators should delay shorting a weak stock until reality, either good or bad, is confirmed at a trigger point.

Usually there are three steps in a long-term downward sloping market. The first step is the initial break where prices decline stunningly swiftly but soon recover during the first technical rally. The second step is a steady stock market decline as business conditions and earnings continually weaken. During the third step, terrible business conditions are evident—resulting in suspended dividends, bankruptcies, mass layoffs and talk by politicians about tax cuts.

The first technical rally in a long-term down market is the safest time to go short. As the market rallies back close to its market high, the ability to short common stock at an advantageous price presents itself.

Stock sold short should conform to the following SEC requirements: 1) the exchange handling the trade must be informed that the order is a short sale; 2) the sale execution must be in conformance with the uptick rule; and 3) the broker handling the sale must have borrowed the stock to make delivery at the time of the sale.

A "hard-to-borrow" short condition indicates that this stock has a very limited floating supply. The SEC uptick rule requires the short sale to take place on a plus tick or zero-plus tick from a prior transaction price. Buy ins and short squeezes are downside hazards for short sellers who should know the stock's float, short interest, short-interest-to-float and short-interest ratio prior to taking a short position.

Short sellers use 10-K and 10-Q reports which explain the business plan and match the financials to the plan to identify the crucial numbers to monitor. Short sellers have an advantage over security analysts on Wall Street because security analysts seldom bother to closely scrutinize financial statements.

Telltale signs of a short-sale candidate include: 1) accounts receivable growing faster than sales; 2) prepaid expenses increasing for no apparent reason; 3) accumulated depreciation dropping quickly; 4) fast inventory growth; 5) deferred charges; and 6) inflated goodwill.

General Motors Corporation (GM) is analyzed as an example of a possible short sale candidate. Expected trigger points on when to short GM common stock are listed and discussed.

Buying Common Stock

The keys to speculative success are: 1) "buy low, sell high"; 2) minimize losses; 3) earn substantial profits; and 4) steer clear of chronic trading. The important concerns for the stock purchase decision are complex and include, in this order: 1) timing, i.e., whether to buy now or later on; 2) identifying which stock to purchase; and 3) what price should be paid for the stock. Making a purchase commitment on a stock is more complicated but less emotional than concluding it.

When buying, the ability to say "yes or no" is paramount. Astute speculators always keep a cash reserve available for extraordinarily rare trading opportunities. Once a position is entered into, it is impossible to remain completely objective because judgment becomes biased due to the very human need of self-justifying the initial commitment. Develop and follow a plan and schedule but let the market action, i.e., trading volume, turning points and stock price tell you if the plan is progressing properly.

Patience is key to making money in the stock market. Waiting for just the right time to purchase stock is often the most important speculative trait to possess. Speculators typically pay too much when buying stock. Purchasing stock at too high a price creates, in the vernacular of Wall Street, a "poor market position." To help counteract this, use buy-limit orders when purchasing stock.

Purchase stock in leading companies in the top 25 percent of industry rankings when the overall market is in stage 2 or 3. Commit to making the required examination of the company's intrinsic, true or fair (ITF) value, market value capitalization, bargain value and margin-of-safety multiple prior to purchase, rather than afterwards. Determine the price to be purchased and what you plan to do if the stock advances or declines in price, write it in your journal, then do it.

Use the following eight rules for purchasing common stock when the market's technical condition is positive and the stock is held in "strong hands."

1. Buy common stock when the S&P 500 Index long-term market trend is making a transition during stage 2 or is trending upward in stage 3.

2. Buy common stock in leading companies that are included in the top 25 percent of industry rankings.

3. At turning points, purchase common stock in leading companies that you know about and understand.

4. At a buying trigger point, purchase only listed common stock on the major exchanges, e.g., NYSE, NASDAQ, or AMEX.

5. Purchase undervalued common stock with a margin-of-safety multiple above 2.0 with good ten additional crucial factors.

6. Purchase high-priced common stock hitting an all-time high price for the first time, the higher the stock's price the better, of at least $10 dollars per share.

7. Purchase high potential companies that Philip Fisher says are either, "prosperous and gifted," or "prosperous because they are gifted."

8. Determine the long-term and intermediate-term technical condition of the market and whether the stock is in "strong hands" or "weak hands"— only purchase common stock held in "strong hands."

Selling Or Covering Stock

The second art of speculation, after correct timing, is knowing how to sell stock or cover a short position once attained. Failure is not the opposite of success in the stock market, when the resulting loss does not knock the speculator out of the game. The fundamental stock selling or covering rule is, "Astute speculators learn to like the act of trading and monetary success more than they fear criticism and/or small failures."

Watching as the stock market fluctuates, the amateur speculator fears completing the trade because that would remove it from the dream state to one of reality. Once having purchased or sold stock short, it is emotionally difficult to sell or cover the position—even for professionals. A major difference between amateur and professional speculators is that when conditions are right to sell or cover, professionals act while amateurs waver.

If the number of persons that Wall Street made rich were written down in books, it would fill only a few volumes. If the number of persons first made rich by the stock market and then subsequently made poor were written down in books, these books would fill an entire library. Those who lose all in the stock market normally have ability and are good traders, but have the fatal character flaw of overreaching or overplaying their position and not selling or covering when they should.

While it is impossible to know when the absolute right time to sell or cover is, the goal is to prevent selling or covering at the much easier to know "wrong time." Selling or covering is prevented at the wrong time, defined as having huge unsustainable losses, by using stop-loss orders which are wonderful defense and offer protection against a trader's non-action tendencies and human weaknesses.

The stop-loss order should always be set to exit long or short positions automatically. Use intraday prices, rather than closing stock prices, to set stop-loss orders no more than a few points or 10 percent away from the transaction price at support or resistance levels. The reward-to-risk ratio should be equal to or greater than four, when either long or short, i.e., expect to make at least four times what is being risked on the stop-loss order.

The stop-loss order price point on a stock is never to be lowered in price if long or increased in price if short. The stop-loss order price point is always to be moved to decrease risk, never to increase the risk on a trade, i.e., speculators, do not second guess yourselves.

Progressive stop-loss orders should be continually raised if long or lowered if short as the stock position becomes more and more profitable, to ensure that increased earnings are captured. Because risk capital is the lifeblood of trading, it is imperative that this capital always be in effective circulation; therefore, use time stops to sell listless stock drifters.

Trigger Points

Markets and stock prices can move based on perceptions and expectations for a better tomorrow over a long period of time. In order to make a major change in investor perceptions, a catalyst or trigger point is required.

High expectations for much better times ahead are often held by the investing public when valuing stock, supported by stock market pundits. Perception of what is hoped for takes on the guise of reality. It is human nature to desire wealth and that is accomplished in the stock market by dreaming about the future. A speculator's perception is often better than reality and a stock's price reaches its highest level when trader's expectations are the highest, not when the ultimate reality is achieved.

When an active stock reaches an all-time high price, not just a fifty-two week price high, this is a good indication that things are going well at the company and an indicator that the company should be further investigated. The investing public rarely, as high as 98 percent, purchases high priced stock that are hitting an all-time high in price. Therefore, a high priced stock (over $100 dollars per share) hitting a new all-time price high is typically held in "strong hands" and is a good purchase trigger point.

A trigger point for an overvalued or undervalued stock is typically the fulfillment of what is expected. Delay purchasing or shorting a stock candidate until reality, either good or bad, is confirmed. Speculator expectations then become frustrated and no longer hold their allure when perceived reality becomes real, realized or not. IPO, single-product company, and bank trigger points are explained. When reality and castle-in-the-air perceptions collide, reality in the stock market always wins.

Tape Reading

The stock market tape is always reliable. Judgment becomes suspect the instant a speculator makes up his or her mind that they know more about the stock market than what is represented on the tape. Successful tape reading is a study in determining whether the buy-side or the sell-side has the most forceful power in the market at that time and then having the courage to participate on that side of the market. Tape reading is an exercise in anticipating price changes based on price and trading volume transactions.

Tape reading is analyzing which direction the stock price is moving, irrespective of momentary reversals. The crucial factor for analysis is the action of the trading volume, price action is secondary, what enlightens is the amount of money going into either the buying or the selling of stock. Unbalanced or asymmetrical bid and offer quotations, i.e., 5000 shares bid and 200 shares offered, as the stock advances in price, is a good sign that interest in this stock is increasing.

Trading Volume

Interpreting what is happening in the stock market is best done by considering trading volume behavior, not simply by looking at stock prices. Price action indicates but is secondary in importance to trading volume which validates the buy-side or sell-side movement. Because the investing public and amateur speculators only concern themselves with price changes, they miss valid stock trends that are confirmed by a significant increase trading volume.

Search for and recognize "good steady volume" activity on the tape. If an inactive stock all of a sudden becomes active for approximately four weeks and the number of shares traded goes up by at least four times normal volume each week—the higher the percentage increase in volume the better—this is an indication of abnormal positive interest in this stock.

Understanding trading volume is crucial to understanding a stock's trend and turning point. It is the amount of money going into the move that chronicles supply and demand imbalances. Trading volume determinations are conditional and best learned by experience.

Turning Points

Turning points may be thought of as the market losing momentum over the long or intermediate-term trend, either up or down. The goal is to make the trade close to the exact turning point when the market or stock then starts going the opposite direction. Turning points typically occur on heavy share trading volume but with no headway in price.

The length of the accumulation or distribution phase in the stock market depends upon the importance of the turn. Long-term turning points take longer to develop than intermediate-term turning points.

The goal of an astute speculator is to recognize the timing of the turn and then to trade along with stock market professionals and not trade on the side of the investing public or amateur speculators.

Stock Market Sectors And Industry Groups

Corporations with shared business characteristics are sorted into twelve stock market sectors. Sectors do not have market diversification but companies within each sector are correlated and display comparable stock price performance.

Companies within sectors are expected to move together over the intermediate term within the long-term stock market trend. Cyclical sectors either lead, are coincident with, or lag the long-term trend in the overall stock market.

Companies within sectors are further sorted into anywhere from 100-225 industry groups. Industry groups are studied because once momentum begins in a industry it tends to continue over the intermediate term, consequently, money can be made by speculating along with industry group trends. Buy leading companies in the top 25 percent ranking of industries and sell short laggard second or third-tier companies in the bottom 25 percent ranking of industries, at the correct time.

Momentum Investing

The foundation of momentum investing is that proven stock winners continue to win while stock losers continue to lose. Momentum investing strategy results directly refute the efficient market hypothesis (EMH), i.e., the thinking that speculating in the stock market is like betting on American roulette where stock prices are independent random variables.

Momentum investing focuses on the momentum of either relative price strength or relative earnings strength. Momentum investing may be called growth investing where media and investor attention feed on itself. Valuations are much less important than other factors such as price movement, i.e., it should not be assumed that a high price-to-earnings (P/E) stock with momentum will not go even higher in price.

Momentum Speculating

There are five major differences between momentum investing and momentum speculating: 1) momentum investing does not concern itself with first identifying the long-term trend in the market which typically leads to disastrous momentum portfolio results once the overall market reverses and goes into a long-term downtrend; 2) momentum investing does not focus on the intermediate term; 3) nor does momentum investing first identify the highest ranking industries prior to investing in a high momentum stock; 4) momentum investing does not calculate a margin-of-safety multiple for each stock under investigation; and 5) momentum investing does not consider taking short-sale positions.

Momentum speculating is recommended and used to identify intermediate-term industry trends for speculative success by looking at the long-term stock market trend, industry ranking, and making the intrinsic value and margin-of-safety multiple calculations for the company. Nine momentum speculating fundamentals for evaluation are listed.

Positive industry return momentum occurs when common stock in that industry outperform the average stock based on relative price or earnings strength. Momentum of an individual common stock on its own, without the benefit of other companies in a high ranking industry, is not consistent enough to make a significant amount of money because the individual stock's trend may quickly change direction due to the company's unsystematic risk, industry momentum or long-term stock market trend.

Past six-month industry price momentum is a good predictor to outsized stock returns up to twelve months in the future and should give astute speculators an intermediate-term planning horizon target to when profits should be taken to lock in the largest speculative gains.

In general, during a long-term upward trend in the stock market, buy the wonderfully managed quickly growing company with sound fundamentals in an exciting new industry and, during a long-term downtrend, sell short mediocre companies with poor fundamentals in distressed industries.

Money Management

Money management focuses upon position size, or how many stock shares should be acquired in relation to the total amount of risk capital available to the speculator, and upon the downside risk of stock trading where speculators plan for the possibility of trading losses by using risk-reduction strategies. There are three main goals in money management: 1) speculators should never put their way of life at risk; 2) only risk as much money as will keep the speculator's mind clear; and 3) keep the money once earned.

Money management rules are emphasized because it is not how much money speculators earn that is most important, instead, it is how much traders do not lose that determines speculative success. Money management rules focus on position size or how many shares should be acquired in relation to the amount of total risk capital available to the speculator.

Money management determines the risk of the trade based on the percentage of the total risk capital put into the trade. The following five speculative money management rules are presented with the highest priority rule listed first:

I. Save Half The Profits: Making money in the stock market is relatively easy, it is the end game of keeping the money earned that is difficult.

II. Learn To "Say No" And Keep A Cash Reserve: An astute speculator has neither the product or industry knowledge of the company trader or the low transaction costs nor the transaction speed of the floor trader, but has one overwhelming advantage—he or she does not have to speculate unless all the probabilities are in his or her favor—the power to "say no" is an invaluable asset. Speculators keep a cash reserve in order to take advantage of extraordinarily rare market conditions when they occur.

III. Protect Capital: Do not focus on just making money, instead, speculators should focus on not losing their risk capital. Success in the stock market is dependent upon not losing a great deal rather than on winning a great deal, i.e., defense not offence is central. Speculators should protect their risk capital, make reward-to-risk ratio calculations that are at least four-to-one and always use stop-loss orders.

IV. Focus Speculating: Not every trade makes money. Drawdown is the term used to describe the probable amount of money lost as a percentage of the total risk capital used during trading in order to achieve the expected returns. The recommended number of companies that astute speculators should trade in at any one time is three, each representing 25 percent of total risk capital. This leaves 25 percent of total risk capital as a cash reserve. Approximately 15 targeted trades are required to earn the astute speculative goal of +33 percent per year.

V. Stay With The Winners: Speculate only in the high ranking industry leader on the way up. The second or third-tier industry laggards on the way up should be the leaders on the way down and sold short. Let both long and short position winners run for large gains.

Money management is concerned with the speculative risk of the trade based upon trade size in relation to the total risk capital, drawdown, reward-to-risk ratio calculations, setting stop-loss order price points and the individual speculator's emotional trading zone.

Program Trading

Program trading is an arbitrage strategy where the purchase of equities on one exchange for instantaneous resale on another exchange captures profits from any inter-market price variations. Institutions rely on program trading to purchase or sell baskets of common stock as efficiently and effectively as possible.

Approximately 59 percent of the trading on the NYSE, NASDAQ and AMEX is program trading performed by a computer based solely upon relative prices from one exchange market to another. The computer programming orders are generated on price divergences only, the reasons are immaterial and the fundamentals of whether the stock is undervalued or overvalued are unknown.

Program trading utilizes computer algorithms to implement the following four strategies: 1) a specific portfolio investment objective; 2) duration averaging; 3) portfolio insurance; and most importantly 4) index arbitrage which is an equalizer between the cash or spot equities markets and the futures & options derivative markets.

As an index arbitrage example, S&P 500 Index futures and the underlying common stock in the S&P 500 Index are at the same fair value, when, new information is foreseen which moves both markets upward. The futures market normally reacts faster than the prices for the underlying common stock, consequently, the need for index arbitrage to bring both stock prices and derivative prices back in line at fair value. The expensive S&P 500 Index futures are sold coincidently with purchasing a basket of the S&P 500 Index common stock.

Character And Personality Traits

The stock market can be beaten for those in the know. The stock market does not defeat the speculator, instead, it is the speculator's own unreasoning instincts and inherent ruinous predispositions that cannot be prevailed over that are ultimately the reason for his or her speculative failures.

A speculator's character and personality determines, as much as anything else, success or failure in the stock market. Traders have to address the unique human vulnerabilities within themselves that jeopardize their own success and find a unique speculative approach that works for their own character, personality and lifestyle, additionally, they have to determine this for themselves. Not always expecting to win and being able to admit a mistake are all crucial for speculative success.

Selecting the strategic approach to speculating should be matched with personal predispositions, motivations, temperament, disposition and ambitions. Ten character traits of the best stock market speculators are summarized as follows:

1) The best speculators have discipline, know the speculative bylaws and have the self-assurance to remain obedient to these bylaws.

2) Success in the stock market is not an option, it is the only legitimate goal, speculators require a passion to succeed.

3) Self-control is used to ensure that in the stock market, money takes precedence over the need for recognition and to save face, consequently, mistakes are freely admitted.

4) One-valued orientations that always require winning, perfection or optimization are rejected and being close enough by attaining the more secure middle two thirds in any market move is embraced.

5) Patience is rehearsed and practiced because the stock market cannot be beaten with chronic trading.

6) Once the risks are known and analyzed, winning traders have the utmost confidence in their judgment and have the courage to act properly— regardless of the trade's eventual outcome.

7) Traders always keep a journal, analyze all their trades and determine in writing what worked or did not work and why.

8) The best speculators never take tips and prefer playing a lone hand by planning and scheduling their stock market operations in order not to trade impulsively.

9) The best speculators practice humility and reject pride of opinion, i.e., the tape confirms what should be done in the market. To achieve success, thinking and beliefs leading to poor results have to be changed, i.e., the best speculators do not stay in an intellectual rut.

10) The best speculators are always reading, always learning and trying to improve their robust methodology and plans and schedules through observation and testing.

Astute speculators resolve to develop the above ten character traits, be completely devoid of all nerves and acquire the iron nerve necessary to be an excellent trader.

Speculative Bylaws

Speculative bylaws encompass trading traditions and regulations that have served stock traders well in the past and are expected to continue to serve them well in the future. The following ten bylaws govern how astute speculators should behave when trading in the stock market. They are vitally important and should be considered commandments.

The speculative bylaws are listed beginning with the most important first. The best strategy to making money is to simply follow the ten bylaws:
1) Keep the mind clear.

2) Have a plan and schedule, do the analysis, do not trade impulsively.

3) Trade at trigger points.

4) Use reward-to risk calculations, stop-loss orders and money management rules. Cut losses quickly and learn to let profits run.

5) Know yourself, select an approach to trading that matches your character, personality and lifestyle.

6) Let trading volume, turning points and market conditions confirm your plan and schedule through tape reading. Discipline your ego by being willing to admit mistakes freely.

7) Judge the news based on your assessment of what the average speculator will think about the average speculator's appraisal of market or stock expectations.

8) Do not trade on margin.

9) Do not be a chronic trader.

10) Do not obsess about making money in the stock market.

Speculators disregard any of these bylaws at their own peril, especially when first starting out as a speculative novice. After many years of trading experience, when speculators know they are experts, the bylaws may be bent—but never broken.

Reinforce The Bylaws

A good way for speculators to reinforce the discipline required to consistently follow the ten speculative bylaws is to sign a contract with themselves. In the contract speculators pledge to follow the bylaws, regardless of the trade's eventual outcome. If the trading outcome is poor, the speculator is not at fault—the bylaws are held responsible. This is a good way to save face with yourself. If the bylaws are broken for any reason, a constructive penalty specified in the contract must be paid upon the speculator's honor.

Do not quickly read and then forget the bylaws. Only a small fraction of stock speculators who try, succeed. The ten speculative bylaws give speculators a huge leg up on the uninformed; however, as Rene Descartes instructs, it is the application of the bylaws that is most crucial. Only skilled speculators will take the bylaws to heart and implement them properly. To only the truly talented will these bylaws become truly advantageous.

Simulator Trading

Mental preparation requires practice runs through all of the potential risks prior to taking the stock position. The best novice traders what to feel they have won the speculative game prior to beginning, consequently, they use simulator trading to practice. Successful simulator trading is considered a final examination before going out into the pure capitalistic world to risk your own hard earned money in the stock market.

Once simulator trading is consistently three times more profitable than the S&P 500 Index over the same time period, speculators may graduate to trading with limited funds. Once small odd-lot trades are consistently three times more profitable than the returns for the S&P 500 Index over the same time period, with trading being made with conviction and no longer jangling the nerves or upsetting the stomach, only then should traders consider themselves a full-fledged speculator and move up to trading round lots.

Speculative Strategies

How each speculator responds to the pressures of trading in a volatile stock market is unique, therefore, it is required that each of us devise a speculative strategy that works best for ourselves. Only we can judge our own nerves and how much stress can be undertaken when trading common stock.

Selecting the strategic approach to speculating should be matched with personal predispositions, motivations, temperament, disposition and ambitions. Because we are our own biggest competitor, knowing who we are and what is the best personal approach when speculating is a crucial factor for our success. The following three successful strategies are presented as possible models:

Strategy A: Panic Or Contrarian Specialist—A transition from investing to speculating. The long-pull semi-investor feels more comfortable waiting until the market hits a long-term bottom and prefers putting his or her risk capital in leading, high-quality companies with stellar track records.

The panic or contrarian specialist combines the margin-of-safety multiple, ten additional crucial factors, the six-step contrarian analysis and the four additional contrarian factors when evaluating leading companies. At the beginning of stage 3, when the market begins its long-term uptrend, allocate equal amounts of the total risk capital (i.e., 33 percent for each stock) when purchasing three leading, high-quality companies with stellar track records.

Strategy B: Box Theory—For the emotional trader who wants to reduce the unwanted, upsetting news of the stock market to zero. Open, high, low and closing prices for each stock tracked are entered into a journal and studied. A "good steady volume" increase of 400 percent for approximately four weeks over normal average weekly volume is excellent evidence of changed circumstances for a stock.

Box theory money management rules are strictly enforced and the "quick-loss weapon" stop-loss order ensures that speculators never lose sleep over a losing stock position. A techno-fundamentalist theory is used which relies on identifying a new vibrant industry and a fundamental assessment of the leading company's high earnings growth rate in that industry.

Stock prices of active issues tend to move within a series of boxes that stack next to one another like an up staircase in an up-trending stock market. Once the dimensions of the box are determined, the stock's price can act anyway it wants within the confines of its box and is considered normal.

Strategy C: Tandem Trading—For the iron nerved speculator who waits patiently until the proof of the correctness of a trade is confirmed and believes that "timing is everything." Tandem speculators have enough experience to look at their journal price and volume entries to see recognizable chart patterns emerge. Changing volume proclaims a new condition or an abnormality is about to occur in the stock market.

Tandem trading requires comparing both the leading company and the second leader sister stock in the same industry. Pivot points or turning points are price support and resistance levels. Reversal pivot points mark the end of a long-term trend. Continuation pivot points are intermediate-term trend reversal points which indicate that a counter trend is ending and the intermediate-term trend will now track along with the long-term trend in the market.

All the tandem trading fundamental and timing conditions have to be in the speculator's favor, including:
1) The market's long-term trend.
2) A high or low industry ranking.
3) Matching the leader and sister stock chart patterns.
4) Purchase the high ranking industry leader or short the low ranking industry laggard company.

5) The prior steps all must support one another.

6) Use reversal and continuation pivot points for clues on timing.

7) Set appropriate stop-loss order price points.

Each speculator may select one of the three successful strategies above to implement, or mix and match different aspects of the three to find a strategy that works best for their own character, personality and lifestyle.

Futures Market

The futures market serves hedgers (producers and end users) and speculators with standardized commodity and financial futures contracts. Hedgers and speculators in the futures market attempt to forecast, for successive months over the next twelve months for most futures contracts, the price of soft commodities (agricultural and food), physical commodities (energy and metals) and financial futures (equity, foreign currency, and interest rate indexes). Both the buyer and seller are committed and obligated to satisfy the terms of the futures contract on its final settlement date.

The futures exchanges bring buyers and sellers together—whether they are hedgers or speculators. The four main duties of a futures exchange are: 1) price settlement; 2) contract standardization; 3) buying and selling liquidity; and 4) the transfer of risk.

Commodity futures require the seller to deliver a particular commodity of a specific grade and quantity to a certain destination on a fixed delivery date, or its cash equivalent. The commodity underlying the futures contract is termed the "spot" and trades in the spot or cash market at the "spot price." Futures contacts use margin.

The seven major futures exchanges and their websites are listed and described, i.e., CME, NYMEX, NYBOT, MACE, MGEX, KCBT and PBOT. The mechanics of the futures trade for each exchange is handled by a clearinghouse corporation.

A hedge fund may invest in common stock, bonds, commodities, equity indexes, interest rate indexes, foreign currency indexes, or in foreign stock markets. Typically the hedge fund manager is permitted to borrow money, buy long or sell short and use futures, options and options on futures.

Hedging is practiced by producers, end users and speculators who attempt to increase profits and/or to reduce their risk by protecting their position in both the futures and the spot or cash market. Hedging only approximates conditions for a producer or end user and only protects against major risk factors in the market. Comprehensive coverage of all risk is not possible using hedging since the risk of commodity price fluctuation is merely exchanged for the smaller risk of a relative basis change between cash and futures prices.

Futures price spread strategies for commodities are based on seasonality. Futures price spreads of the identical commodity between different futures contract expiration dates fluctuate. Prices may not change in an identical fashion on different futures exchanges, therefore, price spread strategies may be used profitably. Example futures price spread strategies include: intra-commodity spread, inter-commodity spread and straddles.

The futures market requires a long learning curve in order to be consistently successful. Unless the speculator is willing to spend their entire professional career understanding and trading futures in a specific commodity, such as agricultural, food, energy, or metals, trading commodities without professional help from a commodities expert is not recommended for astute speculators.

Options Market

A holder of a stock option has the right but not the obligation to either purchase or sell a stock at a predetermined price over a specified time period. Listed options are traded on options exchanges and require the following five pieces of information to describe the option, e.g., "2 INTC Sept 20 call." This is a call option for Intel Corporation for two options contacts each representing 100 shares of the underlying stock or 200 shares total, at a striking price of $20 dollars per share, due to expire on Saturday following the last trading day which occurs on the third Friday in September.

The five major options exchanges (i.e., CBOE, AMEX, ISE, PCX and PHLX) are listed and described where common stock options and equity, industry, foreign currency and interest rate index options are traded. The Options Clearing Corporation (OCC) is the clearinghouse corporation for the above five options exchanges.

The options price, in order of importance, is based upon the underlying stock's price, the options striking price, the length of time remaining until the option reaches its expiration date, the underlying stock's volatility, the risk free interest rate and the cash dividend. Options are termed a wasting asset.

The following call and put strategies are presented and explained: call buying, covered call writing, uncovered call writing, protected short sale, reverse hedge, straddle buying, ratio writing, ratio call spreads, vertical, horizontal and diagonal spread strategies, put buying and collars. Good options strategies with the possibility for unlimited gain and for limited loss are recommended for use: i.e., call buying, put buying, protected short sale, reverse hedge and straddle buying.

Options On Futures

Options on futures are derivatives on derivatives and twice removed from the underlying spot or cash market. First is the commodity or financial cash market, second is futures on the cash market and third is the options on futures on the cash market. Options on futures give the buyer of an option the right but not the obligation to either buy or sell a futures contract at a set price, irrespective of the actual futures contract closing price.

There is a major difference between speculating in stock index futures or stock options and in common stock on the NYSE, NASDAQ, and AMEX stock exchanges. Common stock ownership on the stock exchanges have no fixed expiration dates as with financial futures and stock options which permits time to be the speculator's friend. Put and call stock option premiums are expensive and the same protection is achieved in the stock market at no cost by using stop-loss orders.

Eight Astute Speculator Firsts

The Astute Speculator offers eight speculative book firsts. Approximately forty percent of the material presented in this book has a firm foundation in the referenced classical speculative literature found in the bibliography. The Internet websites listed, to locate data to run models, account in importance for an additional ten percent of the material presented.

About fifty percent of this book represents new material or material presented in a new context. A summary listing of the eight firsts in *The Astute Speculator* are:

Conclusion

1) A stock market taxonomy categorizes the stock market for better communication, category 6 in the taxonomy is covered here.

2) Presentation of the eleven key scientific factors of speculation and the three speculative arts for success are explained and techniques for solution presented.

3) How to use corporate intrinsic values and margin-of-safety multiple calculations to help identify common stock to sell short.

4) The importance of recognizing stock turning points by using trading volume and how to determine trigger points are presented to help accomplish the stock market's primary "art of arts," i.e., correct timing.

5) Momentum speculating is presented for the first time and based on momentum investing but further incorporates long-term trends and industry rankings to identify intermediate-term industry trends. Nine momentum speculating fundamentals are listed.

6) Ten speculative bylaws are presented and explained which should be followed by astute speculators to help ensure speculative success. Sign a contract with yourself to help enforce the bylaws, upon your honor. The ten bylaws may be bent but never broken.

7) Focus speculating uses sound fundamental analysis for selecting undervalued stock to buy or overvalued stock to sell short. The recommended number of companies that astute speculators should trade in at any one time is three, each representing 25 percent of total risk capital. This leaves 25 percent of total risk capital as a cash reserve. Approximately 15 targeted trades are required to earn the astute speculative goal of +33 percent per year.

8) Three separate and distinct strategies, within the context of the astute speculator methodology, are presented to help astute speculators develop a winning strategy for themselves which matches their character, personality and lifestyle.

The knowledge presented in *The Astute Speculator* is practical and self-empowering, helps speculators feel confident in taking control when speculating with their own money and aids in building wealth and a secure future for themselves and their families.

Continued Communication

The astute speculator website address is <u>www.theastuteinvestor.net</u>, go there to read e-market letters, book reviews, articles, press releases and to contact the author.

Glossary

FINANCIAL, INVESTMENT AND SPECULATIVE word definitions are found at www.investorwords.com, www.trading-glossary.com, or by using the referenced dictionary by Barbara J. Etzel.

Accounts Receivable. Customers who purchase goods or services using credit have their payment due amounts recorded in accounts receivable under current assets on a corporation's balance sheet. Accounts receivable become cash when customers pay their bills.

Algorithms. For **program trading,** optimally solves a mathematical model representing a large trading problem by using a goal seeking objective function and a progressive or iterative problem-solving solution methodology. Relies on computers to calculate algorithms designed by human beings, making possible quick decisions to take advantage of the fast changing stock and derivative markets.

Amateur Speculator. Amateur speculators trade based upon incorrect theories or principles that are completely at odds with demonstrated successful practice and scientific study. Amateur speculators do not take the time to weigh facts, learn conditions, or think through the consequences of their actions. Amateur speculators typically sell stock too soon, capitulate and repurchase the same stock at a higher price, buy more stock as the price sinks during a market downturn and finally lose money by selling everything on an impulse at a market bottom. Amateur speculators believe that luck or tips dominate activity in the stock market, willingly overtrade on margin with inadequate capital, take profits too early, trade impulsively and become **chronic traders**. A major difference between amateur speculators and professional speculators is that when conditions are right to sell, professional speculators act while amateurs waver.

Astute Investor. A person who has foresight and is critically discerning, shrewd, subtle, sagacious and keenly aware of what information and facts are the most significant in the field of investing. An investor who plans and knows where to locate website data necessary to run appropriate investment models and how to interpret these models' results for decision making when investing over the **long term**. A seeker of the truth who possesses market vision, investment intelligence and stock market experience while using the practical **ten-step method for investment success**.

Astute Speculator. First and foremost, a person who is an **astute investor**. A speculator in common stock over the **intermediate term**, trading either long or short, who understands the eleven key scientific speculative factors for success and excels at the three **speculative arts**. An astute speculator has foresight, a cool temperament, a clear mind, patience, iron nerve, discipline, is shrewd, humble, keenly aware of what information and data are the most significant in the field of stock market speculation and has the courage to act properly. Astute speculators plan, schedule, work hard and know where to locate data necessary to make necessary calculations and how to interpret model results for proper decision making. Astute speculators are seekers of truth, possess market vision, speculative intelligence, have practical stock market experience and can take appropriate action. Astute speculators recognize the importance of leading, coincident and lagging **sectors** and **industry group** rankings when identifying leading stock for purchase or lagging stock to sell short. Astute speculators follow **speculative bylaws**, use **money management rules**, trade on **turning points** and **trigger points**, perform **tape reading** and realize that price action indicates, whereas, trading volume validates.

Averaging Down. Continuing to add to a losing stock position by naively buying more stock as the stock's price declines in order to lower the average price of a stock previously purchased. Averaging down should be avoided.

Bargain Value Calculation. The **intrinsic, true, or fair value** for a corporation is compared to the **market value capitalization** to calculate its bargain value using a systematic valuation methodology. If the intrinsic, true, or fair value is more than the market value capitalization, then the bargain value is positive. A positive bargain value signifies an undervalued company and a negative bargain value signifies an overvalued company. The calculated **margin-of-safety multiple** and bargain value for each corporation are rank ordered, highest to lowest values, for comparison to make investments based on the **margin-of-safety** principle.

Basic Net Earnings Per Share (EPS). The Basic EPS figure is a fundamental measure of corporate valuation. Ratio of net income (less preferred stock dividends) divided by total shares outstanding. The EPS figure is reported after net income on the income statement [See **Diluted Net Earnings Per Share (DEPS)**]

Basis. The relative difference between the movement of spot or cash prices and futures prices over the term of the futures contract. A perfect hedge has a constant basis.

Bulge. A fast run-up in the price of the stock market, an individual stock price, or a **futures contract** price.

Business Speculation. Because the business endeavor is new, it may seem hazardous; however, the a priori expectation is that the product or service is either necessary or wanted and has the probability of an outsized profit when sold. New product, process, market and financial conditions are systematically analyzed and determined to be beneficial to the speculator.

Buy Ins. The brokerage firm informs the short seller of required higher fees to remain in the current short position or warns that a "buy in" is now possible. Unless the short seller can locate stock to borrow on their own, the brokerage house covers the stock on the short seller's behalf in the open market without the short sellers knowing about the transaction until the next business day.

Buy-Limit Order. An order to the brokerage firm that the customer's transaction be made at a specified price or better. The limit order to buy is set at a limit price below the current price, and all shares are purchased at that limit price or a lower price.

Cash Flow Statement (CFS). Tracks the actual money flow in time through the corporation. The CFS has the following three sections: 1) Cash from Operating Activities; 2) Cash from Investing Activities; and 3) Cash from Financing Activities.

Castle-In-The-Air Theory of Speculation. Expression coined by John Maynard Keynes (1883-1946) to describe how optimistic speculators behave in driving up a stock's price. Regardless of what reality is presently or expected to be twenty years from now, realize that a company's stock price can veer very far from its **intrinsic, true, or fair value**. Keynes' speculative strategy is sophisticated yet subtle: i.e., think about what the average investor will think about the average investor or crowd's assessment of market or stock expectations and trade along with that determination.

Chart Patterns. Traders' human nature does not materially change through time. So while the traders themselves do change, how traders act and react as a consequence of worry, hope, greed, fear and ignorance remains constant. This common reaction to trader's emotions produces recurring shapes or price patterns that constantly repeat themselves when viewed on stock charts or graphs, e.g., a **double top or bottom reversal pattern**.

Chronic Traders. Speculators who feel they have to trade frequently. **Amateur speculators** are obsessed with the idea of having their money working all the time. It is futile to try to force the market to produce profits through chronic trading, instead, only buy into an expected large stock gain. Stock market success is only determined by the amount of money made and kept and not how often trades are made. To trade stock just because cash is at hand is an inexcusable blunder.

Clearinghouse Corporation. A clearinghouse corporation assists in trade executions by conveying money, handing deliveries and certifying the accomplishment of all contracts for members on a **futures exchange** or **options exchange**. Each clearinghouse corporation assumes the responsibility for all trades made on their member's exchange.

Confirming Indicators. To determine the **long-term** trend in the U.S. stock market, follow the **S&P 500 Index Nine Month Moving Average (MA) Trend Line**. Confirming indicators, although not all required, help substantiate the stage 1 through stage 4 **market trends**.

Contingency Orders. Allows a stock or futures speculator to initially put in multiple orders that are dependent upon one another and if one order is completed then the other orders are automatically cancelled, a.k.a., "if-then orders."

Contrarian, Being. An investor who desires, at the correct time, not to invest along with the crowd by purchasing good common stock when prices are low and selling common stock when prices are high. Investors should not use a self-selected market adviser's strategy to being contrarian which is just another form of taking stock tips, but instead use the practical **ten-step method for investment success.**

Current Ratio. Total current assets divided by total current liabilities from a corporation's balance sheet. As a general guideline, the current ratio should be higher than two.

Debt-to-Equity Ratio. A measure of the capitalization structure of a corporation and whether debt is being used wisely. Total liabilities divided by total stockholder's equity which are both available on the balance sheet. A general guideline—although this may change with financial institutions or utilities—is most companies should stay below a debt to equity ratio of 1.00.

Delta. Specifies how much call options will either increase or decrease in value when the underlying stock changes by one point in price, a.k.a., the "hedge ratio."

Diluted Net Earnings Per Share (DEPS). The denominator for the **basic EPS** is expanded to include all convertible bonds, convertible preferred stock, warrants and stock options. If and when these shares are exercised, they dilute the basic EPS figure. This is a caution for investors for that possible eventuality.

Discounted Market Hypothesis (DMH). The discounted market hypothesis (DMH) has the strongest form of market effectiveness—security prices encompass all past prices, all published information and all of the information available to investors anywhere. All expected scheduled news is fully discounted and unexpected news that affects the stock market has already been partially discounted by the marketplace. The **Life And**

Discounted News Theory (DNT). The movement of a stock's price prior to an expected scheduled news occurrence is referred to as **discounting the news**. This explains how the stock market looks ahead to predict coming **political-economic conditions** using the **expected news**

discounting process. All news, whether expected or unexpected, has already been either fully or partially discounted by the stock market, by investors' actions and/or non-actions. The discounted news theory supports the **discounted market hypothesis.**

Discounting. The premise is that the stock market is a "discounting mechanism." Stock markets look ahead to what will happen in the future—at a stock market top, as much as the next six to twelve months—and reacts based on investor expectations. The discounting premise supports **discounting the news.**

Discounting The News. A prior bidding up or selling down of stock prices by professional stock traders, usually over the short or intermediate term, in anticipation of either good or bad news about a company, economic factors, or political conditions. Discounting the news is also practiced when anticipating government pronouncements or actions or any other expected occurrence which affects the stock market. Discounting the news is the premise for the **expected news discounting process** which supports the **discounted news theory**.

Discount Rate, Risk-Free. The rate at which the expected future **free cash flow** is discounted to calculate the corporation's present-worth or **intrinsic, true, or fair value**. The 30-year Treasury bond (T-bond) interest rate is used as the risk-free discount rate because the 30-year T-bond is free of credit risk, exceptionally liquid and extends over the super-long-term planning horizon.

Double Top or Bottom Reversal Pattern. At a market top, a two peak **chart pattern** occurs on a monthly graph at two separate points in time that looks like a upside-down letter W—normally two to six months apart. On a stock chart/graph with almost the same intraday price highs, double tops happen when the S&P 500 Index is rolling over at a long-term market high. At a long-term market bottom, a double bottom occurs on a monthly chart when two troughs that look like the letter W happen on two separate occasions—usually two to six months apart. On a chart with almost the same intraday price lows, double bottoms occur as the S&P 500 Index is forming a base and beginning a overall market upturn. Both are **confirming indicators** to the **S&P 500 Index Nine Month Moving Average Trend Line**.

Drawdown. The probable amount of money lost, as a percentage of total risk capital, during trading in order to achieve the expected returns.

Drawdown increases as the percentage amount of risk capital committed to any one trade is increased.

Due Diligence. Investors are expected to consider properly and thoroughly all possible factors to determine whether an investment or speculative position is suitable immediately prior to the outlay being made. This requires investigating the **political-economic conditions, yield curve** and **industry group ranking** in the stock market, including a company's **intrinsic, true, or fair value**, its **market value capitalization, bargain value and margin-of-safety multiple**. All information and data used for **investing** and **speculating** should be judged for accuracy, omissions and misstatements.

Efficient Market Hypothesis (EMH). The theory of the efficient capital market to describe the overall stock market which relies on the **random walk theory (RWT)** as a way to represent seemingly random daily movements of individual stock prices. The stock market, says the efficient market hypothesis theorists, is efficient because so many skilled participants who possess a collection of all relevant information are setting prices. Because the participants, as a whole know, all the relevant information then the market is competitive and true stock market values always prevail. Consequently, attempting to identify undervalued common stock is pointless because the market has previously priced in information making beating the marketplace unachievable. Results will be as good if common stock for purchase are decided upon randomly, hence the dependence on the RWT. Three versions of market efficiency, weak form, semi-strong form and strong form of the marketplace are offered along with assumptions.

8-K. A report filed with the **Securities and Exchange Commission (SEC)** by a public corporation when a material corporate event that significantly affects the financial condition of the firm occurs.

Equivalent Stock Position. Call or put option positions can be translated into the equivalent number of shares owned of the underlying common stock, either net-long or net-short. The equivalent stock position (ESP) equation is equal to the number of option contacts times **delta** times the number of shares per option.

Expected News. All scheduled news from corporations, from governments, or their agencies. All expected scheduled news, whether meeting or not meeting expectations, that affects the stock market has been fully discounted by professional stock traders using the **expected news discounting process**.

Expected News Discounting Process. Explains how investors with foresight in the stock market constantly look ahead to predict political-economic conditions. This process explains how the stock market operates as a **discounting** mechanism. The recurring scheduled ongoing process of news anticipation, news reality, leading to updated news anticipation is based on Hegel's Dialectic Theory. Expected scheduled news does not startle the stock market or professional stock traders because it has previously been fully discounted.

Fair Value. The fair price at which a stock, option, or futures contract should be purchased or sold. Fair value may be found for stock by calculating its **intrinsic, true, or fair value** while futures, options and options on futures fair values are specified using specific mathematical valuation models.

Federal Reserve. The U.S. central bank which manages the following monetary policy: "to promote effectively the goals of maximum employment, stable prices and moderate long-term interest rates." Creating or withdrawing reserves by the Federal Reserve influences the supply and demand of Federal Reserve Bank balances which adjusts the federal funds interest rate which directly affects **political-economic conditions**. The Federal Reserve sets a target for the federal funds interest rate.

Fill Or Kill (FOK) Order. Directs the floor broker, a.k.a the pit broker, to attempt to fill the order three times at a specified price, after that the order is killed or cancelled if not successful.

Float. Float represents the number of shares in the investing public's hands available for trading, the higher the float the better the stock's liquidity and ease of shorting. A company with a large percentage of shares held by management or owners reduces float because they are less likely to trade their shares. Also, stock holders with brokerage cash accounts may not allow their shares to be shorted by removing them from the street name of their broker's borrowing account which further reduces float. **Buy ins** and **short squeezes** are the reason that short sellers should know the float, **short-interest, short-interest-to-float** and **short-interest ratio** prior to **short selling** a stock.

Focus Speculating. Thoroughly knowing and understanding the few companies that are being speculated in, rather than taking a less knowledgeable statistical diversification approach. Relies on sound fundamental analysis for selecting undervalued stock to purchase or overvalued stock to sell short. The recommended number of companies that astute speculators should trade in at any one time is three, each representing 25 percent of total risk capital. This leaves 25 percent of total risk capital as a cash reserve. Approximately 15 targeted trades are required to earn the astute speculative goal of +33 percent per year.

Free Cash Flow. Free cash flow (FCF) is calculated by adding the normally negative **total capital expenditures** derived from the cash flows from the investment activities portion of the cash flow statement for the year to the hopefully positive cash from operating activities for the year on the **cash flow statement (CFS).** Positive free cash flow (FCF) is considered a benefit for a corporation's stock price because management then has the option of increasing dividends, buying back their own stock, developing promising new products/markets, or meeting competitive challenges — all without the need to raise additional money from outside sources.

Futures Contracts. Hedgers (producers and end users) and speculators in the futures market attempt to forecast, for successive months over the next twelve months for most futures contracts, the price of soft commodities (agricultural and food), physical commodities (energy and metals) and financial futures (equity, foreign currency, and interest rate indexes). Standardized contracts for each commodity traded on the **futures exchange** entails quantity, quality, destination and expiration date. Standardization encourages futures trading and, therefore, market liquidity. Both the buyer and seller are committed and obligated to satisfy the terms of the futures contract on its final settlement date.

Futures Exchange. Its function is to bring buyers and sellers together when trading **futures contracts**—whether they are hedgers (producers and end users) or speculators. The four main attributes of the futures exchange are: 1) price settlement; 2) contract standardization; 3) buying and selling liquidity; and 4) the transfer of risk.

Futures Price Spread Strategies. At certain times of the year, based on commodity seasonality, futures price spreads between different futures contract expiration dates fluctuate. Prices may not change in an identical fashion on different **futures exchanges**, therefore, price spread strategies may be used profitably. Example futures price spread strategies for commodities include: intra-commodity spread, inter-commodity spread and straddles.

Good Till Cancelled (GTC). An open buy or sell order in force now and in the future in the brokerage's system that sets a priority for sale. The GTC order remains in effect until either the customer cancels the order or until it is executed.

Head and Shoulders Top or Bottom Reversal Pattern. This **chart pattern** gets its name because at a market top it looks like the head and shoulders of a person's outline on a monthly graph/chart. Three distinctive market peaks, during a market top, are in evidence. The head is the middle and highest intraday price peak while the left and right shoulders have prices that are approximately equal, but slightly lower in value. For a market bottom, the price pattern is turned upside down. The market bottom head intraday low price trough is the lowest while the left and right shoulder trough price values are approximately equal and not as low as the head's value. Both are **confirming indicators** to the **S&P 500 Index Nine Month Moving Average Trend Line**.

Hedge Fund. An open-ended investment company that large institutions and high net-worth individuals may make an investment. Hedge funds are speculative enterprises whose objective is to earn above market returns and/or to reduce risk, they may invest in the stock, bond, commodities, or foreign exchange markets. Typically the hedge fund manager is permitted to borrow money, buy long or sell short and use derivatives such as futures, options and options on futures—all concurrently.

Higher-Highs and Higher-Lows. When the **long-term** trend line is pointing upward, during Stage 3: Mark-Up - Uptrend; (see Graph 3 - 3), each wave up on the monthly chart depicts successively higher-highs and higher-low prices until Stage 4: Distribution - Topping is attained. This occurrence is a **confirming indicator** for an up trending **S&P 500 Index Nine Month Moving Average Trend Line**.

Index Arbitrage. The most used strategy of **program trading** and involves identifying price inconsistencies among stock baskets, indexes and futures & options contracts on different exchanges. Advanced computer **algorithms** are used to hedge equity positions.

Industry Group. Companies are grouped into twelve **sectors** and further sorted into anywhere from 100-200 industry groups. The primary business pursuit of the corporation determines how companies are sorted into industry groups. Industries display momentum and high or low industry rankings help identify corporate leaders or laggards to either purchase or sell short at the appropriate time.

Industry Subgroups. Large **industry groups** may include as many as 100 public corporations and, consequently, have subgroups of companies that represent a niche within its industry group.

Initial Public Offering (IPO). A company's initial stock sale in the primary market, normally using an underwriter as a manager known as an investment banker—such as Merrill Lynch, Morgan Stanley, Goldman Sachs, Lehman Brothers, JPMorgan Chase, Citigroup and ING Group. The **Securities and Exchange Commission (SEC)** approves and regulates all proceedings of the IPO.

Intermediate Term. In the stock market, a period of time lasting 1, 2, 3, 4, 5 months or longer.

Intrinsic, True, or Fair Value. An intrinsic, true, or fair value calculation for a company is instrumental for the **margin-of-safety** concept and **value investing**. Future yearly expected corporate **free cash flow** (FCF) values are discounted by the 30-year U.S. Treasury bond risk-free interest rate of return which determines the corporation's present-worth or intrinsic, true, or fair value.

Investing. Proper investing requires **investment foresight** and the most beneficial strategies and analysis leading to suitable evaluation and judgment for purchasing or selling common stock or fixed-income securities for either capital appreciation and/or predictable income over a many year planning horizon. Investors should prefer high quality securities at proper or reasonable prices which match the investor's scheduled needs. Investors should believe that all relevant factors are favorable prior to making an investment because the power to decline an investment is his or her most cherished advantage. **Due diligence** and the practical **ten-step method for investment success** should be followed.

Investment Foresight. Foresight for investors requires them to envision or imagine what will happen in the future based on all the necessary information available to them and then to adequately prepare and properly position themselves for the expected consequences. **Discounting the news** and an awareness of **political-economic conditions** are required.

Japanese Candlestick Charting Technique. The open, high, low and closing values form the candlestick. Solid candlestick bodies show the close lower than the open. White candlestick bodies depict the close higher than the open. The thin lines above and below the solid-or-white candlestick bodies are called upper-and-lower shadows and indicate the high and low price range. Candlesticks are figurative and make stock chart illustrations attractive and easy to understand in one glance.

Law of Compensation. Dualism takes place in nature and is the condition of man. Every gain causes a loss; every loss a gain. Look for the silver lining in every dark cloud and the downside that always accompanies an upside experience, i.e., do not let life blind-side you at an inopportune time.

Long Term. In the stock market, a period of time lasting 1, 2, 3, 4, 5 years or longer.

Lower-Highs and Lower-Lows. When the **long-term** trend line is pointing down during Stage 1: Mark-Down - Downtrend (see Graph 3 - 1), each wave down on the monthly chart depicts successively lower-highs and lower-low prices until Stage 2: Accumulation - Bottoming is reached. This occurrence is a **confirming indicator** to a down trending **S&P 500 Index Nine Month Moving Average Trend Line**.

Margin-of-Safety. The Graham-Dodd-Buffett strategy for their prudent **value investment** style. Purchasing stock at suitable prices, as determined by this sound methodology, should triumph over market adversity in the **long-term**. A positive corporate **bargain value** indicates a stock which is undervalued. A company's stock whose **intrinsic, true, or fair value** is at least twice its market value capitalization has a large enough **margin-of-safety multiple** and is a deserving candidate for purchase based on the **margin-of-safety** concept.

Margin-of-Safety Multiple. A company's stock whose **intrinsic, true, or fair value** is at least twice its **market value capitalization** has a large enough margin-of-safety multiple and is a deserving candidate for purchase based on the **margin-of-safety** concept. Margin-of-safety multiples may be rank ordered from highest to lowest, along with their **bargain values,** to select the most deserving corporate stock for investments.

Market If Touched (MIT) Order. Specifies a set purchase price only if the current price drops to the lower set price.

Market Pundit. A so-called expert or investment guru on the stock market or an individual stock who readily offers rationalizations for common stock being either under-or-over valued, all supported by proffered economic justifications using **maps-of-maps**. A stock market sophist known more for plausible but specious arguments then for being ultimately proved correct. In very limited instances—a seeming authority figure making true but nonetheless unprincipled public statements in an effort to manipulate the investing public to do one thing while the market pundit or his associates are doing something else, all motivated by an expected financial gain.

Market Risk. Risk that may be described as systematic factors of **political-economic conditions** that determine overall stock prices. Market risk uncertainties have a tendency to move most stock prices together, thus, market risk cannot be diversified away regardless of the number of companies or types of stock in an investment portfolio. Adequate diversification eliminates almost completely all unsystematic risks associated with individual companies. Market risk is defined as systematic risk.

Market Timing. Expecting to purchase common stock at the very bottom price and to sell at the very top price on any intermediate or long-term move. **Astute investors and speculators** do not assume perfection and believe being close enough by attaining the more secure middle two thirds in any market move is the better strategy and what is expected.

Market Trends. Four main stages defining the market trend over the **long-term** are identified: Stage 1: Mark-Down - Downtrend; Stage 2: Accumulation - Bottoming; Stage 3: Mark-Up - Uptrend; and Stage 4: Distribution - Topping or Rounding Over. Stock markets in the long-term move relatively slowly, monthly data and the **S&P 500 Index Nine Month MA Trend Line** help in determining market stages and trends.

Market Value Capitalization. Calculated by multiplying the corporation's total number of diluted shares outstanding times the current per share stock price. Used with **intrinsic, true, or fair value** to calculate **bargain value**.

Momentum Speculating. Used to identify intermediate-term industry trends by looking at industry rankings and additional fundamental corporate factors. Stock momentum may either be positive or negative depending on intermediate industry and long-term stock market trends, the market stage and **industry group** rankings. **Trigger points** are used to help identify momentum speculating **turning points.**

Money Management Goals. The three goals of money management are: 1) never put one's way of life at risk; 2) only risk as much money on one trade that will keep the mind clear; and 3) be able to keep the money once earned.

Money Management Rules. Money management focuses upon position size, or how many stock shares should be acquired in relation to the total amount of risk capital available to the speculator, and upon the downside risk of stock trading where speculators plan for the possibility of trading losses by using risk-reduction strategies. Money management rules are emphasized because it is not how much money speculators earn that is most important, instead, it is how much traders do not lose that determines speculative success. Speculative money management rules include: 1) save half the profits; 2) have patience, keep cash reserves and have the capability to "say no"; 3) protect capital; 4) use **focus speculating**; and 5) staying with winners.

Moving Average Convergence Divergence (MACD). The MACD for the S&P 500 Index displays two crossing moving averages, the MACD (12,26) line and the MACD EMA (9) line. The monthly MACD is effective as a long-term indicator and should be watched closely at the beginning of each month. The monthly MACD is used as a confirming indicator for the **S&P 500 Index Nine Month MA Trend Line**.

Moving Average (MA) Trend Line. Gives the best perspective needed to observe **long-term** stock market trends.

Naked-Short Position. During a naked-short transaction, one or more of the following **SEC** requirements are deficient: 1) the exchange handling the trade must be informed that the order is a short sale; 2) the sale execution must be in conformance with the **short-sale uptick rule**; and 3) the broker handling the sale must have borrowed the stock to make delivery at the time of the sale. Also, a position in a stock that is not hedged.

Not-Held Order. The brokerage firm is instructed to use their discretion on the timing and/or price when executing either a market or limit order. The floor broker is expected to have a better feel for whether stock prices should rise or fall. The not-held order does not guarantee the customer's order will be filled.

Options. A holder of a stock option has the right but not the obligation to either purchase or sell a stock at a predetermined price over a specified time period. A call option allows the holder to buy the underlying stock at a specific price, called the striking price, and the put option allows the holder to sell the underlying stock at the striking price. Both the call and put options may be traded at any time up until the options expiration date.

Options Exchanges. Where common stock options and equity, industry, foreign currency and interest rate index options are traded. Listed **options** require five pieces of descriptive information, i.e., the basis of the option (whether a common stock option or equity, industry, foreign currency or interest rate index option), if it is a call or put option, the number of options contracts, striking price and expiration date.

Options On Futures. Derivatives on derivatives that are twice removed from the underlying spot or cash market. First is the spot or cash market, second is futures on the spot or cash market and third is the options on the futures on the spot or cash market. Cash-based options on futures, as opposed to commodity based futures options, have no material commodities as a basis for the options contract.

Options Strategies. Call and put options strategies include: call buying, covered call writing, uncovered call writing, protected short sale, reverse hedge, straddle buying, ratio writing, ratio call spreads, vertical, horizontal and diagonal spread strategies, put buying and collars. Good options strategies with the possibility for unlimited gain and for limited loss are recommended: i.e., call buying, put buying, protected short sale, reverse hedge and straddle buying.

Outside Reversal Day (ORD). At a stock market bottom, the **S&P 500 Index** makes a new intraday low for the current move and then closes above the intraday high of the previous day on extraordinarily high share-trading volume. At a stock market top, the S&P 500 Index makes a new intraday high for the current move and then closes below the intraday low of the previous day on extraordinarily high share-trading volume. This confirms a double-top, on the second peak, or double-bottom, on the second trough, of the S&P 500 Index graph pattern. The ORD is a **confirming indicator** for the **S&P 500 Index Nine Month MA Trend Line**.

Pivot Points. Price support and resistance levels define pivot points used with the tandem trading strategy. Reversal pivot points mark the end of a long-term trend for a stock or the stock market, either upward or downward. The reversal pivot point is the ideal psychological time to begin the "long-pull" trade to take advantage of the new major long-term trend in the market. Continuation pivot points are intermediate-term trend reversal points which signify that a counter trend is ending and that the intermediate-term trend will now track along with the market's long-term trend.

Political-Economic Conditions. The long-term stock **market trends** are inexorably tied to political-economic conditions. These conditions are defined mainly by long-term business and political conditions that are not random but irregularly cyclical in nature. The stock market is a symbolic representation of not only the real corporate economy, but also everything that impacts on the real economy. For example, political action by the federal, sate and local governments and agencies that include: the decision to go to war; the policies on fiscal deficits and taxes; currency values; inflation rates; trade laws; decision on the federal funds interest rate; **yield curves**; immigration policy; natural events (e.g., earthquakes, hurricanes, a pandemic disease, etc.); world conditions; etc. The ultimate discovery that most investors make in the stock market is that they must examine political-economic conditions and be able to interpret them to help determine and foresee investment probabilities. Stock market price action discounts **market risk** or systematic political-economic conditions because collectively the millions and millions of investors see more clearly into the future than any one person possibly can. Political-economic conditions are tied to **long-term** stock market stages and are instrumental for the practical **ten-step method for investment success**.

Premium. The absolute price difference in points/dollars, whether positive or negative, between the S&P 500 Index futures contract price and the spot or cash price of the underlying stock in the S&P 500 Index. By knowing "the premium," the market momentum, either up-or-down, is determined.

Price-to-Earnings (P/E) Ratio. Current per share price divided by the corporation's **basic EPS** for a prior period of time. P/E ratios are actual or trailing twelve-month earnings per share divided into the stock price and are usually reported by the financial media. A stock with a high P/E ratio may signify a faster growing company resulting in the investor's willingness to buy at higher prices the same level of annual earnings. Also called *Actual P/E Ratio*.

Program Trading. An arbitrage strategy for inter-market price variations based only on market divergences rather than stock fundamentals. As this is written, program trading accounts for almost 59 percent of the trading on the NYSE and utilizes computer **algorithms** to implement the following strategies: 1) investment objectives; 2) duration averaging; 3) portfolio insurance; and most importantly 4) **index arbitrage**.

Progressive Stop-Loss Orders. Once the trade is profitable, either long or short, the **stop-loss order** is moved so that no loss is incurred on the trade. As the stock price continues to move in the speculator's favor, the stop-loss order is continually moved up if long and moved down if short at a measured distance form the stock's current price so that a larger-and-larger profit is assured if the stock price should then move against the speculator—resulting in the progressive stop-loss order automatically closing out the profitable position.

Proxy Statement. Required **SEC** material sent to existing shareholders, prior to the annual meeting with management, that lists corporate issues to be voted upon—including directorships, the auditing firm, salaries of top officers and major corporate resolutions.

Put/Call Ratio. Tracks speculator sentiment and is calculated by dividing the number of put options contracts traded per day by the number of call options contacts traded on the same day. A put/call ratio (PCR) less than one means speculators are optimistic and expect stock prices to increase. A PCR over one signifies pessimistic options traders who expect a price decline.

Random Walk Process. Movement of a corporation's stock price in the stock market is described in the financial research literature as that of one aimlessly wandering through time as if someone drew by chance a plus or minus number and added that number onto the previous day's closing price. Day to day company stock price movements are seemingly independent from one another and are as random as the flipping of a coin or much like a pure gambling game such as American roulette. Each daily price series for a company's stock acts like a random walk process—no cycles are in evidence. The random walk process supports the **random walk theory** of stock prices.

Random Walk Theory (RWT). The Random Walk Theory (RWT) states that corporate stock prices move randomly, either up or down and that the prediction of a company's stock price is impossible. The RWT is supported by the premise of the **random walk process**. The RWT assumes that prices are set based on random breaking news information which cannot be predicted. Because unpredictable news information comes into the marketplace randomly—it is fully expected that prices respond randomly to this news. The Random Walk Theory supports and is the premise for the **efficient market hypothesis.**

Reaction. A quick dip in price for the stock market, an individual stock price, or a **futures contract** price.

Return-on-Equity (ROE) Ratio. Calculated by taking the annual net income (less dividends on preferred stock) located on the income statement, divided by total shareholder's equity from the balance sheet. Investors want ROE to be a high percentage and improving yearly. ROE is an important measure of management's performance and should be closely monitored when using **value investing**.

Reward-to-Risk Ratio. If the stop-loss order is set two points/dollars below an average priced stock, the expected profits should be at least eight points for this to be considered a good trade. **Astute speculators** should expect to make at least four times what is being risked on the stop-loss order. Assuming a speculator wins 60 percent of the time and loses 40 percent of the time, the probabilities are now in the speculator's favor— total returns are expected to be a positive 30 percent over ten trades, less commissions. Because probabilities are now in the speculator's favor, perfection is not required.

Robust Methodology. Perfection and trying to find the optimal market solution model is counterproductive. Riches and perfection do not go together in the stock market because performing flawlessness in the stock market is impossible. Instead, look for the most robust methodology and stock market models that have been proven capable in practice.

Roth IRA. Taxes are paid on the income and the money going into a Roth IRA. However, at retirement, all of the capital appreciation gained in the Roth IRA is allowed to be withdrawn tax-free at retirement. Some income limits apply.

Scale In-or-Out Orders. An order issued to a brokerage company to execute either the buying or selling of a set number of shares of the same equity at varying prices. The price points are typically set at half-point intervals, either up or down.

Sectors. A stock market sector is a large grouping of corporations with shared business characteristics. Companies on the different exchanges such as the NYSE, AMEX and the NASDAQ are sorted into twelve sectors. Sectors lead, lag or are coincident with the overall stock market. Companies within sectors are further sorted into smaller **industry groups**.

Securities and Exchange Commission (SEC). The federal government board created by the Securities and Exchange Act of 1934 which has regulatory responsibility for the securities industry.

Selling Climax Day. Signifies a market capitulation and occurs at an long-term or intermediate-term support **turning point.** The market opens weak and plunges straight down on very heavy volume. Selling climax volume at a long-term turning point is normally 1.5 times average NYSE volume during a day where stock prices drop precipitously for the S&P 500 Index in a broad market decline. The selling climax day normally coincides with very bad news that causes the investing public and **amateur speculators** to dump their stock holdings at distressed prices while more knowledgeable buyers, who have already discounted the news, now buy the excess supply resulting in higher closing stock prices. A selling climax day turns around the technical condition of the market which changes it from being long or intermediate-term weak to now being a strong market. Also called the "clean out day."

Semi-Investor. A person who keeps four separate financial accounts and is making a transition from investing to speculating and wants to purchase stock bargains in three leading, high-quality companies with stellar track records at a long-term market bottom.

Shares Outstanding. The number of shares of common and preferred stock issued by the public corporation, less the stock later repurchased by the company and held as treasury stock or retired. Outstanding capital stock available for trading.

Short Interest. The total number of a company's shares or positions on the futures exchange that are currently sold short. The higher the short interest the more pessimistic traders are on the common stock or futures position.

Short-Interest-to-Float. The **short interest** divided by the stock's **float.** A high short-interest-to-float percentage is dangerous for short sellers when **short selling** because it shows that a large short position is already in the stock. When putting on a short sale, short sellers prefer not to have too much short-sale company.

Short-Interest Ratio. The **short interest** divided by the stock's average daily trading volume indicates how many days would be required to cover all short-sale shares. When **short selling**, high short-interest ratio stock are more hazardous to sell short because the short position may be too crowded.

Short-Sale Uptick Rule. Assuming the stock shares can be borrowed, The **Securities and Exchange Commission (SEC)** uptick rule 10a-1 of the Securities Exchange Act requires the short sale to take place on a plus tick (increase in price) or zero-plus tick (unchanged price) from a prior transaction price. A trade completed on a plus or uptick is prompted by the buyer while a trade on a minus tick is prompted by the seller.

Short Selling. The common stock or futures contract is sold first without benefit of ownership. "Sell high, buy low" describes the procedure when short selling. As the stock or futures price declines, the short position may be covered at a profit. The speculator, on the short side of the market, is planning to profit from the drop in the price of a stock, commodity, or financial index.

Short Squeeze. A rapidly rising stock or **futures contract** price has the effect of pressuring those in short positions to cover which further increases prices—forcing even more shorts to cover. Examples of events that can cause short squeezes are brokerage house upgrades, buyout or merger Wall Street rumors, intermediate-term swings in the market that go against the short's position and companies that get proactive in trying to squeeze short sellers.

Simulator Or Paper Trading. Simulator trading, paper trading, or virtual trading is a replicated process where speculators practice trading and gain real world experience without risking money. Because there is no risk of loss involved, simulator trading can be an empty exercise if not conducted properly.

Speculating. Stock market speculation is both an art and a science. Eleven scientific speculative factors should be understood and three **speculative arts** should be mastered. Speculators follow **speculative bylaws**, use **money management rules**, trade at **turning points**, use **trigger points**, perform **tape reading** and realize that price action indicates, whereas, trading volume validates.

Speculative Arts. Include: 1) how to time stock buying or short selling over the intermediate-term using **turning points** and **trigger points**; 2) how to sell or cover a stock position by taking the emotion out when using **stop-loss orders** and **money management rules**; and 3) knowing yourself and what strategy will work best for you based on your character, personality and lifestyle.

Speculative Bylaws. Bylaws are necessary because stock market speculation looks relatively easy to **amateur speculators** who incorrectly think of speculation as simply gambling in a large casino called the stock market. Instead, proper knowledge and following tested bylaws are key to reducing risk and achieving market success.

Speculative Goals. Earning +33 percent per year speculating in the stock market, in both good times and bad, and then retaining the profits which is the real end game.

Standard & Poor's 500 (S&P 500) Index. Includes 500 public corporations selected for market capitalization size, common stock trading liquidity and broad industry group representation. The S&P 500 is a value weighted index and represents, as this is written, almost 80 percent of the overall U.S. stock market value capitalization of equities on the NYSE, the NASDAQ and the AMEX stock exchanges. The S&P 500 Index has long been used as a benchmark with which to compare the total returns of other investments and is a good proxy representative of the overall U.S. stock market.

S&P 500 Index Expected Fair Valuation (EFV) Model. The next twelve months of estimated reported earnings for the S&P 500 Index companies are divided by the S&P 500 Index price resulting in a "S&P 500 Index estimated reported earnings yield." Next, the 10-year U.S. Treasury note interest rate is divided by the "S&P 500 Index estimated reported earnings yield" resulting in a S&P 500 Index Value Factor. An expected fair valuation for the S&P 500 Index is calculated by dividing the current S&P 500 Index price by the S&P 500 Index Value Factor. While S&P 500 Index EFV Model is not precise, it gives the astute investor approximate correct forward-looking S&P 500 Index valuations.

S&P 500 Index Nine Month Moving Average (MA) Trend Line. For the **S&P 500 Index**, the monthly trend line gives perspective to identify **long-term** trends in the stock market. Because the stock market, over the long-term, moves relatively slowly, the perspective of monthly data are most appropriate to analyzing long-term **market trends**.

S&P 500 Index Two Month Moving Average Trend Line. Helps identify long-term trends in the marketplace. Used as a **confirming indicator** for the **S&P 500 Index Nine Month MA Trend Line** in the stock market.

Stock Journal. Speculators should study market behavior for stock indexes, **industry groups** and specific common stock by keeping accurate daily journal records. Record significant actual events, i.e., the daily opening, high, low and closing price data, trading volume data, why the trade was entered into and why it either worked or did not work out in practice.

Stop-Loss Orders. Preset instructions to take a trader out of a current long or short position at a small loss when the stock's price moves to a set price level. A sell stop-loss order for a long position is automatically transacted when the stock's price reaches a lower price than which it is currently trading. A buy stop-loss order for a short position is automatically transacted when the stock's price attains a higher price than which it is currently trading. The stop-loss order may be in place for one day, a longer-term time frame, or **good until cancelled (GTC).** A defensive technique to automatically conclude an emotionally charged transaction decision.

Strong Hands. Coming off of a long-term market low during Stage 2: Accumulation, the technical position is strong as strong-hand professional speculators accumulate stock from the **"weak hands"** of the investing public. A strong technical position is in effect at a long-term market bottom because professionals gradually purchase common stock at low prices from the fearful investing public.

Super-Long-Term. Twenty years, two decades, or more in the stock market.

Supply And Demand, Current. Stock price purchase and trading volume figures reported on the tape that indicate the existing supply and demand condition in the stock market. Either buyers or sellers dominate in the market resulting in an upward or downward trend.

Supply And Demand, Potential. Stock prices over the intermediate and long-term move in trends. Looking at a chart/graph, supply and demand points may be described as support and resistance levels. A support level is the price where sizeable new buying demand takes place and may keep the price from falling below this point. A resistance level is the price where substantial new selling supply takes place and may keep the price from rising above this level.

Tape. A scrolling stock market display, through the trading day, of corporate stock symbols, actual transaction prices and the volume of shares changing hands during the transaction. The scrolling electronic tape display is usually available at stock brokerage offices, on cable television and on stock market Internet websites. Also called *electronic tape*.

Tape Reading. Anticipating stock price changes based on price and volume transactions that show up on the electronic **tape**. This requires forecasting stock trends and **turning points** by understanding the consequences of how past price and volume transactions affect future price movements.

10-K. The **Securities and Exchange Commission (SEC)** requires public corporations to file financial information on the firm's operations called 10-K reports. Annual reports going to stockholders are more visually appealing while 10-K reports going to the SEC have more financial detail and incorporate information on management compensation and report on any legal proceedings. The 10-K report is required to be filed 90 days after the close of the corporation's fiscal year.

10-Q. The **Securities and Exchange Commission (SEC)** requires public corporations to file quarterly unaudited financial information on the firm's operations called 10-Q reports. The 10-Q report is a less comprehensive but more regularly filed version of the **10-K** report. The 10-Q report should be filed within 45 days of the close of the corporation's quarter.

Ten-Step Method for Investment Success. The methodology is practical and includes: 1) selecting the correct goal and strategy; 2) identifying **political-economic conditions**; 3) calculating the **S&P 500 Index Expected Fair Valuation Model**; 4) identifying the **S&P 500 Index Nine Month MA Trend Line** using perspective and stock market stages; 5) rational anxiety, non-rational emotions and irrational influences all to be counteracted by proper investment character traits; 6) Graham-Dodd-Buffett **value investing** with **intrinsic, true, or fair value, market value capitalization, bargain values and margin-of-safety multiples**; 7) **yield curve** and interest rate monitoring to identify long-term market tops; 8) news evaluation, **discounting the news, discounted news theory,** being skeptical of **market pundits** and shunning stock tips; 9) avoiding the "**self-selected market adviser's strategy**" to being **contrarian** and being skeptical of conventional wisdom; 10) investors pull all of the information together from steps 1 through 9, to make their own **due diligence** judgments and arrive at their own investment decisions.

Time Stops. Capital is the lifeblood of trading, therefore, it is imperative that risk capital always be in effective circulation. If a stock does not perform as expected, the position is closed out after only a few weeks. It is better to be out of the market and patiently waiting in a neutral cash position for the next superb trading opportunity than have cash locked in a listless stock drifter going nowhere.

Time Value Premium. When a call is out-of-the-money, the call time value premium equals the option premium. The equation is: call time value premium equals call option premium less intrinsic value. The intrinsic value is equal to the stock price less the striking price. When a call option is out-of-the-money, the intrinsic value is equal to zero.

Timing. On Wall Street, timing is the primary **speculative art** or "art of arts." The primary concern for speculators is always "when," the "what" to buy or sell short is always of secondary importance and the stock's price or "how much" to pay or initially receive for the shares sold short is only number three in significance.

Total Capital Expenditures. Total capital expenditures are determined by subtracting the purchase of property and equipment (sometimes called capital expenditures), the acquisition/disposition costs or gains from the purchase or sale of subsidiaries, plus the addition of any proceeds from the sale of assets. These accounts are all located on the cash flows from investment activities portion of the **cash flow statement (CFS)**. Total capital expenditures are important when calculating **free cash flow (FCF)**.

Trader's Market. No well defined upward or downward long-term trend is in evidence during a trader's market during two distinct market phases: Stage 2: Accumulation - Bottoming and Stage 4: Distribution - Topping or Rounding Over. A trader's market is also in evidence during one or more intermediate-term moves that run counter to the overall long-term movement during a Stage 3: Mark-Up – Uptrend long-term advance and during a Stage 1: Mark-Down - Downtrend long-term decline.

Trigger Points. Perception of what is hoped for takes on the guise of reality. It is human nature to desire wealth and that is accomplished in the stock market by dreaming about the future. A speculator's perception is often better than reality and a stock's price reaches its highest level when trader's expectations are the highest, not when the ultimate reality is achieved. A trigger point for an overvalued or undervalued stock is typically the fulfillment of what is expected and is used in **momentum speculating**.

Turning Points. The stock market loses momentum over the long or intermediate-term, either up or down, at turning points. Momentarily, supply and demand are in balance and the market is in equilibrium, however, markets do not stay in equilibrium for long. Turning points typically occur on heavy volume but no headway in price. The **momentum speculating** goal is to make the trade close to the exact turning point when the market then starts going the opposite direction.

Unexpected News. Unexpected news is nonscheduled news with only the likelihood of what, who, where and when the imagined event may take place. The imagined what, who, where and when of unexpected news events cause some investors to modify both their actions and/or non-actions in the stock market. Everything that can be imagined by investors which are determined to affect the stock market are partially discounted by the marketplace.

Value Investing. Buying good securities at a significant discount is the strategy that is expected to triumph over the long-term. Investors should prefer high quality securities at proper or reasonable prices which match their scheduled needs. **Intrinsic, true, or fair value** is a good method for determining a company's present worth and is compared with its **market value capitalization. Margin-of-safety multiples** and **bargain values** for each stock are rank ordered to identify possible candidates for stock purchase based on the **margin-of-safety** concept. Value investing is likened to comparison shopping and looking for terrific stock market bargains.

Wasting Asset. Purchased options are a wasting asset of the "**time value premium.**"

Weak Hands. A market in a weak technical position. At a long-term market peak during Stage 4: Distribution - Topping or Rounding Over when stock is being gradually distributed over many months from "**strong hands**" to the investing public's "weak hands."

Yield Curve. The yield curve is a result of monetary and fiscal policies affecting **political-economic conditions,** over time. A normal yield curve, for federal funds, T-bill, T-note and T-bond maturities, occurs during standard economic growth conditions. An inverted yield curve comes about when both money and credit are restrictive and is a good indicator of a U.S. economic downturn. If the federal funds target interest rate exceeds the 30-year T-bond rate this is a harbinger that the overall stock market may begin to discount a slowdown in the U.S. economy and be close to peaking.

Bibliography

Baruch, Bernard M., *BARUCH: My Own Story*, Cutchogue, New York: Buccaneer Books, 1957.

Bernstein, Jake, *How the Futures Markets Work*, New York: New York Institute of Finance and Prentice Hall Press, 2000.

Darvas, Nicolas, *How I Made $2,000,000 in the Stock Market*, New York: Lyle Stuart Kensington Publishing Corp., 1986.

Edwards, Robert D., John Magee and W. H. C. Bassetti (Editor), *Technical Analysis of Stock Trends*, 8th ed., New York: St. Lucie Press, 2001.

Etzel, Barbara J., *Webster's New World Finance and Investment Dictionary*, Indianapolis, Indiana: Wiley Publishing, Inc., 2003.

Feldman, David, *The Ups and Downs of a Wall Street Trader during the Depths of the Great Depression of the 1930s*, Burlington, Vermont: Fraser Publishing Company, 1997.

Geisst, Charles R., *Wall Street: A History*, New York: Oxford University Press, 1997.

Gibson, Thomas, *The Pitfalls of Speculation*, Burlington, Vermont: Fraser Publishing Company, 1994.

Grossman, Sanford J., and Joseph E. Stiglitz. "On the Impossibility of Informationally Efficient Markets." *American Economic Review*, 70, no. 3, June 1980, pp. 393-408.

Guyon, Don, *One-Way Pockets: The Book of Books on Wall Street Speculation*, Burlington, Vermont: Fraser Publishing Company, 1965.

Hoyne, Thomas Temple, *Speculation: Its Sound Principles & Rules For Its Practice*, Burlington, Vermont: Fraser Publishing Company, 1988.

Kelly, Fred C., *Why You Win or Lose*, Burlington, Vermont: Fraser Publishing Company, 1998.

Lefevre, Edwin, *Reminiscences of a Stock Operator*, New York: John Wiley & Sons, Inc., 1994.

Liveright, James, *Simple Methods for Detecting Buying and Selling Points In Securities*, Wells, Vermont: Fraser Publishing Company, 1968.

Livermore, Jesse, added material by Richard Smitten, *How to Trade in Stocks*, Greenville, South Carolina: Traders Press, Inc., 2001.

Loeb, Gerald M., *The Battle for Investment Survival*, New York: John Wiley & Sons, Inc., 1996.

Mackay, Charles, *Extraordinary Popular Delusions and the Madness of Crowds*, New York: Barnes & Noble Books, 1989.

Magazine of Wall Street, *Fourteen Methods of Operating in the Stock Market*, Burlington, Vermont: Fraser Publishing Company, 1968.

Bibliography

Magee, John and W. H. C. Bassetti (Editor), *Winning The Mental Game on Wall Street*, Boca Raton: St. Lucie Press, 2000.

Malkiel, Burton G., *A Random Walk Down Wall Street,* 8th ed., New York: W. W. Norton & Company, 2003.

Mamis, Justin, *When To Sell*, Burlington, Vermont: Fraser Publishing Company, 1999.

Mamis, Justin, *How To Buy*, Burlington, Vermont: Fraser Publishing Company, 2001.

McMillan, Lawrence G., *Options as a Strategic Investment*, 4th ed., New York: New York Institute of Finance and Prentice Hall Press, 2002.

McNeel, R. W., *Beating the Stock Market*, Wells, Vermont: Fraser Publishing Company, 1987.

Moskowitz, Tobias J., and Mark Grinblatt. "Do Industries Explain Momentum?" *Journal of Finance*, 54, no. 4, August 1999, pp. 1249-1290.

Neill, Humphrey B., *Tape Reading & Market Tactics*, Burlington, Vermont: Fraser Publishing Company, 2000.

Nison, Steve, *Japanese Candlestick Charting Techniques*, 2nd ed., New York: New York Institute of Finance and Prentice Hall Press, 2001.

Norris, Frank, *The Pit*, New York: Penguin Books, 1994.

O'Neil, William J., *How to Make Money in Stocks*, 2nd ed., New York: McGraw-Hill, Inc., 1995.

O'Neil, William J., *24 Essential Lessons for Investment Success*, New York: McGraw-Hill, Inc., 2000.

O'Shaughnessy, James P., *What Works On Wall Street*, New York: McGraw-Hill, 1997.

Oz, Tony, *The Stock Trader*, Oak Park, California: Goldman Brown Business Media Inc., 2000.

Prentis, Eric L., *The Astute Investor*, 2nd ed., Houston, Texas: Prentis Business, 2006.

Prentis, Eric L. "Discounted Market Hypothesis: Empirical Study 1928-2005." (forthcoming).

Schabacker, Richard W., *Stock Market Profits,* Great Britain: Prentice Hall, 1999.

Schwager, Jack D., *Market Wizards: Interviews With Top Traders*, New York: New York Institute of Finance, 1989.

Selden, G. C., *Psychology of the Stock Market*, Burlington, Vermont: Fraser Publishing Company, 1996.

Staley, Kathryn F., *The Art of Short Selling*, New York: John Wiley & Sons, Inc., 1997.

Tape, Rollo, *Studies in Tape Reading*, Burlington, Vermont: Fraser Publishing Company, 1997.

The Trader, *Commonsense Speculation*, Burlington, Vermont: Fraser Publishing Company, 1992.

Tracy, John A., *How to Read a Financial Report,* 5th ed., New York: John Wiley & Sons, Inc., 1999.

Watts, Dickson G., *Speculation As A Fine Art And Thoughts On Life*, Burlington, Vermont: Fraser Publishing Company, 1979.

Williams, Frank J., *If You Must Speculate Learn the Rules*, Burlington, Vermont: Fraser Publishing Company, 1970.

Wolf, H. J., *Studies in Stock Speculation*, Burlington, Vermont: Fraser Publishing Company, 1990.

Wolf, H. J., *Studies in Stock Speculation, Volume* II, Burlington, Vermont: Fraser Publishing Company, 1998.

Wyckoff, Richard D., *Stock Market Technique, Number Two*, Burlington, Vermont: Fraser Publishing Company, 1989.

Wyckoff, Richard D., *Stock Market Technique, Number One*, Burlington, Vermont: Fraser Publishing Company, 1990.

Wyckoff, Richard D., *How I Trade and Invest in Stocks & Bonds*, Burlington, Vermont: Fraser Publishing Company, 1998.

Index

G